Doing and Writing Qualitative Research

Second edition

REFERENCE

Doing and Writing Qualitative Research

Second edition

Adrian Holliday

SAGE Publications
Los Angeles • London • New Delhi • Singapore

First published 2007

Reprinted 2008

SAGE Publications Ltd
1 Oliver's Yard
55 City Road
London EC1Y 1SP

SAGE Publications Inc
2455 Teller Road
Thousand Oaks, California 91320

SAGE Publications India Pvt Ltd
B 1/I 1 Mohan Cooperative Industrial Area
Mathura Road, New Delhi 110 044
India

SAGE Publications Asia-Pacific Pte Ltd
33 Pekin Street # 02-01
Far East Square
Singapore 048763

British Library Cataloguing in Publication data

A catalogue record for this book is available
from the British Library

ISBN 978 1 4129 1129 0
ISBN 978 1 4129 1130 6

Library of Congress Control Number 2006927474

Typeset by C&M Digitals (P) Ltd., Chennai, India
Printed in Great Britain by TJ International Ltd, Padstow, Cornwall
Printed on paper from sustainable resources

To Mehri and Shabnam, my most important readers

Contents

● ● ● ● ● ● ● ●

Figures and Tables   IX
Preface   XI
Acknowledgements   XIV

1 Approaching Qualitative Research   **1**
Qualitative and quantitative   1
Schools and approaches   15
Writer as stranger   20
Summary   21

2 Starting Out   **22**
Researching everyday life   23
Determining the area   26
Establishing a research question   28
Defining the research setting   33
Summary   41

3 Showing the Workings   **42**
Introductions   44
Conceptual framework   47
Describing procedures   50
Significance of research strategy   57
Articulating issues   58
Summary   59

4 What Counts as Data   **60**
Overview of qualitative data   60
Artefacts revealing the unfamiliar   68
Arising from social settings   71
Thick description   74
Approaching thick description   77
Summary   88

5   Writing about Data   **89**
From data to written study   91
Organizing and presenting data   93
Degrees of explicitness   102
Preserving original richness   107
Photographs as co-constructed text   111
Caution   112
Summary   113

6   Writer Voice   **114**
The struggle with convention   114
New thinking   120
The author writes back   123
Creating coherence   129
Personal orientation, history and narrative   132
Achieving credibility   135
Summary   136

7   Writing about Relations   **137**
Reflexivity   138
The small culture of dealing   139
Setting up relations   145
Establishing relations   153
Behaving appropriately   156
Using experience as data   159
Disciplined learning   162
Summary   163

8   Making Appropriate Claims   **164**
Allowing 'ordinary' voice   164
Cautious detachment   167
Suspending judgement   173
People in relationships   181
Summary   182

Topics for Discussion   **183**
Written Studies Used as Examples   **187**
References   **189**
Index   **196**

Figures and Tables

──────────────────────────────── Figures ────────────────────────────────

1.1 Trails of necessity   17

2.1 Interconnectedness of data   35
2.2 Small culture selected for qualitative research   40

3.1 Written study, structure and functions   43
3.2 Positioning the researcher – a conceptual framework   48
3.3 Coding used for reference to data   55

4.1 Egyptian university students   67
4.2 Greek news still   68
4.3 Building a picture of a headmistress   74

5.1 From data to writing   90
5.2 Constituents of thick description   103
5.3 Managing perception   107
5.4 Posing   112

6.1 Discourses and genres of qualitative research   115

7.1 Culture of dealing   140
7.2 Entering into the culture of dealing   151

──────────────────────────────── Tables ────────────────────────────────

1.1 Two paradigms   6
1.2 Sources of validity   9
1.3 Paradigms, strategies and methods   16

2.1   Research questions   29
2.2   Criteria for research settings   34

3.1   Examples of conceptual framework   49

4.1   Types of data   62

7.1   Shopkeeper research   142

Preface

● ● ● ● ● ● ● ●

The second edition contains all the same elements of the first edition with some important additions concerning the nature and use of visual data, personal narrative, core and periphery data, and data reconstruction and fictionalization, all of which raise deeper issues of representation in an essentially subjective discipline. Greater attention is therefore given to issues of validity and the complexity and layering of voices, and to the relationship between the researcher and the people in the research setting. Throughout there is a general tightening and updating of the text, and the adding of new textual examples of researchers' writing.

The overall focus continues to be on how the principles of doing qualitative research are realized in the structure, conventions and language of the written study, while addressing the inevitably difficult task of squeezing the rich experience of the shifting realities of social life into a written product that demonstrates scientific rigour. Part of the fascination with qualitative research is that experienced researchers continue to revisit and struggle with the same problems that preoccupy those who are starting out. They require a postmodern awareness of who the people are that we are daring to research, who we are to be researchers, and on what basis we can begin to understand what is going on between us. And indeed they are not unlike the problems of how to make sense and to communicate that face all of us in everyday life. Mastery is not immediate.

A book on qualitative research cannot be a simple manual. The content is designed in such a way that the first part of each chapter is more accessible for novice researchers, with simple advice about where to begin and how to proceed, supported by discussion questions at the end of the book. For the experienced researcher, each chapter then moves rapidly to an interrogation of more problematic issues concerning the social, cultural and political complexities which every step involves. It is with the novice in mind that I look at the very first steps of starting a research project in Chapter 2 – but not until some of the basic principles of what research is and how it is ideologically situated are mapped out in Chapter 1. At the same time, the experienced researcher can revisit the basics of her craft, and then find the deeper discussions in which they are embedded. The book maintains this duality of depth by being both technical and academic. It is technical in the way it looks at the close detail of how qualitative research writing is constructed, from the use of specific words and phrases to the way in which texts are planned and organized. It is academic in the way it makes reference to the broader discussion. The novice too needs to be aware of the broader perspective in order to gain a sociological imagination of what she is doing.

A variety of audiences are addressed: undergraduate and master's students who are writing anything from very short assignments to dissertations; doctoral students who are writing lengthy theses; colleague professionals and academics who are writing papers for publication – all relating to issues that arise in tutorials, in qualitative research classes, in doctoral vivas, in discussion with colleagues, and in the recurring struggles we all face in the writing of assignments, dissertations, theses or research papers. Throughout is the conviction that clarity in the composition of the written product means clarity in thinking, and that writing must be in ongoing dialogue with the research itself.

A second important element in the book is my own vision of what qualitative research should be, and how it can be realized in writing. In Chapter 1 I align myself with a postmodern approach, which combines critical, constructivist and feminist principles. However, while shunning the more naïve expectations of postpositivist naturalism, that we can simply describe things as they are by 'being there', I maintain that the researcher does not have to fall into the abyss of cultural relativism. She can maintain rigour through careful articulation of who she is, what she has done, and how this has responded to the particular exigencies of the cultural setting. Writing thus becomes the basis for scientific accountability. Showing the workings of the research in this way is a major focus of Chapter 3 and continues as a theme throughout. Chapters 4 and 5 contain a detailed discussion of how the researcher as writer articulates her data and then uses it as the basis for argument and discussion within the guiding principle of thick description.

Unlike many of the commentators in this area, I have written this book as an applied linguist. I look at the writing of qualitative research as an artefact of language in society. My concern is with academic writing as a discourse that is culturally and ideologically located. In Chapter 6 I emphasize how the writer becomes a player in this discourse. I present her as someone who must simultaneously participate in and creatively assert her own space and presence in this discourse, making it work for her and perhaps changing it as she goes. Discourse is a living social force which can be dangerously predatory and imperialistic, and at the same time malleable. Again, it is impossible to suggest how to write qualitative research without increasing the researcher's awareness of the ideological struggle she is getting herself into.

As someone who has spent much of his career in international language education, which has involved interaction between the constructs of Western English and other people's societies, I bring with me a preoccupation with intercultural matters. My own and my students' research is mainly concerned with the question of linguistic and cultural imperialisms. From this comes a more general concern with how we all perceive, and can so easily reduce, the 'foreign' Other through culturally chauvinistic description, whether in other societies or in our own. I see the role of the researcher, within a cultural space that belongs to people who are not researchers, very much in these terms. My concern with the presentation of the person of the researcher as writer in Chapter 6 is balanced with an analysis, in Chapters 7 and 8, of how she must struggle with the realities of the people she encounters within the boundaries of a research project she has constructed.

The book is itself based on qualitative data. From Chapter 2 onwards I base my discussion of how qualitative researchers write on a corpus of around 20 examples of good writing which are listed in the section 'Written Studies Used as Examples' preceding the References. These include undergraduate student assignments, master's dissertations, published papers and doctoral theses. Partly because so much of what is written elsewhere in the area comes from education, but also because there is an increasing interest in qualitative research from other academic and vocational areas, I have made a very conscious decision to reduce my use of education examples as far as I can. The corpus thus includes written studies in sports science, health care, fine art, media and women's studies. However, because I felt it important to use the work of my own students or colleagues, and indeed my own, which gave me the added insight of knowing the researchers and the issues with which they struggled, several of the works are in international language education. I was able to interview some of the writers to get further background to why they did what they did. To enhance representativeness of the field, the corpus also includes work from German, Turkish, Swedish, Cypriot, Japanese, Chinese, Greek, Iranian and Pakistani, as well as US and British researchers. All of this is written in English, either because it is published in international, English-medium journals or books, or because it is written for assessment in English-medium universities. I make no attempt to address qualitative research beyond the domain of an English-speaking world.

It is not my intention to present the corpus as a random sample of qualitative writing. I have purposely chosen good examples; but at the same time I have followed the principles of submission and emergence, which I introduce in Chapter 7, and allowed the corpus to speak to me in such a way that a productive dialogue was set up. What I found in the corpus was not always what I expected, and it served to change significantly many of the ideas I had on how qualitative research writing is actually done. My analysis of the examples is not however 'critical' in the sense that I do not get into a critique of their academic content. There are only two cases, in Chapter 8, where I include real examples of what I consider 'culturist' writing, as something to avoid; I take one from my own writing, and keep the other anonymous.

On a technical note, where I refer to people in the abstract, rather than using politically correct devices such as 'he/she', I always use the female, and then the male where it allows convenient distinction. This break from the default discourse of placing male first falls within the principle of qualitative research to problematize everything (cf. Clark and Ivanič 1997: 171, citing Cameron). My citations from interviews with researchers are virtually verbatim – i.e. edited for coherence. Hesitations, sequences on other subjects and my own words are not included.

I use the word 'data' as an uncountable noun – e.g. 'data is' instead of 'data are'. I use the uncountable form because to me it signifies a *body of experience*. This is a conceptual break from quantitative research which sees data as a number of items.

Acknowledgements

· · · · · · · ·

I wish to acknowledge the researchers whose work has made up the corpus of written studies from which I take my examples, who are listed separately in the bibliography, some of whom also agreed to be interviewed. I am also especially indebted to the research students who attended my Thursday lunchtime discussion meetings, and the research seminars in Mexico City and Guanajuato over the last six years, and to those who attended the qualitative research seminars at Eötvös Lóránd University, Budapest, and to colleagues in Education, Sport Science, Media, Fine Art, Health and Language Studies at Canterbury, all of whom have helped me to interrogate the boundaries of what can be done in qualitative research.

CHAPTER ONE

Approaching Qualitative Research

Within the broad context of doing qualitative research, about which much has been written, I shall focus quite a lot on writing. This is as an equally problematic area for novice and experienced researchers alike; and there is much to be learnt about the process of doing research by keeping the issue of writing in mind. In this chapter I will begin with the broader context. I am establishing a state of affairs which will be referred to in the discussion of examples of writing from Chapter 2 onwards. From the start I take the view that there is the potential for considerable rigour and discipline in qualitative research, that there *is* science within its complex nature, but that this rigour largely resides in the way in which the research is expressed in writing. I shall argue that qualitative research presents a statement about reality and social life that has to be continually argued and reaffirmed. It is this need for constant articulation that makes writing as important as other aspects of doing the research.

I shall begin with a standard comparison between qualitative and quantitative research, and then move on to the way in which qualitative research has to be carefully managed as a social activity which is as ideological and complex as those it studies. Finally, in a brief tour of schools and approaches, I shall locate the writing task as presented in this book. A point of terminology: in the ensuing chapters I shall base my discussion of writing in qualitative research around a corpus of examples of writing. They range from short undergraduate assignments to master's and doctoral dissertations and theses to published papers. For the sake of clarity, when I talk generally about the written product of research, I shall refer to all of these types of writing collectively as 'the written study'.

Qualitative and quantitative

It is fairly standard to introduce qualitative research by distinguishing it from quantitative research. This is an unadventurous way to begin, but necessary because, when asked 'What is research?' most people refer to the more familiar, traditional quantitative research. Also, it is often argued that a major binding feature of qualitative research is its opposition to positivism, the philosophical basis for quantitative research. There needs however to be note of caution with regard to these distinctions, here and throughout the book. Social research is a complex area, and attempts to divide it into hard categories will always suffer from oversimplification. Qualitative research will always involve quantitative elements and vice versa.

Surveys and experiments

Quantitative research concerns counting. A straightforward example might be:

EXAMPLE 1.1   CAR SURVEY

To find out the *proportion* of Ford cars to Peugeots in a particular country. This would entail counting the number of each. If it is not possible to find every single occurrence, a sample may be taken. Statistical analysis tells us both how many, or what percentage of each, and how valid the sample is in representing the whole.

The next example is not quite so straightforward:

EXAMPLE 1.2   CAR EXPERIMENT

To test the *hypothesis* that more Ford cars will be bought if prospective first-time buyers are exposed to advertising that says they are safer. A sample of first-time buyers is exposed to the advertising; another sample is not; and the degree to which each group buys Fords is measured. A variety of techniques are employed to control variables to reduce contamination. For example, the age and social class of the subjects are kept constant.

Here we can see that a lot of effort is made to reduce the effect of variables other than that of exposure to advertising. The overall aim is to control so that the experiment can be replicated with different groups to test the hypothesis time and time again. However, this will always be difficult. The people taking part in the research would need to be isolated from all other influences on their attitudes to cars, influences that nowadays pervade every aspect of society, if contamination is to be totally prevented.

At first sight, the next example seems as straightforward as the car survey in Example 1.1:

EXAMPLE 1.3   EYES SURVEY

To calculate the proportion of brown to blue eyes within a particular nationality. The occurrence of each is counted within a statistically valid sample.

However, on reflection, the definition of 'blue' and 'brown' is not as straightforward as the definition of 'Ford' and 'Peugeot', which have clear proofs of manufacture to distinguish them. Indeed, in different places and among different types of people, the meaning of and therefore distinction between 'brown', 'blue' and other colours of eyes may vary according to language and social values. Colour when related to human appearance is not neutral. This is certainly true of skin colour, which carries racial connotation for many people and is attributed poetic value by others. 'Blond' hair and 'blue' eyes are not neutral phrases for many people as they relate to images of popular beauty that resonate beyond simple physical descriptions. An apparently simple survey is therefore made complex and less reliable by the social qualities attributed to definitions of colour. The next example addresses this issue by trying to find out what these qualities are:

EXAMPLE 1.4   EYES QUESTIONNAIRE

Within the population in Example 1.3 to find out what people mean by, and what their attitudes are to 'brown' and 'blue', and what sort of social values underlie these meanings and attitudes.

There are well-known problems with questionnaires – how the mode of question influences the mood of response; how far people tell the 'truth'; how far they understand the question anyway; how far the social impact of a questionnaire will influence perception. Bell (1993: 58) skilfully guides us through the potential minefield of questionnaires, looking at issues such as memory, leading questions and presentation. Again, the aim is to control variables as much as possible. The difficulties increase as researchers get into closer contact with the people they are researching, in interviews, or when questionnaires are delivered face-to-face. The following example from my own experience confirms this:

EXAMPLE 1.5   EGYPTIAN INTERVIEW

I was sitting in an Egyptian university faculty common room listening to a lecturer answering survey questions about the timetable in her department. The American interviewer was going through the questions with her, perhaps to ensure good researcher–subject relations. Later on the lecturer 'confided in me that what she had told him bore little relation to reality, but that she had not wished to disappoint him by telling him that she could not answer most of the questions'. This was part of a nation-wide survey carried out by a US curriculum agency, upon which policy decisions in educational aid were based.

I do not think that the lecturer felt that she was 'lying'. I feel that she was sincere in her response to what she considered a social commitment to being polite which outweighed the fact that she did not have all the information the researcher wanted. On the other hand, in this particular context educational resources were scarce; and she probably did not wish to reveal to this outsider that the official course timetable could never be maintained because lecturers spent all their time travelling by bus from the capital (Holliday 1992a: 409). This is only my interpretation of her behaviour. The point I wish to make is that people's reasons for responding in the ways they do to questionnaires and interviews can be both far from what the researcher expects and mysterious.

For readers not from that part of the world, the Egyptian setting of Example 1.5 might imply 'foreign' society and therefore 'exotic' behaviour. The strangeness it invokes lends credence to the notions that things may not be as they seem and that there is a mysterious element in human behaviour. It is, however, a major tenet of qualitative research that all scenarios, even the most familiar, should be seen as strange, with layers of mystery that are always beyond the control of the researcher, which need always to be discovered. To avoid cultural chauvinism, or culturism, which I shall talk about in Chapter 8, we must apply the discipline of seeing all societies and settings, including our own, as equally strange and complex. Indeed, observing what the Egyptian lecturer in the example says may make a British researcher begin to realize that it is not so different to what might happen in her own university when reporting to external quality assurance agencies.

The qualitative areas of social life

I have moved quite a distance from the quantitative Example 1.4 to Example 1.5, which is in effect qualitative data in embryo, in that it describes actions within a specific setting and invites rather than tries to control the possibility of a rich array of variables. Example 1.5 presents research in terms of human relationships and invokes the need to discover as much about how research subjects feel about the information they provide as about the information itself. Indeed, the people about whom the research is carried out are less 'subjects' than just people who happen to be in the research setting. (See my discussion of 'subjects' and 'participants' in Chapters 7 and 8.)

It is these qualitative areas in social life – the backgrounds, interests and broader social perceptions that defy quantitative research – that qualitative research addresses. Qualitative research does not pretend to solve the problems of quantitative research, but does not see them as constraints. Rather than finding ways to reduce the effect of uncontrollable social variables, it investigates them directly. So examples of qualitative research about brown and blue eyes and Ford car buying might be:

EXAMPLE 1.6   EYES STUDY

An exploration of what people mean by, and what their attitudes are to 'brown' and 'blue' eye colour, and of what sort of social values underlie these meanings and attitudes. The residents of three households of different classes and ethnicity in a provincial town are studied. They are interviewed in groups on topics related to human attractiveness as displayed in their daily life, in advertising and in the media. The interviews are open-ended, allowing relevant topics and themes to be developed. They are followed up with further interviews to which the residents are invited to bring photographs of family and friends, advertising and the media as props, and with observation of interaction in settings that emerge as significant, e.g. wedding parties.

EXAMPLE 1.7   CAR STUDY

An exploration of attitudes to Ford car adverts. An advert is played on video in three public houses frequented by members of the target first-time buyer group, and their comments recorded. This is followed up with group interviews which explore topics arising from the comments. The public houses are revisited one year later and the same people are interviewed about which cars they bought and what this means to them.

The whole orientation of these two examples of qualitative research is quite different to that of the quantitative examples. Rather than controlling variables, these *studies* are open-ended and set up research opportunities designed to lead the researcher into unforeseen areas of discovery within the lives of the people she is investigating. Also, they look deeply into behaviour within specific social settings rather than at broad populations (Chapter 2). It also becomes apparent that the written study for qualitative research must account for how the research steps interact with the individual setting.

These differences, summarized in Table 1.1, comprise two paradigms of research. By 'paradigm' I mean a whole way of thinking about something. Indeed, by suggesting two paradigms, I am suggesting that quantitative and qualitative research do represent very different ways of thinking about the world.

The beliefs listed in the table hint at the philosophy underlying each paradigm. The belief in quantitative research that reality can be mastered by the right research

Table 1.1 Two paradigms

Quantitative research	Qualitative research
Activities	**Activities**
Counts occurrences across a large population	Looks deep into the quality of social life
Uses statistics and replicability to validate generalization from survey samples and experiments	Locates the study within particular settings which: provide opportunities for exploring all possible social variables; and set manageable boundaries
Attempts to reduce contaminating social variables	Initial foray into the social setting leads to further, more informed exploration as themes and focuses emerge
Beliefs	**Beliefs**
Conviction about what it is important to look for	Conviction that what it is important to look for will emerge
Confidence in established research instruments	Confidence in an ability to devise research procedures to fit the situation and the nature of the people in it, as they are revealed
Reality is not so problematic if the research instruments are adequate; and conclusive results are feasible	Reality contains mysteries to which the researcher must submit, and can do no more than interpret
Steps	**Steps**
First decide the research focus (e.g. testing a specific hypothesis)	Decide the subject is interesting (e.g. in its own right, or because it represents an area of interest)
Then devise and pilot research instruments (e.g. survey questionnaire or experiment)	Go into the field to see what is going on
Then go into the field	Let focus and themes emerge
	Devise research instruments during process (e.g. observation or interview)
Rigour	**Rigour**
Disciplined application of established rules for statistics, experiment and survey design	Principled development of research strategy to suit the scenario being studied as it is revealed

instruments (Table 1.1) is *normative*. It maintains that there is a normality that we can fathom and understand, and master by statistics and experiment. The universe is organized in such a way that can become clear to scientists. It therefore maintains that with the correct use of technique, it is possible to reveal *objective facts*. The qualitative belief that the realities of the research setting and the people in it are mysterious and can only be superficially touched by research which tries to make sense (Table 1.1) is *interpretive*. It maintains that we can explore, catch glimpses, illuminate and then try to interpret bits of reality. Interpretation is as far as we can go. This places less of a burden of proof on qualitative research, which instead builds gradual pictures. The pictures are themselves only interpretations – approximations – basic attempts to represent what is in fact a much more complex reality – paintings that represent our own impressions, rather than photographs of what is 'really' there. They are created by collecting a number of instances of social life. In the eyes study in Example 1.6, the whole research enterprise is designed around researchable instances – groups talking about human attractiveness – which in themselves point to further instances – groups referring to artefacts they bring with them. The same is true of Example 1.7.

There is however the very problematic burden of how to manage *subjectivity* in such a way that scientific rigour is preserved, and also how to account for this management in the written study.

Managing subjectivity

Qualitative research is increasing in use in a wide range of academic and professional areas. It develops from aspects of anthropology and sociology and represents a broad view that to understand human affairs it is insufficient to rely on quantitative survey and statistics, and necessary instead to delve deep into the subjective qualities that govern behaviour. One reason for this growth may be that it is becoming apparent to everyone that the statistical quantitative statements of opinion polls, government, opposition and 'independent' scientific reports, and what 'research has shown', can tell many quite different stories and be at the mercy of political 'spin'. Characteristic of this realization of the limitations of prescribed method is the following extract from educational research:

> [A] careful, objective, step-by-step model of the research process is actually a fraud and ... within natural science as well as social science, the standard way in which research methods are taught and real research is often written up for publication perpetuates what is in fact a myth of objectivity. (Walford 1991: 1 citing Medawar)

Instead, what actually happens is very different to the apparently regular methods that are reported. Day-to-day research comprises shortcuts, hunches, serendipity and opportunism. Walford's account of Watson's research into DNA reveals how his findings developed from 'the lucky turns of events, the guesswork, the rivalries between researchers and personal involvement and compromise' (1991: 1). Walford states that qualitative researchers have also contributed to an illusion of objectivity in previous years by making their procedures appear more straightforward than they really are. Research needs to be accompanied by accounts of how it was really done (1991: 2). His collection of papers is a breakthrough in that it involves researchers revisiting previous projects to reveal how they negotiated complex procedures to deal with the 'messy' reality of the scenarios being studied. It is a celebration of the way in which qualitative research works through ongoing dialogue with different social worlds. This is relevant to the issue of writing because, as a result of this breakthrough, qualitative researchers are increasingly expected to come out and tell it as it really happened.

Developing rigour through writing

As Table 1.1. shows, while the prescribed steps of quantitative research make it difficult to respond to uncontrolled variables, qualitative research invites the unexpected. Decisions about research instruments are made in gradual response to the nature of the social setting being investigated as its nature is revealed. This means that every qualitative research design will be different. Whereas the rigour in quantitative research is in the disciplined application of prescribed rules for instrument design, the rigour in qualitative research is in the principled development of strategy to suit the scenario being studied.

Whereas in quantitative research the source of validity is known, qualitative research has to *show its workings* every single time (Chapter 3). This concept of 'showing one's workings' reminds me of doing maths problems at school. One was never allowed just to give the right answer, which was not considered valid unless the steps taken to get to it were very clearly and properly laid out. Showing the method one had used was the proof that the answer had not been copied from the key at the back of the book or got from someone else.

Table 1.2 shows what sorts of things the researcher in each paradigm needs to tell the reader of the written study. Where the quantitative researcher needs to report details of established procedure, the right-hand column shows that the qualitative researcher needs to justify every move – demonstrating particularly how the overall strategy is appropriate to the social setting and the researcher–subject relationships within it, and the steps taken for thorough engagement.

Judicious balance

This concern with how far research strategies are appropriate to the setting and the people in it will be a recurring theme throughout this book. For the moment it is necessary to talk briefly about the nature of the balance this demands.

There are two sides to qualitative research. To meet the exigencies of the social situation being studied, freedom is needed to explore creatively the best way to approach the scenario. In the eyes study in Example 1.6 there are many possible ways to go forward. On the other hand, the researcher must be prepared to account carefully for every move made. These two sides represent the judicious balance between *taking the opportunity* to encounter the research setting while *maintaining the principles* of social science.

Consider the car study in Example 1.7. The writer of this research would have to explain in the written study why *three* public houses were visited, and why a *particular* three. It may be that the three were selected not just because of the clientele, but also because the researcher had access to and a relationship with them which would enable her to play videos without undue disruption. This is *opportunism*; but the *principle* of maintaining appropriate relations with people in the research setting is fulfilled. Then comes the question, why show the videos in pubs anyway? Here the researcher needs to explain the principles behind exposing the people in the research setting to the videos when they are in a familiar setting that is also relevant to the discussion of car buying.

Table 1.2   Sources of validity

Quantitative research	Qualitative research
Need to tell the reader of the research:	Need to tell the reader of the research the rationale for:
Details of the population (in samples)	*Choice of social setting:* how it represented the research topic in its role in society, how feasible and substantial it was (e.g. access, duration, depth, breadth)
What sort of questions (in survey questionnaires)	*Choice of research activities:* how they suited the social setting, how they were appropriate to researcher–subject relationships, how they formed coherent strategy
Which statistics The composition of groups (in experiments)	*Choice of themes and focuses:* how they emerged, why they are significant, how far they are representative of the social setting
Which variables are being included and excluded	
What groups are exposed to in experiments	*Dedication to and thoroughness of fieldwork:* how and to what extent the field was engaged with (e.g. strategies for 'being there'), how data was recorded and catalogued
	Overall need to articulate a judicious balance between opportunism and principle

Important data here could be observed behaviour while watching the video. On the other hand, there might be no opportunity to show the video to so many people in any other location. There is also the question of on what basis video watching was followed with interviews, and why group interviews. It would not be sufficient to say that group interviews are established research tools per se. Nothing is done in qualitative research simply because it 'is done'. The researcher would need to demonstrate how the data collected from the video stage led her to interviews of a particular type and content. Bailey et al., talking about the role of qualitative research in social geography, make the point that 'there is a need for most researchers to be more explicit about their research processes: to offer a rationale and further detail on issues such as respondent selection, key changes in research direction and analytical procedures' (1999: 169, citing Baxter and Eyles). This *accountability* for opportunities taken is also demonstrated in the *protocols* of research writing which govern the syntax of referencing and citing evidence (Chapters 3 and 5), and making appropriate claims (Chapter 8).

Research as social action

There are several issues involved in the balance between creative opportunity and maintaining scientific principle: (a) creative exploration makes qualitative research akin to the research we all do in everyday life; (b) as in the rest of everyday life, researchers, like other people, are ideologically motivated; (c) approaching the research setting appropriately involves interaction between the culture of the setting and the culture of research; (d) accounting for the research strategy, to demonstrate how the judicious balance is maintained, requires careful articulation which resides in the conventions of research language; (e) all in all, qualitative research is learning culture. I shall look at these issues in turn. Taken together they support the notion that research, like many other aspects of professional and private life, is part of social action. As Cameron et al. comment, 'researchers cannot help being socially located persons' (1992: 5). By 'socially located' they mean part and parcel of all the influences and interests of society. Researchers cannot put themselves above other people. They must struggle as people to interact with people. Thus, the written study also becomes an account of personal struggle to make sense of complex human situations within which the researcher herself often becomes implicated.

Research and everyday life

In many ways qualitative research is what we all do in everyday life. We have continually to solve problems about how we should behave with other people in a wide range of settings. To do this we need to research not only how others behave but also how we should behave with them. Schutz (1964) characterizes this natural research as what happens when a 'stranger' approaches a social group which she wishes to join or to deal with. It might be taking a new job or dealing with car mechanics for the first time and having to learn new rules of behaviour. This would involve analysing behaviour and language, working out how and when to be formal or informal, learning new technical terms, specialist turns of phrase, what constitutes humour, when to be serious and when not – attitudes, values, relative status. An instance of this is learning the culture of the common room in the institution where I currently work.

EXAMPLE 1.8   COMMON ROOM

I first encountered my colleagues as a group in the common room at coffee time. Although they were my compatriots, of a similar class and educational background, and although I had worked in similar institutions before, there were cultural features peculiar to this particular setting which I needed to observe. For example, colleagues came and went without greetings or leave-taking. It seemed understood on leaving that there was a pressing work engagement which needed no explanation. Also, talk about work had to be announced first. Much of this could not be learnt just by watching. It was necessary to watch for clues, form *hypotheses* – calculated guesses – about appropriate behaviour, then try things out, observe the result, then confirm, adapt or reject the hypothesis.

Another true case I shall always remember because of the persistence and courage of the person involved is as follows:

EXAMPLE 1.9   RESTAURANT

A young Egyptian woman was living in the capital for the first time. She had never been to a restaurant before. In order to work out how to do this, she first watched customers coming and going from across the street. As she gained confidence she went and stood just inside the door of the restaurant, which was sufficiently large and crowded for her not to be noticed. Here she watched and listened to how customers sat down and ordered. Eventually she learnt enough to sit down and order herself – to try out the hypotheses she had formulated as a result of her observations.

This example from Egypt shows a particularly varied society in which movement from province to capital precipitates startling cultural difference and demonstrates the acuteness of the need for personal research.

It can be appreciated that the 'interpretive practice' implicit in qualitative research is the 'work of everyday life' and involves 'the constellation of procedures, conditions, and resources through which reality is apprehended, understood, organized, and represented' (Gubrium and Holstein 1997: 114). We have to interpret the behaviour of others, and do qualitative research whenever we interact with them.

A significant factor here is what the researcher brings to the situation. Even in Example 1.9, where there was no prior experience of restaurants, the researcher brought with her a wealth of social knowledge from her previous experience of how people behave in all institutional situations. She has a knowledge of how culture works which she can apply to any setting. Lankshear et al. explain that 'whatever particular set of institutions and social relations a given human being is born into, s/he is thereby born into a cultural milieu, a discursive universe' which provides 'resources' with which 'to engage in meaning-making activity' (1997: 18, 19). In other words, everyone has an innate ability to research culture, the resources for which are already present in existing cultural experience.

Discovering and doing culture

To understand the nature of this innate cultural competence and how the researcher is as involved in culture making as anyone else, it is necessary to explore for a moment what is meant by 'culture' – which is a difficult task because there are many ways of looking at it. In my view of qualitative research, 'culture' does not relate to prescribed or 'essentialized' ethnic, national and international features (Holliday 1999). This perhaps popular view of 'culture' is as a countable noun referring to a physically bounded entity – 'this culture', 'that culture', 'Chinese culture'. Thus, '*a* culture' is like '*a* sea' or '*a* water'. It refers to physically bounded entities such as river X, Y ocean or Z sea. These are socially constructed entities that exist only in the way in which people operationally (politically, economically, scientifically) divide up the world. Qualitative research must avoid this prescriptive view of culture because it implies how things are before the research begins and does not allow meaning to emerge. I shall look at this issue in more detail, within the context of reducing people in the research setting to prescribed stereotypes, in Chapter 8.

Within an interpretive paradigm, a more minimal, small, operational notion of culture allows the differentiating characteristics of groups to be *discovered* rather than presumed. Here, 'culture' is an uncountable noun that refers to cohesive behaviour as a basic feature of the human condition – 'this is an example of cultural behaviour'. It is rather like 'water', which flows, drips, collects in pools and rivers, can evaporate and freeze. It is more like a molecular state than a political construct. As such, it exists as a social fact in that it is there wherever there are people coming together in groups. Qualitative researchers can nevertheless speak of 'a culture', but only in the sense of *the* specific piece of society they have chosen to draw boundaries around for the sake of their research. 'Culture' therefore refers to the composite of cohesive behaviour within any social grouping from a neighbourhood to a work group (Beales et al. 1967: 8). When a researcher looks at an unfamiliar social grouping, it can be said to have 'a culture' when there is a discernible set of behaviours and understandings connected with group cohesion.

Culture in this sense is a dynamic, ongoing group process which operates in changing circumstances to enable group members to make sense of and operate meaningfully within those circumstances. According to Beales et al., 'the outstanding characteristic of a cultural system is that it is in process; it moves' (1967: 5). It is 'the sum total of all the processes, happenings, or activities in which a given set or several sets of people habitually engage' (1967: 9). As an uncountable qualitative aspect of group life, culture constitutes a social 'tool-kit' which emerges to 'solve problems' when required (Crane 1994: 11) in a continually shifting milieu. It is this tool kit which the researcher also uses, which is brought to the common room and the restaurant in Examples 1.8 and 1.9. Culture making and culture research are integrated in the same competence; and indeed, as soon as the Egyptian woman approaches the restaurant, she is also contributing to its culture as it adapts, perhaps only very slightly, to her presence. I shall look at this latter issue in Chapter 7.

The researcher approaching the new cultural setting, whether a group of colleagues or a first restaurant, has as much affinity with it as the people already there. She may be a 'stranger' for a while, but will gradually be seduced into all the 'thinking-as-usual' that makes them feel secure. There is a danger here for the qualitative researcher. She has to work hard to discipline herself to capture the essence of being a stranger at the moment when everything is noticed and seems strange, before the new culture being approached becomes too familiar. She has to learn how to deal with how it might change because of her presence. Schutz conceives a particular methodology in the stranger's attempts to proceed without sharing the 'thinking-as-usual' ability of the members of the new group, thus seeing what is behind the cultural symbols for behaviour which have become routine and tacit in the group. The stranger 'becomes essentially the [woman or] man who has to place in question nearly everything that seems unquestionable to the members of the approached group' (Schutz 1964: 96).

A basic difference between everyday qualitative research and scientific qualitative research is that the researcher must take on the discipline of *making the familiar strange*. Even where the research scenario is familiar, the researcher must find ways of recovering the stranger position. This is central to qualitative research; its impact on how the researcher applied caution in writing will be addressed in Chapter 8. As well as having implications for the way in which the researcher must discipline her perceptions, this also has implications for the written study, where she must take care to communicate to the reader the sense of strangeness of what she has seen. This involves a highly strategized articulation of carefully selected data (see Chapters 4 and 5).

Research as ideological practice

Lankshear et al. link the natural learning and doing of culture with the acquiring of social literacy, showing the connection between cultural competence and discourse:

> How do human beings become capable of classifying, conceptualizing, and generally making sense and meaning out of their experiencing? The short answer here is that they *learn* to do so through sociocultural process which initiates them into, or apprentices them to (what have been called) 'forms of life', 'domains of social practice', or 'Discourses'. (Lankshear et al. 1997: 22, their emphasis)

Whereas the common notion of 'discourse' is of 'just stretches of language'. Here, it is defined as 'a way of "being together in the world"':

> Social groups organize their lives around concepts, purposes, values, beliefs, ideals, theories, notions of reality, and the like. Through Discourse human life is organized into shape and form which can be recognized and understood – it can be 'read' as having 'meaning' – by ourselves and by others. (Gee 1997: xv)

Fairclough (1995: 135) similarly refers to discourse as 'language use conceived as social practice'. I refer to the role that discourse plays in culture because, when the researcher approaches the new culture, she brings with her residues of her own cultural background. Discourse is a major physical artefact of culture which carries much of its power (Holliday 1999: 251). The type of power I am concerned with here is that which connects with ideology, not necessarily in the sense of political movements such as Marxism or fascism. It can be any 'systematic body of ideas organized from a particular point of view' (Kress and Hodge 1979). Ideology can thus be present in everyday '"common sense" assumptions' that certain states of affairs or being, often represented by 'relations of power', are 'natural' (Fairclough 1989: 2). The power that discourse can have in carrying this type of ideology is experienced whenever one finds oneself with a group of people who are indulging in sexist language. Their discourse, or way of talking, forces one to choose between joining or remaining an outsider and eventually being excluded from the group. The discourse and the ideology it carries is a basic tool in enforcing the boundaries of the small culture to which the speakers belong.

Within the context of qualitative research, the ideology that is particularly relevant is that of the scientific community. I have already referred to the way in which political 'spin' can influence research and how scientific method can never claim full objectivity. It is also becoming understood in a postmodern world that how science, along with other technologies, is done depends very much on the ideology of the people who do it (Lankshear et al. 1997: 2). Within social science, Kuhn's (1970) treatise on how the internal politics, culture and ideology of a scientific community can influence the development of scientific thinking has had a major impact. Kuhn helped establish the notion that science is characterized by a series of paradigms which display 'universally recognized scientific achievements that *for a time* provide model problems and solutions' to a scientific community of practitioners (1970: viii, my emphasis). This community bases its reputations, standards, hierarchies and modes of work on the concepts produced by the paradigm – until eventually an 'anomaly' emerges and brings about a 'crisis' that precipitates revolution. Then a new paradigm is formed, often completely overturning established structures. In this way, the changing paradigms of science can be likened to other forms of social and indeed cultural change (e.g. Schutz 1964: 96).

The postmodern recognition of the deeper ideological complexities embedded in the discourses of social life gives qualitative research a major impetus. This throws doubt on whether any method or theory can be privileged over another (Denzin and Lincoln 2000b: 3, citing Richardson). A very important irony is, however, that qualitative research must recognize the ideology which is embedded in its *own* discourse, method and theories. Qualitative researchers spin their own constructions of reality through their own ways of talking about it. Gubrium and Holstein describe these discourses or areas of '*method talk* as knowledge factories – places where the work of knowledge construction takes place' (1997: 3, my emphasis). Their tour of qualitative research thus becomes its own 'sociology of knowledge' (1997: 5).

That qualitative research is itself dangerous ideological practice is now well understood. There has been considerable effort to liberate it from the sins of nineteenth-century anthropology, where simplistic cultural definitions of subject peoples were used to justify European colonization and 'an objective way of representing the dark-skinned Other to the White world' (Denzin and Lincoln 2005: 1; also Morawska and Spohn 1994; Comaroff and Comaroff 1992; Asad 1973; Nzimiro 1979; Sangari 1994; Sarangi 1995). 'Conventional anthropology allowed "the power of topography to conceal successfully the topography of power"' (Schudson 1994: 37, citing Gupta and Ferguson). Kabbani thus connects 'the forging of racial stereotypes and the confirmation of the notions of savagery' as 'vital to the colonialist world view' (1986: 4). 'It was the colonial cataloguing of goods; the anchoring of imperial possessions into discourse' (1986: 62). Chapter 7 of this book deals with how the discourse of the researcher can dominate the research setting, and Chapter 8 with how the cultural behaviour of people in the research setting can be reduced and 'othered'. A fascinating example of how this distortion could happen is reminiscent of the complex research relationships I describe in Chapter 7. There is evidence that 'local' researchers who were employed by British gazetteers to collect data, presumably to ensure its authenticity, produced the information they believed the British wanted rather than 'true' accounts of what was really happening (Barua 1996).

Research, language and writing

It becomes clear from this tour of qualitative research as social action that the writing of qualitative research is not going to be an easy task. Looking again at the right-hand column of Table 1.2, one can now see that showing one's workings, being as transparent as possible about how the research is constructed in relation to the research setting, enables evaluation of its cultural and ideological appropriateness. This is not enough, though. Because the writing of the research is a product of a discourse community which cannot avoid ideology, it has to be carried out in a very self-conscious way. Atkinson asserts rightly that 'sociologists pay close attention to their own textual practices, as well as those of the people they study' (1990: 6) because:

> Texts do not simply and transparently report an independent order of reality. Rather, the texts themselves are implicated in the work of reality construction. ... There is no possibility of a neutral text. The text – the research paper or monograph, say – is just as much an artefact of convention and contrivance as is any other cultural product. (Atkinson 1990: 7)

Hence the purpose of this book – an exploration of how to write as 'simply and transparently' *as is possible* within the ideological minefield of qualitative research. The academic writing conventions of social research will thus be presented as a highly refined language and code of conduct designed to achieve this result.

Furthermore, it can be argued that the very act of interpretation within qualitative research is itself integrated with the act of writing. Denzin, largely following Lévi-Strauss's notion of 'field-worker-as-*bricoleur*', describes how 'moving from the field to the text to the reader' is central to the whole qualitative research process in which 'interpretation requires the telling of a story, or a narrative that states "things happen this way because" or "this happened, after this happened, because this happened first"' (Denzin 1994: 500). So 'the problems of writing are not different from the problems of method or fieldwork' (1994: 501, citing Clough). Denzin and Lincoln cast this as a 'crisis of representation' in which 'issues such as validity, reliability, and objectivity, previously believed settled, were once more problematic' (2005: 18).

Schools and approaches

Any venture into the literature will reveal that qualitative research is presented under a confusing array of different and variable headings. Denzin and Lincoln's (2000a) encyclopaedic *Handbook of Qualitative Research* is very useful in that it organizes the field under the macro categories of paradigms, strategies and methods. Table 1.3 broadly follows their categories. The purpose of the table is not to provide an exhaustive catalogue, but to show how some of the more commonly encountered headings relate to one another, and to provide a partial map on to which the novice can place other headings as they are encountered.

Table 1.3 Paradigms, strategies and methods

Paradigms and perspectives	Strategies of enquiry	Methods of collecting and analysing data
LARGEST ⇐ ⇐	all items usable by all items in other columns	⇨ ⇨ SMALLEST
NATURALIST QUALITATIVE **Postpositivism, realism** Reality is still quite plain to see	**Case study** study of a specific 'bounded system' – e.g. person or an institution (Stake 2005: 444)	Interviewing
Deeper social reality needs qualitative enquiry	**Ethnography** explores 'the nature of a specific social phenomenon'	Observational techniques Interpreting documents
Probable truth is supported by *extensive*, substantiated record of *real settings*	'unstructured data', 'a small number of cases', interpretation of the meanings and functions' and 'participant observation' (Atkinson and Hammersley 1994: 248)	Content analysis Semiotic analysis
Researchers must not interfere with real settings	**Ethnomethodology** 'focus on how members actually "do" social life ... the mechanisms by which they concretely construct and sustain social entities such as gender, self, or family' (Holstein and Gubrium 2005: 486)	
POSTMODERN QUALITATIVE **Critical theory, constructivism, postmodernism, feminism**	**Phenomenology** 'focus on the ways that the life world – the world every individual takes for granted – is experienced by its members'	
Reality *and* science are socially constructed	'attention to this life world is to first "bracket" it', to 'set aside belief in its reality in order to bring its apprehension into focus' (Holstein and Gubrium 2005: 485)	
Researchers are part of research settings		
Investigation must be in *reflexive*, self-critical, creative dialogue	**Grounded theory** 'theory that is grounded in data systematically gathered and analysed'	
Aims to problematize, reveal hidden realities, initiate discussions	'continuous interplay between analysis and data collection' (Strauss and Corbin 1994: 273)	
	Participatory action research 'emphasises the political aspects of knowledge production' (Reason 1994: 328)	
	'involves the individual practitioner in continually reflecting on his or her own behaviour-in-action' so that 'other members of the community do the same' (Reason 1994: 331)	

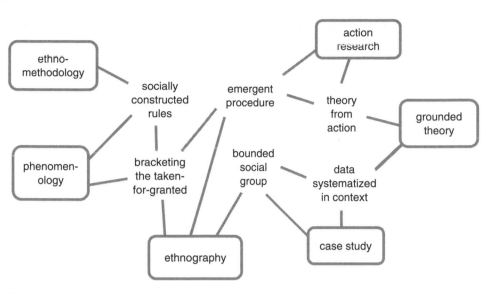

Figure 1.1   Trails of necessity

A fluid picture

Taking strategies first, Denzin and Lincoln (2000b) make it very clear that there are no tight categories. For example, you do not have to choose between case study, ethnography and grounded theory. Case studies can be ethnographic or not, and do not have to be qualitative at all. Whether or not to do a case study 'is not a methodological choice but a choice of what is to be studied'. It is 'defined by interest in an individual case, not by the methods of enquiry used' (Stake 2005: 443). Although ethnography is often associated closely with participant observation, 'it has been argued that in a sense *all* social research is a form of participant observation' (Atkinson and Hammersley 1994: 249). While focusing on ethnography, Hammersley and Atkinson (1995: 31) build on the ideas of Glaser and Strauss, usually associated with grounded theory, and talk about 'cases' as a specific phenomenon within or across social settings (1995: 41). Each of the writers cited in the table takes great pains to show the approximate nature of the areas they describe. It is also clear from Table 1.3 that there is significant overlapping and commonality, with the items in each column fully available to each other. There is a strong sense, in all the strategies of enquiry, of a movement away from 'traditional' forms of social research, of locating research within the meanings people give to their worlds, and of allowing this meaning to emerge. The term 'interpretive' appears in almost every strategy. Terms like 'method' appear at all levels.

This interplay of different strategies of enquiry is shown in Figure 1.1. Connecting them are investigatory principles which they share. It is a little bit like looking out over the same terrain from different mountain tops. In many ways, each strategy necessitates bringing others with it. They could be related in different ways; and other areas and principles could be added to the figure. It is noticeable that among the investigatory principles there is a definite coherence of approach – perhaps more pragmatic towards the right of the picture and more philosophical towards the left. This is only a tendency. An exception is where phenomenology has been transmuted into a tightly methodical pragmatism in some professionally oriented research, for example in some health studies. I would place my own personal approach towards the centre of the field, looking more from the vantage point of ethnography.

The division between paradigms and perspectives (Table 1.3, column 1) is slightly more critical, because they do involve very different attitudes to qualitative research. I have distinguished two major paradigms, *naturalist or postpositivist,* and *postmodern.* I use the latter term in the same way as Guba and Lincoln (2005) to incorporate a wide range of critical and constructivist approaches.

Naturalism

Naturalism, or postpositivism, is a more 'traditional' paradigm in qualitative research, much closer to positivism, in that reality is seen as relatively straightforward (Table 1.3). In many ways, 'positivist and postpositivist traditions linger like a long shadow over the qualitative research project' (Denzin and Lincoln 2005: 11). The research setting is a physical, geographical 'place', which the researcher can describe simply by 'being there' long enough and ensuring 'authenticity' by focusing on what 'local characters' say in interview, personal accounts and conversation. The hardest form of data thus becomes verbatim transcripts of local people's actual words (Gubrium and Holstein 1997: 19–33). As with positivism, there is much concern with representative sampling and substantiation. Although the deeper social world is not quantifiable, its 'real' nature can be established with sufficient weight of description. Substantiation is gained via minimal researcher interference and bias – e.g. through objective coding of verbatim accounts and an unobtrusive 'fly on the wall' approach. Hence, written studies tend to minimize the authorial presence of the researcher.

In naturalism, the researcher gets fully involved in the setting for a sustained period. She continues in the field until representativeness and exhaustiveness are confirmed, i.e. when the same features begin to emerge again and again. The data thus needs to be collected until it tells nothing new, as evidence that there is maximum coverage and that nothing has been overlooked. Thus, 'in its most characteristic form it involves the ethnographer participating, overtly or covertly, in people's daily lives for an extended period of time, watching what happens, listening to what is said, asking questions' (Hammersley and Atkinson 1995: 1). This is the view from the heartland of anthropology, where the tradition is to study whole geographic neighbourhoods and communities (Gubrium and Holstein 1997: 19). Hence, written studies tend to be exhaustive accounts.

Although it presents a critique of the 'realist-positivist view of science' as 'oppressive' (Scott and Usher 1999: 15), postpositivist naturalism shares many of the principles of positivism. Confusion is thought to be caused by the carrying over of a quantitative, positivist view of validity into the qualitative domain (Janesick 2000: 393). At the institutional level, it can still be quite difficult for postmodern researchers to assert their voice in university departments where naturalism has become the established norm, which may indeed create a 'negative drag' on the development of postmodern methodology (Miller et al. 1998). A particular area of conflict here is the degree to which researchers come out and present their own voice in writing (1998: 401) (see Chapter 6). Postmodernists thus criticize naturalists for naïvely overlooking inevitable ideological and cultural influences on the research process, actually believing that it is possible to minimize observer effect and see a virgin setting '"like it is" without biasing preconceptions or theoretical prejudices' (Gubrium and Holstein 1997: vi).

The postmodern liberation

In contrast, postmodern qualitative researchers 'portray people as *constructing* the social world' and researchers as 'themselves constructing the social world through their interpretations of it' (Hammersley and Atkinson 1995: 11, their emphasis). So whereas naturalists believe that meaningful social worlds can be discovered by 'being there', postmodernists 'argue that there is no "there" until it has been constructed' (Gubrium and Holstein 1997: 38). 'Every act of "seeing" or "saying" is unavoidably conditioned by cultural, institutional, and interactional contingencies' (1997: vi).

The naturalist position that validity is related to degree of saturation may therefore be oversimplistic. When a researcher has the opportunity for long-term exposure to a setting, it is easy to see the quantity of data as a major factor. However, it may be that this model obscures other sources of validity. At the opposite end of the spectrum to extended ethnographic study, there are also very small studies, such as Monsey's ethnography of how people interact with vending machines (Spradley 1980: 54). Much of the qualitative work featured in the corpus of written studies I use as examples comprises shorter, smaller, more 'micro' studies, in professional and study-oriented research where there is often insufficient time, access or opportunity for saturation.

Also, because she reflexively seeks to acknowledge in what way she is the arch designer of data collection, and how she disturbs the surface of the culture she is investigating, the postmodern researcher is in a position to dig deeper and reveal the hidden and the counter. This paradigm shift in qualitative research parallels the way in which anthropological ethnographers have become critical of their long tradition of unselfconsciously 'writing culture' and have begun to acknowledge how the authorial voice 'inscribes' the making of 'polished' texts (Clifford 1986: 2; Emerson et al. 2001: 352).

Qualitative research has thus grown from both interminglings and divisions, resulting in a complex family of interrelated methods and approaches. There are not only different paradigms. In the preface to their *Handbook*, Denzin and Lincoln reveal that different academic and professional groups, such as nurses and cultural anthropologists, have their own 'disciplinary networks' which may not 'cross each other, speak to each other or read each other'. The 'field of qualitative research' contains 'essential paradigmic differences and inherent contradictions among styles and types of research' (2000a: xi). Yet, all these different threads 'have a great deal in common regarding the [qualitative] research enterprise as a whole' (Gubrium and Holstein 1997: 10).

Nevertheless, amongst this complexity a clear direction is emerging. The postmodern break from naturalism does enable a far greater variety in procedure and scope, in which data is presented more creatively, with more openness about who the researcher is and how she spins validity through argument (Chapter 5). This makes it possible to devise a qualitative research approach for almost every conceivable scenario. It is therefore very clear that one does not *begin* by choosing a method. Methods can be sufficiently flexible to grow naturally from the research question, and in turn from the nature of the social setting in which the research is carried out. Janesick warns against the dangers of what she terms '*methodolatry*, a combination of *method* and *idolatry*, to describe a preoccupation with selecting and defending methods to the exclusion of the actual substance of the story being told' (2000: 390, her emphasis). Her association between qualitative research and dance illustrates well the mixing of creativity and discipline. The major point is that it is in the writing of the research that sense is made of how the research is crafted to suit the question and the setting, and how the rigour of the process is then made clear and accountable.

Writer as stranger

To demonstrate the essence of qualitative research I have used Schutz's notion of the stranger approaching a new culture. In this chapter I have tried to 'approach' qualitative research in a similar way. In the rest of the book I would like to think of the researcher as writer 'approaching' her own research experience in the same way. Essential to Schutz's phenomenology is allowing nothing to be taken for granted. Like the stranger learning culture, the qualitative researcher as writer should see every part of what she has done in the field as a fresh phenomenon. The same 'bracketing' – setting aside judgements about the expected 'nature', 'essence', 'reality' of things (Schutz 1970: 316) – should be applied to the research experience itself.

Because their research is known to be ideological and ethnocentric, and in itself a culture of institutional behaviour, qualitative researchers must never forget to approach their own actions as strangers, holding up everything for scrutiny, accounting for every action – and seeing how they speak and write what they have done as integral to the whole. In this way they should gain, in the words of C. Wright Mills, a 'sociological imagination' by *locating* themselves and their actions critically within a wider community or world scenario. 'In a word, by their reflection and by their sensibility, they realize the cultural meaning of the social sciences' and of their place within this meaning (Mills 1970: 14).

Summary

A major task of qualitative researchers is to manage the subjectivity of their work. An important purpose of the written study is to account for how this is done, in the following ways:

- Through showing the workings of the research, the written study establishes the rigour of the research process.
- The written study must show how the research has responded to the social setting in which it takes place.
- The written study must communicate the sense of strangeness and culture learning encountered in the research process.
- The writing of qualitative research is as ideologically problematic as the research itself. The researcher must be very vigilant in monitoring her own ideology in the language of the written study.
- Postmodern research no longer accepts the need for the writer to remain an invisible presence, and allows her to state her position and argument in the first person 'I'.
- The great variety of possible research procedures allows for greater scope in the type and size of written study.
- The qualitative researcher as writer must see her own research experience as strangely and freshly as she does the social setting in which she is working.

CHAPTER TWO

Starting Out

In this chapter I shall consider the first stage of qualitative research, that of finding a topic, forming research questions and establishing a research setting. My major aim is to look at how researchers write about these aspects, usually in the introductory part of the written study; but the chapter will also serve as a useful guide for getting into the whole business of doing qualitative research. Dealing with starting to write and starting to research in the same breath will emphasize the need to see these as one integrated activity. I shall also take up the idea introduced in Chapter 1 that a central part of this activity is working with opportunities while being accountable, in writing, to sound principles.

I shall begin by looking at the principles of opportunism, within the context of daily professional or academic life, and then deal with determining the research area, questions and setting. Throughout I shall refer to examples from my corpus of written studies.

Getting into qualitative research is very often about grasping opportunities that address a good idea or longer-standing preoccupation. Unlike quantitative research, which requires very specific and controlled research settings, qualitative research settings are difficult to control; and we have to capitalize on those that are available to us. It will rarely be possible to pre-design research conditions or even to find the conditions we want. Opportunism is therefore of the essence of the qualitative research. 'Opportunistic research' is to be considered neither second best nor deceitful, but central to the way in which research can address reality (Hammersley and Atkinson 1983: 40), given that the principles and rigour of research are maintained. Indeed, much qualitative research, even within formal educational settings, is in response to problematic or otherwise puzzling social realities that people find around them, whether personal, professional or institutional. It is the responsibility of qualitative research to find ways to investigate these realities in whatever form they present themselves and through whatever means this necessitates.

Researching everyday life

I have already broached the notion, in Chapter 1, that qualitative research integrates deeply with everyday life. More and more people are doing qualitative research in connection with their daily life, work situations or the social issues with which they are concerned. In effect, they are transforming the natural research of everyday life into the more rigorous, accountable activity which characterizes formal research. Within an academic setting, research might often be undertaken in order to satisfy assessment, get an academic qualification or increase one's list of publications. However, there is always another, intrinsic reason, which might be a concern with issues that have arisen through previous experience – some sort of problem, inconsistency or shortcoming which has led to a desire to look into the issue further. For example Broadley (1999), an undergraduate sports science student, became interested in the world of body builders at a local gym where he got a part-time job.

Researching at work

Other people do research as an integral part of their daily routine – perhaps as part of their work within their normal professional role. Examples of this are common and well established in management – 'on management teams, in pharmaceutical laboratories, and in other R&D [research and development] departments' where researchers could be 'computer systems analysts, chefs at gourmet restaurants, or specialists at the New York Stock Exchange' as well as 'many types of consultants' in accountancy, advertising, law or engineering (Gummesson 1991: 6). In nursing, 'a flustered young nurse practitioner ponders, "Why does this 80-year-old woman with a hip pain for 6 years insist on seeing me now?"', generally asking the question, 'What is going on here? How can I explain it?' (Crabtree and Miller 1992: xiii). This group may well include part-time students who use their work situation as a source of data. Especially in post-experience, professional development programmes, mature part- and full-time students often bring with them experiences and agendas which they wish to follow up; and in some cases the requirement of the programme that they have to do research stimulates professional memories that become meaningful research projects.

In many cases daily work and research can merge. Gummesson is 'fascinated' by how the work of the management consultant is very similar and sometimes indistinguishable from that of researcher (1991: ix). I had a similar feeling while working as a full-time, higher education consultant in Egypt. I shall talk later about how my research and work often became the same thing – assessing institutional resources, interviewing lecturers and administrators and observing classes. In education, the idea of 'teacher as researcher' – someone who must integrate research with work in order to do the latter properly – is now common (e.g. Nunan 1990; Ruddock and Hopkins 1985). It can be argued that this integration of research and work in many professions, which often takes the form of 'participatory action research, and action enquiry', is part of 'an emerging world view, more holistic, pluralist and egalitarian, that is essentially participative' in which not only professionals but a wide variety of people, including 'disadvantaged people in Asia, Africa and South America; factory workers in the United States and Scandinavia', come 'to understand their own worlds' and take ownership of knowledge and 'define the reality' (Reason 1994: 324–325).

Using work to research

Especially for people who have always worked, but never imagined how they could also research, it might be helpful to consider the double work–research role from the other way around. It is well known that undercover detectives and spies often take on a real work role in order to get the information they want. The way that the undercover cop in *Donnie Brasco* gets too involved with some of his subjects in the Mafia, with ethical and life-threatening consequences, is indicative of the interpersonal issues that beleaguer many ethnographers (Chapter 7). Detective work has much in common with qualitative research – looking for something, pursuing leads, not always knowing what will come up next and what significance it will have, and being prepared to change direction when a new lead emerges. A common theme in television crime dramas like *Colombo* is that the idiosyncratic investigation strategies of the successful detective remain mysterious to other people until the end.

Ethnographers also often carry out their research during the course of normal jobs or roles within society. For them, the 'dual role' is '(1) to engage in activities appropriate to the situation and (2) to observe' (Spradley 1980: 54). In the case of Monsey's study of the way people interact with vending machines:

> As a participant observer she made frequent purchases from Coke machines. To all outward appearances, she did what others did, but she approached each vending machine with an additional purpose: to watch her own actions, the behaviour of others, and everything she could see about the social situation. (Spradley 1980: 54)

Spradley cites other cases where researchers have taken employment in restaurants, or the role of customers in shops (1980: 51). For example, Kruft found an ideal role – that of blood donor – where long waits in queues enabled her to take field notes (Spradley 1980: 52).

Capitalizing on existing roles

Whereas ethnographers who are first and foremost researchers by profession have to fabricate 'normal' roles, people doing research as part of their job have the huge advantage of starting out with a normal role within the environment in which they work, which can double as a research role. The 'pre-existing social routines and realities' (Hammersley and Atkinson 1983: 94) of their jobs allow for wide movement and the type of behaviour characteristic of the researcher. Teachers are normally expected to observe and assess the behaviour of their students; they can give them questionnaires and interview them as part of classroom activities. In many contexts, all parties are expected to collect information to assess their work as part of quality assurance and reflective practice. Here, though, over-indulgence can be a problem. For example:

> When nurses or midwives do research, they are already part of the setting and know it intimately. This might mean, however, that they are over-familiar and could miss important issues or considerations. To be able to examine the world of the participant, the health professional must not take this world for granted, but must question his or her own assumptions and act like a stranger to the setting. (Holloway and Wheeler 1996: 5)

This invokes the notion of researcher as phenomenologist, making the familiar strange. Where the work situation does not allow access to data – often the case with classroom observation of other teachers because of professional taboos or institutional regulations – the teacher is no worse off than the ethnographer, who often has to enter the situation with whatever licence she has managed to negotiate, which is often insufficient.

Taking and creating the opportunity

For some students the normal work situation has never existed, or has been left behind, and research opportunities have to be created less naturally from social settings or other people's work situations which they find around them, over relatively short periods of time. Among the authors of my corpus of written studies, Anderson (2002) went back to a language school which was a previous work situation and made it the site of his three-year doctoral project. Scholl (1999), for his undergraduate assignment in cross-cultural studies, compared the behaviour of tourists in three churches: in Canterbury, England, where he was studying, and in Speyer and Trier, Germany, near where he lived. Celik (1999), for her assignment in cross-cultural studies, investigated the behind-the-counter culture of the local McDonald's where she had taken a part-time job.

In short, many would-be researchers, in their jobs and daily lives, are already in, or can find around them, situations that have the advantage of presenting ready-made research settings. What they need is to take the opportunities available. What I wish to show is how the *additional purpose* of formal research can be achieved. I am now going to show how some successful researchers have taken or created such research opportunities, thus embarking upon the first steps of qualitative research.

I shall divide this initial phase of the research process into three stages, which may well overlap or even change order in some circumstances: (a) determining the *area or topic* – broadly what is going to be studied; (b) determining the *research question* – the researcher deciding what she wants to find out; (c) determining the *research setting* – the location and boundaries within which the research will take place. As with all categories of this nature, each interacts with the others. Although I shall take them in the order presented here, each could also precede or be simultaneous with the others. For example, the whole research process might be precipitated by a fascination with a particular setting in (c), as with Celik's (1999) fascination with the behind-the-counter culture in the McDonald's in which she worked, which led to other things. Throughout this whole book, the organic nature of all the relationships within qualitative research must be remembered.

Determining the area

The choice of area or topic can relate to a number of things, such as previous interests or concerns, or even elements deep in the biography of the researcher. Linehan, in my corpus of written studies, is a language teacher who works in a university language centre. For several years she has noticed a lack of attention to the teaching of writing; but this concern goes back further. She makes the following statement in the introduction of her master's dissertation:

> My interest in writing owes something to my own language learning experience. As a child brought up in a Greek speaking community I learnt to write English relatively late. Greek was not my mother tongue, but the first language I learnt to read and write. As a result I have some sympathy with the orthographic experiences [of] some students. (Linehan 1996)

Similarly, Herrera writes of an encounter on her first morning in Egypt, when she woke up in her student hostel to loud noises from a neighbouring building. From this her interest in an ethnography of Egyptian schooling grew:

> [A] loudspeaker ... and the military-like responses of girls, drum beats and off-tune accordion blared into my room. ... Irritation turned suddenly to fascination. 'What on earth are they doing over there?' I wondered. 'What are they saying? Who are they? What does it all mean?' ... I wandered into the hall, still in pajamas, and asked an Arab student ... what the ruckus was about. She ... said, emphasizing the obviousness of it, 'it's a school'. A school. And yet its sounds were so unfamiliar. (Herrera 1992: 6)

Already she is asking ethnographic questions.

Quite differently, Celik's decision to 'investigate the principal factors relating to the organization, universally known as "McDonald's"' is precipitated by the fact that she has a part-time job there. However, she also feels an overriding concern that she has, and her readers might have, with regard to such a universally important phenomenon. She writes in her introduction – 'Its impact is felt far beyond ... the United States in the fast food business. It has influenced a wide range of undertakings, indeed the way of life of a significant portion of the world' (Celik 1999). Similarly, Broadley's interest in hard-core body building developed from a short exposure to a particular setting:

I just went down the gym initially – I just do strength training – and got a bit into it – got to know the manager quite well – and he ended up offering me a job – and I just got into the training side of it – and once I got into the body building rather than straight weight training – I just got to know about and made a study of it. (Interview)

What he found interesting was:

How different it is – what they actually practise and what they portray. Outside the gym they portray shirt off and down the beach. Behind the scenes it's all talk of doing [body building] drugs, strict diets and never missing a workout. They talk and give a *picture* of health, but practise otherwise. It's not about health; it's about creating an image of the body. (Interview, his emphasis)

What turns these interests into research is again the opportunity. In the case of the above, the opportunity was in a sense forced by the need to write a dissertation or assignment. This made the students set out to look for research scenarios in which to realize their investigations. Being confronted with a formal request for research can thus force a liberation of latent research ideas. Broadley goes on to explain that he was able to choose a topic for his 5,000-word assignment from anything in sports science within the areas of 'sociology, physiology or psychology'. His choice was driven by his desire to 'base it on body building in the gym' that he 'was going to'. He explains:

I was looking at physiology to begin with, but that meant bringing in subjects, blood tests and things like that for the drugs, but it wasn't going to work. The next thing was just to write about what they portray – and that's sociology based. So I chose my area first, and it just fell into it. (Interview)

What is very significant here is that Broadley's natural entrance into the body builders' world not only structured the investigation itself, but led him into a new way of (sociological) thinking. The development of 'interviews and participant observation' seemed a natural progression from working in the gym.

Research done by academics may also grow from their life and professional experience. One of the authors of Maguire and Mansfield's (1998) study of the construction of the female body in aerobics classes states that her orientation to the subject grew from her sporting and aerobics background and, like Broadley, from part-time work, which culminated in the revelation of a particular anomaly:

My own involvement in sport and exercise – I could go into my whole sporting biography – that was where the involvement came. Involvement in the aerobics context came because I had been teaching aerobics and involved in doing aerobics for a number of years, and when I came to teach it, it struck me that the reasons I was doing it for, which in the main had to do with improving my fitness for the sport I was playing in a very fun way, it was very social for me – plus I was a student at the time, it was supplementing my income then – *but* it struck me that the people who I was teaching seemed to be doing it for *very very* different reasons. (Interview, her emphasis)

She then goes on to explain how this interest was taken up by academic work with a distinct train of developing thought:

> Then as I was doing my master's work it crystallized itself into a project, into a dissertation, in a formal way. I did a master's degree on aerobics specifically. My PhD, which I'm in the middle of really, again is focused on the women's experiences of exercise, sport and physical activity, but in a broader social sense. But it is focused on what people do at health clubs, fitness clubs. (Interview)

Cynics might believe that many academics only publish as a result of institutional pressures. On the other hand, such pressures may indirectly drive them to focus more critically on the realities that surround them; and the reading which accompanies research will lead them to critique the ways in which the these realities are represented in the literature. Thus, Maguire and Mansfield seek to address their conviction that 'traditionally, the body has been overlooked in sociology and the sociology of sport. Sociological analyses have tended to adopt a disembodied approach, and until recently, bodies have remained a secondary concern in social theory' (1998: 112).

Talbot, in her article on how gender is constructed in a teenage magazine, seeks to 'empower' her audience 'in the sense of giving them greater conscious control over aspects of their lives'. She therefore invites her readers to look at the language of the magazine with her, themselves to join with the researcher in '"making strange" conventions which usually seem perfectly natural to people' (Talbot 1992: 174).

Because, in all these cases, aspects of the researcher's own life history influence what they decide to investigate, and indeed (as we shall see in Chapter 6) how they go about it, some degree of discussion of personal orientations becomes a significant part of the written study.

Establishing a research question

The researcher also needs to determine what she wants to find out within the area or topic she has chosen. For some this is quite difficult as it requires a very specific formulation. When I asked a group of master's students to formulate the questions they were asking and three points they were making in fairly short group research projects for which they had already collected data and begun to determine findings, it took them about an hour to produce this information. They found it extremely difficult to reduce the richness of what they were doing to a few precise statements. Even at the outset, when perhaps no more than the topic has been determined, the researcher's thinking will already be very rich and difficult to reduce in this way. This is characteristic of research which is an exploration of the quality of social life. Qualitative research does not conjure the same type of precision required by quantitative research: it is intent on expanding rather than controlling variables. Table 1.1 illustrates how qualitative research invokes notions such as 'all possible social variables', 'exploration', 'foray',

Table 2.1   Research questions

Questions	Specificity	Agendas
In what ways can open learning (self-access) help develop writing skills? (Linehan 1996)	Relationship between an educational process and an outcome	Writing suffers from lack of (self-access) open learning.
How is teenage femininity constructed in a magazine for teenage girls? (Talbot 1992: 174)	Relationship between a social configuration and a discourse site	Critical analysis can 'empower'. Teenagers' 'femininity *is* constructed for them'. (174)
What are the lived, embodied experiences of women who participate in aerobics? (Maguire and Mansfield 1998: 109)	Relationship between a social group and an activity	'The separation of sexes in the local "health" club setting reflects a patriarchal organisation' (112). 'Women are not able to ignore the sociocultural images of feminine beauty' (114).
What is the world of hard-core body builders like? (Broadley 1999)	The nature of a small culture	There is an interesting duality between what they say and do.
How do people who work in McDonald's behave? (Celik 1999)	The nature of a small culture	McDonald's has a world cultural impact.

'emergence' and 'mysteries', rather than 'reduce contamination' in the quantitative column. Nevertheless, the rigour of qualitative research is in managing what has the potential to be a very messy subjectivity; and central to this managing at the outset is the formulation of research questions – *even if they are likely to change* – a possibility which I shall discuss in a moment.

Finding out

Research questions in qualitative research can be as varied as the topics and scenarios being investigated. Speaking about education, Janesick suggests that 'in general, questions that are suited to qualitative enquiry have long been the questions of many curriculum researchers and theorists, sociologists, anthropologists, students of organizations and historians' (2000: 382). Basically, they are the questions we all ask about things which fascinate, puzzle, anger and shock us about social life.

The examples mentioned above produce the questions in Table 2.1. The first thing to notice is that, reading from top to bottom of the middle column, the questions move from fairly specific, to not very specific. This is of course just my interpretation; but when I try to map these questions on to Figure 1.1, thinking of overall orientation rather than particular methods, the specificity of particular settings and processes in the first two projects places them more towards action research, grounded theory or case studies, with a tendency to be more *instrumental* in seeking to solve a particular problem. Linehan's project does indeed take on an action research mode seeking the very practical, professional outcome of an improved pedagogy. She writes, 'the aim of this study was primarily to improve practice by finding an appropriate context, through self-access, to assist students with their writing skills' (1996: 20). Talbot's project, although not calling itself a 'case study', is tied specifically to the case of a particular magazine. In contrast, the final three projects are asking more general questions about the nature of a small culture and the way in which the meanings and values of society are constructed per se, which moves them more in the direction of ethnography, phenomenology or ethnomethodology.

Another observation is that despite the more open-ended, exploratory nature of the questions towards the bottom of the table, there are specific fascinations and concerns which set an agenda in all the questions. Summaries of these are listed in the right-hand column of Table 2.1. When I asked one of the authors of the third study (Maguire and Mansfield 1998), how she viewed their own very strong points of view in relation to what was allowed to emerge from the research setting, she said that they were very relevant to the study because 'they reflect a lot of the literature on gender, sport and exercise' and 'they are certainly things that I have observed [in the past], that women, at least the ones I've interviewed, have talked about' (interview). At the same time she is wary of balancing 'presuppositions or preconceived knowledge with the importance of taking a step back from the situation that you are observing'. Each question is nevertheless sufficiently open-ended to allow open-ended exploration and the emergence of factors and issues which the researcher might not have previously thought about, allowing the 'quality' of each topic to speak for itself. This is quite different to questions in quantitative research, which must be sufficiently narrow to allow maximum control.

The place of hypotheses

This brings me to the issue of hypotheses, which can be confusing to newcomers to qualitative research because the different disciplines or strategies of enquiry of qualitative research have different views on the subject. Bell maintains that 'many research projects begin with the statement of a hypothesis', and cites Verma and Beard in defining a hypothesis as 'a tentative proposition which is subject to verification through subsequent investigation', and explaining that 'in many cases hypotheses are hunches that the researcher has about the existence of relationship between variables' (Bell 1993: 13). The first of these two roles for hypotheses represents a very specific building-block in controlled quantitative enquiry in which the aim is to test a precisely stated relationship between two variables (e.g. buying, advertising, statements about safety). Great care must be taken here to ensure that the hypothesis is mathematically falsifiable. Such a hypothesis is stated in the car experiment in Example 1.2 – that more Ford cars will be bought if prospective first-time buyers are exposed to advertising that says they are safer. This hypothesis can be tested statistically. Moreover, if it is proved false, it can be precisely modified (e.g. to state 'to advertising which shows an accident' or 'safer for children') until something verifiable is found.

Taking these broad principles, hypotheses do not have to be restricted to the controlled world of quantitative research. They can be used in qualitative research when a relationship between several entities is being investigated in a systematic way. This is the case in the first three projects in Table 2.1, where such relationships are specified very carefully. Also, hypotheses do not have to be formulated explicitly. Whether or not hypotheses *are* stated may depend on the degree of instrumentality in the study. They would need to be more explicit within a more instrumental action research discipline in which investigators seek 'to consider their original research propositions and hypotheses in the light of experience, modifying, reformulating, and rejecting them, adopting new hypotheses and so on' (Reason 1994: 327). Here, the staged modification of hypotheses enables an identifiable progression of understanding in dialogue with research action. McNiff (1988), following the work of others, provides a very clear account of how this can be done. She refers specifically to education, but with principles that can be transferred to all disciplines.

Hypotheses played an important role in my own doctoral research. On the one hand, my quest was less instrumental. I asked the general question – *Why is innovation in the foreign language curriculum so often rejected by the institutions into which it is introduced?* – which was pursued through an ethnographic study of local and expatriate lecturers in Egyptian university classrooms. On the other hand, the research followed the progress of action research that I was carrying out simultaneously in my professional capacity as a curriculum consultant. Research and consultancy were thus merged and informed each other in such a way that the staged hypotheses of the action research became part and parcel of the development of understanding in the ethnography. Thus, instead of being the starting point, as would be the case in quantitative research, altogether eight hypotheses were generated during the process of the research; and some of them continued to be reformulated as the research progressed. Hence, at an early stage in the data analysis it was possible to formulate this one of several hypotheses: 'Hypothesis 4: Classroom events are characterized by a ritualistic formality which would not lend itself either to change or to collaborative, community learning' (Holliday 1991: 281). After more data analysis:

> The evidence in this chapter of an overall collectionist perception of the role of the lecturer ... is consonant with and further underlines a generally formal attitude to education in the local educational environment as a whole. Therefore, it is possible to modify hypothesis 4: – *Hypothesis 4a:* (1) Classroom events characterized by a ritualistic formality and (2) a collectionist perception of 'lecturer', would not lend themselves either to change or to collaborative, community learning. (Holliday 1991: 385)

It is thus more common to produce, rather than begin with, hypotheses in qualitative research. The eight hypotheses that emerged by the end of my research comprised the basis for recommending future professional action. Being able to say 'these are the likely relationships' was in effect the findings of my research.

Towards the middle of the spectrum between more and less instrumental approaches (Figure 1.1), in my interview with one of the authors of Maguire and

Mansfield (1998), in Table 2.1, I asked if the stated relationship between women and aerobics classes could be expressed as a hypothesis. She responded – 'They are not something that sit very well with me. They're something I associate with the natural sciences. In terms of what I want to find out, the knowledge I am trying to build on, I don't think they're useful to me' (interview). When I asked how far she was seeking to validate the statements, she continued, 'I would say not. I'm not looking to see if anything is valid or true. I'm looking to see what emerges.'

At the opposite end of the spectrum (in Figure 1.1) to action research, the notion of exploration rather than validation becomes even more prominent. It is normally thought inappropriate to use hypotheses in ethnography, which is seen as 'exploring the nature of particular social phenomena rather than setting out to test hypotheses about them' (Atkinson and Hammersley 1994: 248). Nevertheless, this can depend on how naturalistic ethnography is seen to be. Hammersley and Atkinson argue that naturalist ethnographers believe 'all perspectives and cultures are rational' and will provide all the structure necessary for exploration, with little need for hypothesis testing (1983: 12–13). However, within a more reflexive ethnography, in which 'social researchers are part of the social world they study' (Hammersley and Atkinson 1995: 16), 'data should not be taken at face value, but treated as a field of inferences in which hypothetical patterns can be identified and their validity tested' (1995: 19) (see also Barton and Lazarsfield 1969: 176–196.) I shall look in more detail at reflexivity in Chapter 3. Spradley also concedes that ethnography can be 'hypothesis-oriented' (1980: 31, citing Hymes). He gives the example that 'hypotheses about the influence of child-rearing practices on adult personality have oriented numerous ethnographic projects in anthropology. ... The research still follows the [ethnographic] cycle ... but the initial selection of a project and data collection are influenced by a set of hypotheses' (1980: 31).

Developing questions

In the same way that hypotheses develop and adapt throughout the research process, research questions can also change as the research moves on from the initial concept. Initial questions lead the researcher to investigate in a certain direction; but within this process there will be unforeseen discoveries which raise further or different questions. In some cases the whole focus of the research may change.

Anderson had this experience as his doctoral project developed. His initial question – *How do social and psychological factors affect how students learn when they are involved in task-based group learning?* – seemed unrealistic when, in the initial stages of data collection, he found it was difficult to detach what was happening in task-based groups from other factors in the classroom environment as a whole. He therefore developed a new question which would consider group work in broader terms – *How is group work organized, constructed and run in the classroom and for what purposes?* The themes that began to emerge from the data collected to answer this question led him to address the broader question concerning the culture and discourses of teaching itself. As part of his justification for this movement, Anderson states in his thesis:

The initial focus was only a potential route that could be taken and was not set in stone. It was a set of possibilities, not fixed absolutes. As my approach to the classroom observations was to note everything I saw, to start with a tabula rasa, it was unsurprising if categories and themes emerged that diverged from the original proposal. (Anderson 2002: 125)

Interestingly, in the final written study, the term 'research question' does not appear at all, clearly having outlived its use. Generally speaking, research questions may cease to appear explicitly in the written study, their purpose having been served.

There are also *ethnographic questions* which can only emerge once the researcher has entered the social setting she is investigating (Spradley 1980: 31). In many ways these are the natural questions one asks when approaching any new or strange social group – e.g. *What is going on here? What are the rules of engagement? Who is in charge? How is power managed and distributed?* – which help to unlock what is meaningful and appropriate for members of the group. Answering these questions reveals what one needs to know in order to gain membership and operate within its culture. Within this type of questioning, hypotheses will also come into play, as is evident in my example of learning how to behave in the common room in Chapter 1 – *If I leave the group without saying goodbye this will be acceptable because pressing work engagements need no explanation.* In this sense, the precise nature of research questions cannot really be determined until the social setting has been determined and the research encounter has begun.

Defining the research setting

Another very important task lies in establishing the research setting – exactly where, when and with whom the research will take place. In opposition to the notion of survey in quantitative research, the aim is to go deep into a definable setting in which phenomena can be placed meaningfully within a specific social environment. Such an environment can be groups of people, institutions, cases, geographical areas, communities, texts and so on. This setting can in itself motivate the research. For Broadley, Scholl and Celik it was the fascination with the setting they were already in, the gym, the church as tourist site and McDonald's, which led to the research question. In other cases the setting is connected closely to the research question in that it provides an environment in which the questions can be addressed. For some research projects it is harder to find the research setting than for others. A series of criteria need to be considered (Table 2.2). In the following pages I shall look at how these criteria are met in my informants' research projects.

Boundedness and richness

It is important that the scenario has clear boundaries (criterion 1 in Table 2.2) so that the readers of the research can be clear about exactly what is going on and in what sort

Table 2.2   Criteria for research settings

Criteria	Details
1 The setting must have a sense of boundedness.	Time, place, culture
2 The setting should provide a variety of relevant, interconnected data.	People to watch or interview, artefacts (e.g. displays, clothing, decoration, implements)
3 There should be sufficient richness.	Different instances, facets and viewpoints – a microcosm of the research topic in wider society
4 The setting should be sufficiently small.	Logistically and conceptually manageable
5 There should be access.	For the researcher to take whatever role is necessary to collect data

of context. I am purposely leaving the notion of setting as open as possible. It is common to think of a setting as a group of people who share a specific interest. However, ethnographers in particular would require the setting to be a culture (Spradley 1980: 13). As I argued in Chapter 1, my own ethnographic orientation leads me to visualize all qualitative research settings as cultures, where research is essentially culture learning. In my view, taking a minimal definition of culture as those aspects of social cohesion, values and artefacts that distinguish one social group from another, only a small culture can provide the network of meaning for the social phenomena found as data.

Cultural boundedness thus enables the data to be *interconnected* (criterion 2). This is demonstrated in Figure 2.1, where, on the left, the three people interviewed and the observation of workplace behaviour do not come together as meaningful data. On the one hand, there is not the quantity of data to amount to a survey. On the other hand, what three people say and what a group of employees do can be of little consequence, even if they do belong to the same profession or occupation, unless they are somehow bound together. On the right-hand side of the figure, the interviews and observations are socially located within a bounded setting, and become valid because they interconnect via an environment which contains other actions, events, icons and so on which give them meaning.

The way in which different fragments of data can be interconnected in this way is demonstrated in the eyes study, Example 1.6. People are interviewed within the context of their household, which provides an environment in which the photographs of family and friends and advertisements, which they are asked to bring to the interviews, take on rich meanings as they interconnect with the existing meanings that each participant brings to the situation. This can also be seen clearly in the way Celik's interview with the McDonald's manager links with her observation of employees' dress and behaviour and their feelings about their work which she herself experiences as an employee:

> The last point is the definition of 'hustle'. In my view, hustle is the most important key element at McDonald's. My manager pointed out that hustle is

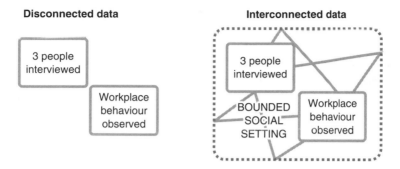

Figure 2.1   Interconnectedness of data

the efficiency, which is attained from safe and appropriate use of the three popular 'Cs', that is 'Communication, Co-operation and Co-ordination'. He also stressed that you should not mistake hustle for rushing or even running. Unfortunately this is not in accordance with the truth. But you have no other choice. In lunch time, everybody is running there and back. (Celik 1999)

This apparent duality between official statement and reality connects with her observation that throughout the setting work and morale are regulated through an array of institutionalized phrases and acronyms. Similarly, Scholl links what a tourist in the English church says about smoking with his tacit knowledge about the overall culture of tourist behaviour in churches:

I asked an Italian tourist who was on his own for a lighter. We stood in the middle of the crypt. I obviously wanted to smoke, cigarette on my lips. ... The man apologized and said 'No, sorry, I don't smoke'. He then walked away a few steps, turned round and said 'I don't think you can smoke in the church.' ... There are no signs in the crypt which state 'smoking prohibited'. The Italian just transferred his knowledge about the culture in a church in Italy to the unknown Canterbury Cathedral. ... We collect more and more data and add it to our picture of a culture. If there had been another one asking him for fire [*sic*], or he had seen somebody smoking, the Italian might have believed or 'added': 'In English churches smoking is allowed'. (Scholl 1999)

Here Scholl is not only learning about the culture of church tourism, but about how culture develops in general. These examples also show the necessary richness of multifaceted data (criterion 3, in Table 2.2). In another case, a group of undergraduate cross-cultural studies students made their research setting a coffee shop on the top floor of a bookshop. Here, their interconnected data comprised analysis of text written by regular customers in the 'visitor comments' book, as well as observation of customer behaviour.

Maguire and Mansfield (1998) similarly *locate* their interviews with women about exercising within what they observe of them in the aerobics class. The interviews connect with women's body image issues in the wider society (e.g. 'physical activity in childhood and their experiences of education and sport' [interview]) and also with their aerobic class behaviour. The setting of the aerobics class is thus a 'microcontext' for the 'wider "exercise-body beautiful complex"' (1998: 110) – which again fulfills criterion 3. Indeed, Maguire and Mansfield relate their research specifically to the principle in 'figurational (process) sociology', in which there is a 'network of independent, mutually oriented people. In the case of the 'exercise-body beautiful complex', this involves 'diet technicians, fitness "scientists", media personnel, and exercise consultants' which to some extent reproduces a 'patriarchal ideology' (1998: 110).

Talbot's study is particularly interesting in these terms. Her social setting is the *text* of the teenage magazine. Here the text is established as similar to other settings, in people and behaviour, by the way in which the interactants within it are visualized:

> What I intended to do is look at some of the 'population' of a two-page feature. But I will not be looking at the text in a traditional way as the product of a single author containing a clearly defined cast of characters or *dramatis personae*. Instead I will examine it as a 'tissue of voices', a mesh of intersecting voices of characters inhabiting a text. ... We can examine a text's population by looking for traces of people addressing one another, traces of characters' words or thoughts. (Talbot 1992: 176)

Constructing the setting

Maguire and Mansfield's research project is different to those of Celik and Scholl, who were each fascinated by a ready-made setting, in that they have an agenda to explore and a research question to ask which leads them to look for a suitable setting. The difficult nature of this search is evident in my own doctoral research (Holliday 1991). My research question about the nature of curriculum innovation (see above) involved looking at a whole curriculum project on a large national scale. Following criterion 4 of Table 2.2, that the setting should be manageable, this very large setting was too unwieldy. I therefore needed to select a *core setting* within it which would be a suitable microcosm of the whole while fulfilling all the other criteria.

The different elements of the whole project setting are: (a) *classes* of 60–500 in 17 universities with 4-year degree courses; (b) *expatriate lecturers* trying new pedagogy in the universities; (c) *working groups* with volunteer Egyptian curriculum developers; (d) *expatriate curriculum developers* – convening working groups to develop new pedagogy and visiting universities; and (e) aid *agencies*, the Ministry of Education, and the academic establishment.

All potentially qualify as core settings in that they are all bounded, rich, and are to different degrees microcosms in that within each one most of the issues of the whole project are acted out (criterion 3 in Table 2.2). The 'working group' would have been a good choice in that it had clear boundaries (criterion 1), was small and manageable (criterion 4), was a rich example of local and expatriate interaction, the former carrying trails from their larger cadre of academics in the universities, the latter representing the conflicts between the expatriate lecturers and curriculum developers, each with their local and agency interests, and so on (criterion 3), contained the critical artefacts of curriculum documents and materials, and the physical arrangement of the working group setting, furniture, seating arrangements and presentation technology, which would reveal the many-faceted cultural ideologies of the different project players (criterion 2). However, although I was a member of the 'working group', the politics were too sensitive and combustible for me to have sufficiently problem-free access (criterion 5). The cultural conflicts and sensitivities of the whole project were so much focused on the 'working groups' that it would have become difficult to manage when compounded with those of researcher–participant relations (Chapter 7).

I finally chose the university classes as my core setting. There was sufficient richness and easy access, as it was part of my job to attend other people's classes as an observer and to interview lecturers – 'The professional-academic and other relevant local cultures would come into play and be observable within the confined situation presented by the classroom, to which I, as a curriculum developer, could have easy access' (Holliday 1991: 197). Classrooms are in themselves particularly good locations for research. The way in which they mirror the world outside is verified by the interest taken in them by 'a variety of disciplines: sociology, anthropology, social psychology, communicative ethnography' (Allwright 1988: x, citing Candlin). They possess special features, such as routines and scripts that occur in a controlled context, which make them especially attractive to researchers (Van Lier 1988: 9–10).

However, the classrooms I was concerned with were spread over the 17 institutions covered by the project; and the logistics of my work role meant that I was not able to get to any of them more than once or twice. This meant that I had to *construct* the notion of a classroom culture around the resources at my disposal rather than use a single real classroom as my core focus. Spradley provides a precedent for this:

> It is often useful to think of a social situation as a *kind of place*. For example, one beginning ethnographer began observing on a specific bus that ran along Grand Avenue in St. Paul Minnesota. However, it soon became clear that she could not do all her research on that specific bus, so she treated all the 'Grand Avenue busses' as a single kind of place. She could have enlarged this category to 'city busses' and treated them all as a kind of place, a social situation with various actors and activities. (Spradley 1980: 40, his emphasis)

And indeed such 'kinds of place' could be as diverse as internet chat rooms, a period in history, an individual life history and so on. Hammersley and Atkinson also acknowledge the possibility that 'the more settings studied the less time can be spent in each', and that 'the researcher must make a trade off here between breadth and depth of investigation' (1995: 40). Hence, I argued my case for a composite classroom culture in my thesis as follows:

> Every classroom has its own individual culture, but a wider, average culture for a particular educational institution can be ascertained by observing a large number of cases. Initially it was hypothesized that all the 17 faculties of education could be treated as one institution with a meaningfully common classroom culture. It should be remembered that the description of the classroom culture would be made up of a conglomerate of ideal typologies ... and that the intention would not be to produce a description of *the* real culture, but to use the concept of culture operationally in order to find the information needed – 'Let's treat the classroom as a culture and see what it shows us'. (Holliday 1991: 197–198)

This statement is also important in that it is *showing my workings* (Chapter 3). What I did may appear eccentric, but it is valid in that I did it in a disciplined way, appropriately deriving research strategy from the broader setting as it emerged, and articulating it well within the study. I shall follow the progress of how I did this in Chapter 5. This focus enabled me to compare similar, well-defined events over a large geographical area. Teachers, methodologies and institutions were different but there was the overriding constant of undergraduate language students following a national curriculum. Some of the politics of dealing with 'a strategically selected locale, treating the system as background ... without losing sight of the fact that it is integrally constitutive of cultural life within the bounded subject matter' is discussed by Marcus (1986: 172).

Moving between core and peripheral data

Focusing on a core-bounded setting does not however preclude the importance of data which is peripheral to the setting. Whereas in my research the core data was classroom behaviour, data was also collected outside the classroom in seminars, meetings and even, on one occasion, on a university bus carrying commuting lecturers to work (Holliday 1991: 205). Such peripheral data serves to connect the core setting with the important context of a wider society, community or history, in respect to which it is of course not peripheral, thus enabling the critical 'sociological imagination' referred to at the end of Chapter 1.

The productive dialogue between core and peripheral data is demonstrated in Honarbin-Holliday's study of two Tehran university art departments in Iran. Whereas her core setting comprised the classrooms, studios and corridors of the two departments, she had to acknowledge that 'the site of observation is an evolving and fluid space, with the possibility of shifts in locations and more abstractly, shifts in perspectives'. She therefore also included 'university car parks, ateliers, galleries, researcher's studio, coffee shops, taxis, and other public or private spaces where the processes of enquiry might continue' (Honarbin-Holliday 2005: 44).

A particularly powerful source of data was conversations with taxi drivers on her way to the core setting, because they represented a key link between the core setting and the broader society. She writes:

> Their participation in the discussion is my way for further reflection and contextualization, and/or cross-referencing, the socio-political analysis given by the participants at the two universities in Tehran. … [The taxi driver's] oral histories of recent and distant pasts, their collective text, comes from the 'outside' world, the margins of my research site, but speaks from the heart of society in Iran. (Honarbin-Holliday 2005: 36)

Her reference to the margins of experience reminds us that it is often these potentially unnoticed margins which tell us the most. She takes the idea of learning from juxtaposing 'the "not included", the "marginal", or "the insignificant"' against her core data from Derrida's notion of *différance*, which in my view forms a basis for thick description (Chapter 4). Another example is in Duan's (in process) study of the impact of the national university entrance exam on the lived experience of Chinese high school students. Travelling from Britain, where he was a full-time research student, to his core research site at a school in China, he found it helpful to prepare himself by beginning to collect data on his long journey from Beijing, which comprised overheard conversations in the airport, on the train, and while stopping off at his sister's house.

Such data sources external to the core setting also provide an external viewpoint from which to see with the *stranger's* fresh eyes. Before embarking on his journey, Duan practised his observation skills in the strange environment of his daughter's primary school classroom in Britain. This provided him with an unexpected view of schooling which enabled him to see the familiar school in China differently:

> My experience of research in an English School, alongside my own three-year experience of English society, would help in shaping and changing my ideology and viewpoint. This facilitated … the raising of my 'critical awareness' when doing research in a Chinese educational and cultural setting, assisting me in striking the necessary balance between detachment and involvement … and particularly in making the familiar strange. (Duan in process)

Applying culture

Hammersley and Atkinson make the key point that 'settings are not naturally occurring phenomena, they are constituted and maintained through cultural definition and social strategies' and that 'their boundaries are not fixed, but shift across occasions, to one degree or another, through processes of redefinition and negotiation' (1995: 41). I would take this further. My earlier phrase 'Let's treat the classroom as a culture and see what it shows us', implies that determining the research setting is at least partly in the mind of the researcher (Holliday 1999). Figure 2.3 illustrates this process. In actuality the social world is a seamless mélange of complex behaviours. This perception is central to the interpretive principles of qualitative research. The researcher does not presume to define, a priori, the social world in one

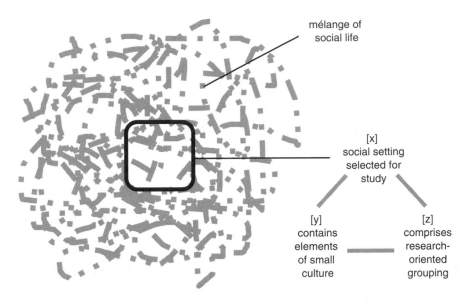

mélange of
social life

[x]
social setting
selected for
study

[y]
contains
elements
of small
culture

[z]
comprises
research-
oriented
grouping

Figure 2.2   Small culture selected for qualitative research (Adapted from Holliday 1999: 255)

way or another, and is thus scientifically humble in the face of its complexity. The defining of a particular social setting (x in the figure) involves taking a section of this mélange and drawing an operational boundary around it. By 'operational' I mean for the purpose of research. The social setting does not necessarily have a reality other than that created by the researcher. The social setting has to contain the elements of small culture (y in the figure), fulfilling the criteria in Table 2.2. However, the grouping which makes up this small culture is essentially defined and constructed by the research (z) – picked out from many other possible small cultural groupings for the sake of the research project (Holliday 1999: 254).

In the case of my own research project described above, other possible groupings than the ones listed above might have been the small cultures of individual student groups, the student body of a particular university, the faculty of a particular university, or the cadre of expatriate curriculum developers, all of which overlap and interact. The same applies to other studies cited in this chapter – for Celik, possible other groupings could have been a group of teenage customers or the managers of McDonald's in a particular region. Maguire and Mansfield could have chosen aerobics instructors or a particular sub-group of women. The term 'grouping' is important, to remind researchers that it is *they* who have grouped the people in their research projects as a construction of the research. Whether or not this 'grouping' equates with the perceptions of 'group' held by the individuals within it is to be discovered rather than assumed. Small cultures do not exist except in the minds of the people who conceptualize them (Holliday 1999: 255). This small culture is not a 'cause of behaviour' (Baumann 1996: 11), but a structuring within which behaviour selected for study may be understood. It is a means to investigation rather than an end in itself. Hence, 'as interworked systems of construable signs ... culture is not a power, something to which social events, behaviours, institutions, or processes can causally be attributed; it is a context, something *within* which they can be intelligibly – that is thickly – described' (Geertz 1993: 14, my emphasis). It is crucial here for the researcher to remember that the grouping she has defined must not be reified into something it is not. To forget this is to be in danger of culturism – reducing real people to the definitions we construct for them – just as sexism reduces women to the stereotypes constructed by others (Holliday 1999: 245). I shall take up this issue in Chapter 8.

Summary

In this chapter I have presented fairly summarily the wide range of possibilities, in a wide range of circumstances that make qualitative research a realistic option. I have also shown how researchers write about these. In the next chapter I shall concentrate more on how to *write* about the questions a particular researcher may have chosen to ask, and the options she has chosen to turn these questions into research.

The following points have been made in this chapter:

- Qualitative research can develop from experiences and issues from life and work contexts.
- The contexts both provide and structure opportunities for research. The researcher must capitalize on and work with these opportunities in determining the area of research.
- Research questions vary from very specific and instrumental to the broad and exploratory. They may change and develop as the research proceeds.
- Hypotheses tend to be used where the research is more instrumental.
- The research setting provides richness and boundaries. It provides an environment within which to interconnect data. But we must not forget other data that may connect it with a broader community of society.
- Settings are not always ready-made or easy to find. Their choice will depend upon the complex logistics of the broader environment. They may well be the construction of the researcher.
- 'Culture' is used within qualitative research as an operational, heuristic device. Researchers must be wary of reducing reality to the 'culture' they themselves construct.
- Researchers need to write about the above issues in the introduction to their written studies, as they explain the initial orientation of their various research projects.

CHAPTER THREE

Showing the
Workings

I have already argued in Chapter 1 that a significant aspect of qualitative research is the need for researchers to show their workings, to reveal how they have managed the subjectivity inherent within this research paradigm. This is the major way in which rigour can be maintained, and it makes the writing of the research a central element in achieving accountability. Moreover, where the writing of the research undeniably constructs its own reality (Atkinson 1990: 7), it is all the more important for the researcher to be aware of this and to *show* how she is constructing this reality. This chapter will concentrate on how qualitative researchers construct the reality of their research through the way in which they show their workings.

Explanations of the workings of the research are placed strategically throughout the whole of the written study. Figure 3.1 shows a structure which is common in many written studies, and where the workings of the research are found. This structure can be taken as a useful default while realizing that there are a variety of ways of departing from this model, as will be demonstrated below. Some argue that this model is rooted in the positivistic paradigm; but I feel that it still works well within qualitative research. The boxes on the left of the figure are the major parts of the written study. Their size reflects the extent of each part. Whether or not they correspond to individual chapters will depend on the length of the piece of work. Indeed, the discussion of data, which is large in relation to the other parts, may comprise several 'data chapters' in longer pieces of work. I have placed 'literature review' and 'research methodology' in one combined box because although the former looks at the topic of the research and the latter at the principles underlying how the research will carried out, they both require an assessment of current thought and both result in the researcher establishing her own position in the form of a conceptual framework. I hesitate to use the common term 'literature review' because literature is also reviewed in the discussion of research methodology and may continue to be cited throughout the rest of the study. Listed on the right of the figure are the details of what has to be covered in each part of the written study to show the workings. They

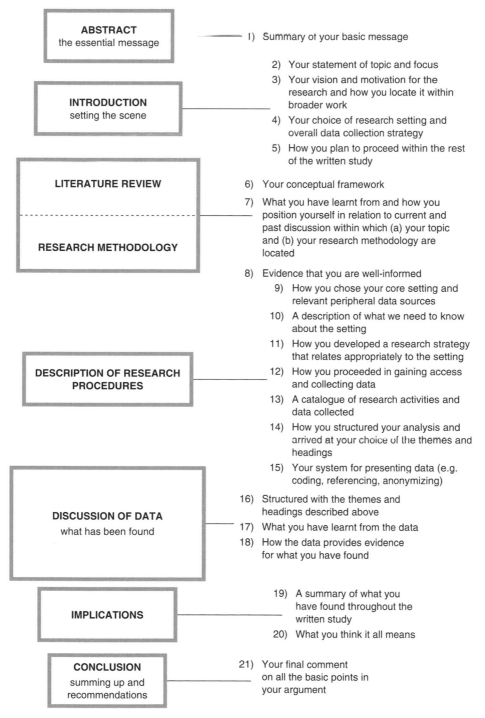

ABSTRACT
the essential message

1) Summary of your basic message

INTRODUCTION
setting the scene

2) Your statement of topic and focus
3) Your vision and motivation for the research and how you locate it within broader work
4) Your choice of research setting and overall data collection strategy
5) How you plan to proceed within the rest of the written study

LITERATURE REVIEW

RESEARCH METHODOLOGY

6) Your conceptual framework
7) What you have learnt from and how you position yourself in relation to current and past discussion within which (a) your topic and (b) your research methodology are located

8) Evidence that you are well-informed

DESCRIPTION OF RESEARCH PROCEDURES

9) How you chose your core setting and relevant peripheral data sources
10) A description of what we need to know about the setting
11) How you developed a research strategy that relates appropriately to the setting
12) How you proceeded in gaining access and collecting data
13) A catalogue of research activities and data collected
14) How you structured your analysis and arrived at your choice of the themes and headings
15) Your system for presenting data (e.g. coding, referencing, anonymizing)

DISCUSSION OF DATA
what has been found

16) Structured with the themes and headings described above
17) What you have learnt from the data
18) How the data provides evidence for what you have found

IMPLICATIONS

19) A summary of what you have found throughout the written study
20) What you think it all means

CONCLUSION
summing up and recommendations

21) Your final comment on all the basic points in your argument

Figure 3.1   Written study, structure and functions

deal with what the researcher did, what the study does, and how the whole research project achieves what it does; thus in effect they represent the infrastructure of the research. They are metastatements – standing outside the hurly-burly of the research process and pointing at it, acting as a map or guide. The terms 'you' or 'your' are emphasized throughout this list because showing the workings of the research requires the researcher to declare her agency – what *she did* in order to carry out the research. (I shall return to the importance of agency and voice in Chapter 6.)

During the rest of this chapter I shall demonstrate how different researchers express a number of the themes on the right of the figure. While they all maintain the principles of the items, there are differences in order and detail, and how they relate to the whole, depending on the length and style of the written study. While maintaining a common discipline within the genre, there is also room for creative difference. Indeed, an advantage of qualitative research is the possibility of considerable variation in the way the study is organized and sequenced. In a sense, it is this creative articulation of approach which carries the study and makes it valid. There will also be considerable variation in detail and extent depending on the level and readership of the study – e.g. whether it is an undergraduate assignment, a doctoral thesis or a published paper.

Introductions

Whereas some shorter works, or chapters in books, may not have abstracts, they all set the scene within an introductory chapter or section.

Explaining why and how

Maguire and Mansfield (1998), in their study of aerobics classes, follow the order of 2, 4, 3, 2, 5 in Figure 3.1; and they insert, in several places, discussion and detail which might 'normally' be left until later in the paper. They thus maintain the principle of showing the *way* in which the research is carried out, and *how* this interacts with the setting expressed. They begin by stating their topic and focus in the form of a research question: 'The principal aim of this paper is to examine the lived, embodied experiences of women who participate in aerobics (exercise to music)' (1998: 109). After a comment on the status of this aim, they then go on to state the research setting, showing at the same time the type of data they will use, 'drawing on evidence from participant observation and interviews, the significances of techniques, practices and rituals of women who participated in a particular aerobic class are mapped out' (1998: 109). This is followed immediately with an explanation of how their work relates to other studies:

> Informed by a feminist-figurational framework, several issues are discussed. The main theme in our findings is that women's bodies are sites for studying the interrelationships between power and gender, discipline and control, and

gendered identity construction. In this respect, our work confirms studies conducted over the past decade. (1998: 109–110)

This is supported by a list of references to the studies, and then a statement about issues to be dealt with in this paper: 'Here, however, we want to emphasize the contribution that a feminist-figurational perspective can make' (1998: 110). After a page of discussion on this point, the authors return to the default format to lay out the structure of the rest of the paper: 'There are several other sections within this paper that frame our case study. A selection of literature is reviewed that examines the lived experiences of active women' (1998: 110). After a little background, they connect the literature with the data they collect – 'This leads to an examination of the complex and dynamic network of power relations, generated by and characteristic of the aerobic class. We utilize the Eliasian concept of established–outsider relations in our analysis of ...' (1998: 111). Then, after further detail on how they do their analysis, the introduction is rounded up with a brief discussion of the final part of the paper, beginning with the statement: 'In the final part of the paper, we connect long term "civilizing processes" to problems of deeply layered gender identities' (1998: 112).

Establishing key terminology

In the introduction to my own doctoral thesis I cover 3, 4, 5 in Figure 3.1. It is in the region of 1,200 words – much longer and more detailed, in balance, with a much more extensive study. However, regardless of this, it is characterized by an early establishing of terminology that will be used throughout the study. The initial statement of motivation based upon professional experience declares that: 'The motivation of this thesis is the occurrence of *tissue rejection* in ... curriculum projects' (Holliday 1991: 1). This is followed with 60 words explaining the technical term 'tissue rejection'. I then go on to introduce the setting and means of data collection:

> As with tissue rejection in organ transplant operations, the reasons for tissue rejection in [... curriculum] projects are complex and deep. In order to find out what these reasons are, it is necessary to carry out extensive investigation, not only of the host institution, but of the host educational environment. ... *Ethnography* was employed in this investigation both to test an ethnographic approach and to provide a methodological base. (Holliday 1991: 1)

This is followed by 600 words on the suitability of ethnography, how this characterizes the overall approach to the research, the subsequent relationship between the role of researcher and that of ethnographer, the resulting applied nature of the ethnography, and the way in which it is adapted to the professional setting. In presenting how the thesis is going to be structured, I begin with the chapter which deals with the major outcome of the research: 'Proposals at the level of principle for transferring findings and methods from the case study to other [curriculum] projects are set out in the penultimate chapter' (1991: 4). The proposals are then listed in a brief explanatory discussion – a further 150 words. Finally comes the summary of what each chapter is about, beginning with:

> The structure of the thesis is as follows. The first chapter surveys the problem of *tissue rejection* in EFL curriculum projects, and the extent to which this can be attributed (a) to the nature of the host educational environment, and (b) to the difficulty which curriculum developers have in finding out about it. (Holliday 1991: 5)

Contextualizing the research

A very different way of doing this is seen in Herrera's master's dissertation, which comprises a study of a girls' school in Cairo. Her introduction follows the order 3, 1, 4, 5 in Figure 3.1. She begins with a long preamble about the under-resourced conditions of education in Egypt: this is immediately detailed, with references to relevant literature. The reason for this is that the bulk of her dissertation, from the preamble onward, is devoted to data analysis. The preamble serves to set the scene to the extent that when she announces the research she did on the third page, it is already well contextualized:

> An ethnographic study of a school enables one to deal with the everyday reality of individuals involved in the process of education and address some very practical questions. Questions such as how, in actuality, does a government school function; how is it organized, what are its dynamics. (Herrera 1992: 3)

She continues to list more questions, and then explains – 'A case study can open up a world, but the reader must be aware of the very particular world being exposed. A number of different factors would alter any given school atmosphere in Egypt' (1992: 3). She lists these factors briefly, then describes the parameters of her particular setting, demonstrating how logistics and opportunity overcame her initial plans:

> Both personal interest and political pragmatism influenced the designation of this particular school as my universe of study. Entering any government institution as a researcher necessitates security clearance, which in this case would be issued by both the Ministry of Education and its Security Office. Although initially interested in studying a school serving the urban poor, I was told that obtaining a security clearance was highly unlikely. It was instead suggested by some Egyptian educators whom I consulted, that an upgraded school in a middle class area would be more suitable for this purpose of conducting research. The prospect of studying a better school, as opposed to one of Cairo's worst, was also appealing as it would allow less room for sensationalism. (1992: 3)

A positive tone is adopted to deal with the choices being made for her by the bureaucracy. She goes on to describe in a further page how she finally got an introduction to a school, and briefly what sort of school it was – its level, type of location, type of student body and the background of the parents. Finally comes the structure of the study, which is described in such a way that a sense of development is clear:

> This study is divided into six chapters which attempt to incorporate different aspects of the school and of education in general. Chapter one deals with my own orientation as a researcher in the school, and by so doing, attempts to orient the reader as well. ... The focus shifts in chapter two from the school itself to the most influential individual in it, the Headmistress. ... Continuing with the attitudes and practices of the Headmistress, but extending them out to encompass a general philosophy about education ... Chapter three ... (1992: 5)

Thus, though very different to the first two examples, all the essential features of the introduction, setting the scene, stating issues, questions and structure plan are covered. Again, however, there are different degrees of detail in different places, to the extent that the more detailed description of setting, which one might expect in the description of research procedures (10 in the Figure 3.1), is brought forward.

Conceptual framework

Throughout the literature on qualitative research, passing reference is made to various types of conceptual framework relating to different aspects of research projects. Robson, speaking of case studies, defines a conceptual framework as covering 'the main features' of the research design and their 'presumed relationships', and says that it 'forces you to be explicit about what you think you are doing' (1993: 150). My interpretation of this is that a major function of the conceptual framework is to position the researcher in relationship to the research (6–7 in Figure 3.1). It is also a place where the issue of ideology inherent in qualitative research can be addressed. Janesick explains this as follows:

> Qualitative researchers accept the fact that research is ideologically driven. There is no value-free or bias-free design. The qualitative researcher early on identifies his or her biases and articulates the ideology or conceptual frame for the study. By identifying one's biases, one can see easily where the questions that guide the study are crafted. (Janesick 2000: 385)

It is therefore a pivotal part of the written study. Figure 3.2 shows how the conceptual framework comprises a major aligning of the key elements of the research project. The methodological approach is positioned ideologically with respect to current discussion and issues as well as to the research setting (1, 3 and 4 in the figure). This enables the characterization of two important points of direction in the research – the *ideological position* and the *impact* on the research setting. The conceptual framework thus states that the researcher's ideological position results from her agreement or disagreement with current discussion and issues (2 in the figure). It then states how, because of this position, her own ideology is defined, directs her research methodology and thus has

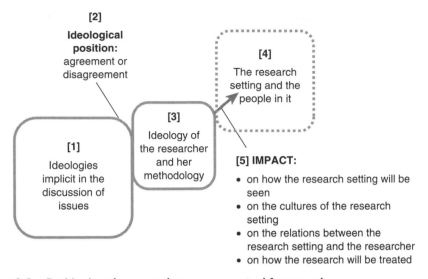

Figure 3.2   Positioning the researcher – a conceptual framework

a certain type of impact on the research setting and the people involved, in terms of all aspects of how she sees, interacts with and treats it (5 in the figure).

It is difficult to find good examples of the conceptual framework because many researchers find it difficult to *see* their own ideological positioning easily. Furthermore, only parts of the framework can be seen in different studies. Examples of this, from the studies consulted in this book, are shown in Table 3.1. Column A in the table first of all shows that although the location of the conceptual framework may be partly in the introduction, it does frequently appear between the discussion of issues related to the subject and the methodology of the research, as suggested in Figure 3.1.

The other interesting thing to note in the table is the distribution of full and empty boxes. In column A, all but one of the authors make explicit statements about their ideology. Indeed, all the works cited are critical works which wish to make statements against the establishment and therefore need to state their own position. The empty boxes in columns C and E indicate that fewer of the researchers found the impact of their ideology on how they saw or treated the setting sufficiently important to make an explicit point, lack of space being a major consideration in shorter works. However, in each study it is possible to see how these boxes may be filled by reading between the lines. In column C, Hayagoshi sees the classroom as a place where behaviour is misinterpreted; and she prioritizes data which reveals this (1996). Maguire and Mansfield and Shaw see the aerobics class and the media, respectively, as battlegrounds between the individual and hegemonic control; and the implications of this are stated in column E, where they prioritize what the individual has to say.

The whole of column D is empty, implying that the impact of researcher ideology on the culture of the research setting and researcher–participant relations is of even

Table 3.1 Examples of conceptual framework

Research study	[A] Location in the written study	[B] Statement of ideology	[C] Impact on how the setting will be seen	[D] Impact on setting cultures and relations	[E] Impact on treatment
Celik 1999	Introduction	'McDonald's has maintained cross-cultural domination.'	'You have to consider how individuals are subsumed into McDonald's corporate identity.'		
Hayagoshi 1996	End of chapter discussing research subject issues	'At this point I shall summarise the position I believe about Japanese students [*sic*] ... Most British teachers still have stereotypical ideas about Japanese students ... which are totally different from how they are now.' (9)			
Maguire and Mansfield 1998	Beginning of discussion of methodological issues	'Our feminist-figurational position emphasises that women are active in interpreting and attaching meaning to their experiences in social settings.' (118)			'On this basis our analysis of the aerobics exercise class gives priority to what these women have to say.' (118)
Talbot 1992	Introduction Beginning of discussion of methodological issues	'Looking at language critically ... can help to "empower" people, in the sense of giving giving them greater conscious control. ... Written mass media texts construct social identities for readers.' (174)	'I will not look at the text in a traditional way as a product of a single author ... [but as] a "tissue of voices" ... of characters who inhabit the text'. (176)		'I have found it helpful to divide the "population of characters" into three categories: interactants, characters, and subject positions.' (177)

(Continued)

Table 3.1   Continued

Research study	[A] Location in the written study	[B] Statement of ideology	[C] Impact on how the setting will be seen	[D] Impact on setting cultures and relations	[E] Impact on treatment
Shaw 1998	During discussion of methodological issues	'The choice of method was also shaped by feminist approaches ... (10)			... placing women at the centre of the research process.' (10)

lower priority for these researchers to write about. It may indeed be that this was felt to be unproblematic. In the case of Talbot, only documents are being dealt with. In interview, one of the authors of Maguire and Mansfield talks at length about her impact on the setting – showing that she was very aware of this during the research process, but that there was no perceived relationship issue:

> To them, because I became open and honest about what I was doing, initially I was a teacher of aerobics, a participant, because not only was I teaching, I would go to other people's classes. To the people who were teaching I was a colleague. But also they then realized that I was doing research, that I was at the local university, that I was doing a study, that I was interested in speaking to people. And interestingly a lot of them, because they volunteered to be inter-viewed, were interested and fascinated by the topic area and were keen to say something. ... In some situations I was an insider and in some situations I was an outsider. I never acted out a role. (Interview)

For other researchers there are significant issues in this area, which do need to be accounted for. At the risk of creating a cliffhanger here, I shall deal with this in detail in Chapter 7 in my discussions of field relations.

Describing procedures

The more practical description of research procedures (9–15 in Figure 3.1) can be dis-tinguished from the more theoretical research methodology part of the written study in the following way. *The research methodology chapter or part* deals with the broader questions of approach – why qualitative research is relevant to the research project, why a particular qualitative approach is used (e.g. why a case study or why action research; why it is justified to look at multiple sites or at the behaviour of one small group). It involves literature review, thus placing the methodology against current theory and issues in social research. *The description of research procedures* applies the principles set out in the discussion of methodology to the practicalities of the day-to-day realities of the setting and structuring of activities by means of an account and cataloguing of what was done and why – usually in the past tense.

Condensed and factual

An example which fits the default picture in Figure 3.1, following the order 10, 9, 13, 11, 14, is Shaw's study of women's images of the body. Her explanation of procedures comes at the end of the section in her paper entitled 'Research questions and methodology', after she has established the theoretical relevance of qualitative research. She begins with a detailed description of setting:

> Three groups of women participated: two 'body' groups and one 'non-body' group. These groups consisted of a diet group (members of 'Weight Watchers'); a fitness group (members of a 'Step Aerobics' group); and a 'non-body' or 'alternative identity' group (members of a Christian organization 'Navigators'). The total number of participants was twelve in each group. (Shaw 1998: 10)

The style here is condensed and factual, very different to the more discursive style that would appear in the discussion of methodological issues which precedes it. Shaw goes on, beginning with citations from literature, to justify the selection of women in each group that made up the setting:

> The selection of women was based on a form of 'theoretical sampling' (Strauss, 1987), guided by the question, 'Where can I find instances of women for whom the body is potentially more or less important in their self-identities?' The women in each group were chosen to exemplify different positions in relation to the body as a 'project'. (Shaw 1998: 10)

She continues in this vein for a further half-page, accounting for each group in turn. Although she now supports her justification with reference to literature, the style is still descriptive. The use of the past tense denotes that she is describing what she *did*.

The next part of the section conflates the catalogue of research activities and indication of dialogue with the setting: 'The interviews were carried out in the home of each participant, and lasted between forty minutes and one hour. The schedule aimed to cover the three main research questions, but interviewees guided the agenda by the extent of their enthusiasm for topics' (1998: 11). This continues with details of how the interviews were taped and transcribed. That Shaw sees no need to justify the interview in terms of its appropriateness to the culture of the setting, presumably indicates that this procedure is not problematic, and is established in her field of study. She is satisfied that it allows the women to 'guide the agenda'. She has stated earlier, in her partial conceptual framework, that her methodology follows feminist principles in placing women at the centre (Table 3.1).

Dialogue with setting is however implicit in the way in which she allows themes to emerge, which are coded and then form the structure of her analysis:

> Gradually, with repeated readings of the data, particular topics became apparent ... and these were assigned a code. The transcripts of the coded passages were scrutinized again, and broader themes identified. The coded phrases were placed under each of these themes. (Shaw 1998: 11)

After some further detail about this procedure, she explains that 'early analysis of the data was fed back to some of the participants for comment' to ensure 'validity', again referring to literature for support. She then concludes by saying that the data analysis in the next section is 'organized according to ... the emerging themes' (1998: 11).

Scholl, in his much shorter undergraduate assignment studying tourist behaviour in churches, still manages to follow 9, 10, 13, 11 in Figure 3.1. He makes a very brief description of setting and activities:

> The location of the churches is in each case in the very middle of the city centre. They are all ... visited by hundreds of thousands of tourists each year, throughout the seasons. Included in the case study are not only the interiors but also churchyards and entrances. Data has been collected in very many ways. The biggest part has been observing people and spotting their behaviour. This has been achieved by sitting in benches and merely observing, wandering around or joining the stream of tourists through the churches. Another good means of survey was to follow a person from the very beginning [from when] he or she entered or paid at the cashier, till the end of the round when he or she left the church. (Scholl 1999)

He continues briefly to add to his catalogue of interviews, drawings and plans to show where people moved and collected, descriptions of surroundings, and 'asking provoking questions to tourists' (an example of the last is discussed in Chapter 2). He demonstrates dialogue with the setting in the way in which he takes notes:

> Most of the observation results were put down immediately, some however had to be written down from memory a few minutes later. As one can imagine, there was not always the possibility given to take out pen and paper and begin scribbling [especially during] provoked interactions with tourists. (Scholl 1999)

Because he carried out this research in a public place, and he takes on the role of mingling with tourists, his dialogue with the setting is no more than that of any other member of the public.

Within the limitations of his short assignment, Scholl does not talk about how his analysis is structured; and neither he nor Shaw goes into the detail of how their data is presented (15 in Figure 3.1). For Shaw this is probably because it is a published study which does not require such detail in showing the workings. Description of how data is presented is however very important in dissertations and theses where emphasis on accountability is greater.

The placing and nature of the description of procedures are sometimes specified by publishers, journals or university departments. For example, in the nursing journal, *Image*, the abstract takes the form of a prescribed catalogue of key aspects of the whole paper under the headings, 'Purpose', 'Design', 'Methods', 'Findings' and 'Conclusions'. Under the first two headings, Berman, in her study of children grow ing up in violence, writes:

> *Design*: Critical narrative and descriptive. Data were collected, 1995–1996, in Canada, from a convenience sample of 16 refugee children of war and 16 children of battered women.
>
> *Methods*: Participants were asked open-ended questions about the violence in their lives, their feelings about what occurred, their thoughts about the reasons for violence, and their ways of surviving and growing. Common themes were identified and validated. (Berman 1999: 57, her emphasis)

There is also a section within the article which deals with procedures, in which more detail is given. The basic default function of the abstract, to provide the essential message (Figure 3.1), is maintained, though a precise catalogue of procedural elements is clearly seen as being a key part of this message, which in turn reflects the technical rigour required by nursing science.

Qualitative researchers, perhaps seduced by notions of intuition and creativeness, can easily underestimate the need for detail in their description of procedure, thus overlooking an important aspect of the demonstration of rigour. One area that requires such detail is the degree of engagement with the setting (Table 1.2), which falls within item 11 in Figure 3.1. Honarbin-Holliday, in her study of two Iranian university art departments, demonstrates the rigour of her engagement in the section of her thesis entitled 'Deconstructing the researcher's methodological behaviours' as follows:

> The process of collecting data depends on meticulous time keeping and constant planning and re-planning, always looking ahead in order to be ready for diversions. It is my experience that diversions do emerge and no matter how well prepared, events do not necessarily develop according to plan. ... The fact was that I felt privileged to be a researching artist, and since I had been given the permission to be at these institutions I wished to adopt strategies that would enable me to use my time in the best possible way. Making sure that I would arrive a few minutes earlier and leave when they [teaching staff and students] did helped my status as a colleague, and a co-worker. I kept to a schedule of two full days per week at Tehran University and two mornings, or one morning and one afternoon at Al-Zahra University. These could not always be the same days, since different tutors came in on different days. I did try to keep at least one day per week at Tehran University, and one afternoon at Al-Zahra University as a constant. These became my days when the students or the tutors could locate me on the campuses, should they wish to discuss particular issues. (Honarbin-Holliday 2005: 47–48)

There is a demonstration here of an important methodological politeness which touches on another area that requires detailed accounting – the sensitive business of developing and maintaining appropriate relations with the people in the setting, which is dealt with in detail in Chapter 7.

Codes and references

Detailed accounting is also important in the cataloguing and coding of which data was collected when, and how it is going to be referenced. A major feature of the 7,000-word description of procedures in my thesis is a table which catalogues all the items of data collected (Holliday 1991: 117). It shows clearly that there are 70 observations in 17 different university sites of 26 class groups, who was teaching, who else was present, and who else was observing along with the researcher. A section of this is displayed in the centre of Figure 3.3, which shows how the information in the table becomes a centrepiece for the way in which the data is referenced in the data discussion chapters. Column 1 shows the position of each observation within the total number. In column 2, LG = local lecturer G, BE = British lecturer B, and Self means that I was teaching myself. In column 4 we see that in observation 33 I had two co-observers, local lecturers B and H, and that in observation 35 I was accompanied by local lecturer G and also videoed (V) and photographed (P) the class. The final column indicates the nature of the event described. All of this information is provided in a key at the foot of the table.

This catalogue also makes the subsequent discussion of the validity of the different types of observation much clearer. For example:

> As [the] table ... shows, the involvement of co-observers was only in fact achieved in 20% of the observations of local lecturers, 30.7% of the observations of expatriate lecturers and 9% of my own lessons. This did not alter the fact that much of value was learnt from observing the behaviour of the local co-observers and their relationship with the class lecturer, in what was for them a very novel experience. (Holliday 1991: 118)

The role of the catalogue in how data is referred to again in the data discussion chapters (Figure 3.3) is explained in a footnote at the beginning of the first of these chapters, to set the scene for how to read the chapters, and also to state the policy on reference to gender:

> A comprehensive catalogue of the observations is in table. ... References to the data will be by the number and the site number of each observation. Lecturers will be referred to as LA, LB etc. (for local lecturers), AB, AC etc. (for American lecturers), and as BA, BB etc. (for British lecturers). No reference is made to the gender of the lecturers because this is not considered relevant to the findings, unless there is specific reference to gender-related elements such as dress. (Holliday 1991: 1251n)

On the right of Figure 3.3 A and B are examples from the data analysis chapters (1991: 231, 332) which refer to items 32 and 35 in the table, showing how the coding is used as reference. There is some variation depending on the type of event. Policy decisions were clearly made not to include subject/event in references to lessons (B), or lecturer in references to other events (A).

A

On one occasion, when inviting a local lecturor to give a seminar:-

[I] had not been able to inform her/him [that there was no overhead projector] before the presentation because s/he had not been at home and the university lines are too crowded for me to get her/him at work. (Obs.32, site 17, seminar)

Obs. no.	Site	Class lecturer	Observer	Subject/ event
32	17	LG		seminar
33	17	LG, self	LB, LH etc.	seminar rehearsal
34	11			university bus
35	13	BE	LG, (V) (P)	*Essay-Composition*

B

The two photographs (6.6–7) from the same lesson show the front rows involved in group work; and in my notes from the presence of the camera:-

There was little evidence that the students were behaving differently to what they would normally do–as experienced in other observations of the same class in the same room. (Obs.35, site 13, BE)

Photo.6.6: Obs.35, site 13, BE

Photo.6.7: Obs.35, site 13, BE

Figure 3.3   Coding used for reference to data

Protocols such as these will be dealt with again in Chapter 6, but it can be noted here that the indented quotations from the data, the references in brackets and the 'Photo' captions, are equivalent to quotations from literature with their references in brackets (e.g. Holliday 1991: 221), and to captions for figures or tables. Thus, the data catalogue table is equivalent to a bibliography in that it provides the master list for referencing in the body of the study.

Integrated with other parts of the study

The description of research procedures is not always located in the same part of the study. This is especially true of pure ethnographies, where the researcher is immersed in the research setting for an extended period. Here the development of research strategy grows gradually with the process of learning about the research setting, and the data is less compartmentalized – essentially the researcher holistically observes everything. Once the principles of ethnography have been accepted, the issues in this type of qualitative research are not so much which data to collect when and involving whom, but the overall developing of access, relationships and acceptable researcher presence. Thus, in Herrera's dissertation, discussion of procedure is integrated within her first proper chapter (i.e. after her introductory preamble) in which she describes the 'newcomer's orientation'. Here she takes on a very personal tone and describes how her overall acceptance in the school and access to classes depended on her being taken seriously as a married woman with children (Herrera 1992: 12–15). I shall look further at this type of data in Chapter 7, and in detail at what happened to Herrera, and how this in itself provided valuable reflexive data, in Chapter 8. Here, however, we should note that at the end of her first chapter, 'Newcomer's orientation', she explains how procedures for data collection were helped along by her developing relations with the teachers in the school, and she explains how these procedures developed at the same time as she writes about relations with people in the setting. She thus emphasizes the degree to which this research interacts with the research setting (item 11 in Figure 3.1):

> After obtaining permission to tape-record interviews at the school [from the Headmistress] four months after arriving there, a time when I began more systematically gathering information based on the experience of some months of observation ... I developed a friendship with a group of teachers, four in particular, who took an interest in the study, and opened my eyes to the salient issues of the school. Although the anthropological literature would label these individuals with the impersonal title of 'informant', I prefer to put our personal and professional relationship in the context of education, and call them my supervisors, or *moshrifeen*, as they are called in Arabic. These teachers, although my peers in age, patiently and enthusiastically oversaw my work, just as their more experienced and senior advisors did for them. They helped me compile informal questionnaires and gather statistics, reviewed my notes and evaluated my progress. (Herrera 1992: 16)

Here can also be seen the movement from broad to focused research characteristic of ethnography (e.g. Spradley 1980: 34), showing how this was not so much the choice of the researcher as precipitated by the way in which the setting responded to her presence.

Another case in which explaining research procedures was integrated with data analysis is in Kyeyune's (1996) doctoral thesis on education in Uganda. A surface look at her contents page gives the impression that only a very small part of her thesis is devoted to data analysis, and a large part devoted to research methodology and procedure. However, closer inspection reveals that the latter chapters are in effect data analysis, which has the dual role of informing research methodology and procedure.

In shorter studies the explanation of procedures can also be integrated with the discussion of methodological issues. This can be seen in Broadley's study of body builders, in his chapter entitled 'Methods of research', where he writes, supporting what he says with reference to literature:

> The reason for only investigating male bodybuilders and not females is because, as was found by Padfield and Proctor (1996), a better detailed response is given when a male interviews males and when a female interviews females. Therefore, as the author is male, males only were selected for interviewing. (Broadley 1999: 17)

Significance of research strategy

The concern with showing the workings of research procedure, demonstrated so far in this chapter, can go right through to the final stages of the study. The part where the implications of the research are finally discussed (items 19-20, Figure 3.1) can look at *procedural* as well as *substantive* issues. In other words, answering the question '*What does it all mean?*' could be to do with the substance of social life and may read like this:

> I have discovered something about the *substance* of particular phenomena within a particular social setting. How important is this something? What does it contribute to our understanding of phenomena and social life, and to this type of phenomena and social setting?

And also with procedures for looking:

> Throughout my research I have developed a particular methodological *procedure* for addressing particular questions about a particular social setting. What are the implications of using this procedure? How effective has it been? Have I developed a way of looking, and of interacting with the social setting, which has enabled me better to understand the types of phenomena I am interested in? Is there something significant in this procedure which could be of interest to other researchers? What contribution can it make to understanding how to do qualitative research?

Whether or not researchers give this sort of attention to procedure will depend on the overall aims of their research and the extent to which their procedure is innovative or has had a noteworthy effect on what they found out. Attention could be given in a small way. For example, Scholl notes that, in his study of tourist behaviour in churches, 'working all alone had some undeniable advantages'. He 'could easily mix with tourists and talk to them without being suspected of doing research'. On the other hand, he notes that 'there was but one perspective available'; moreover that a larger-scale research project, which might include interviewing staff, would have found much more (Scholl 1999). Shaw says more about the importance of using a qualitative approach to the female body in the media:

> Finally, the research described in this paper also contributes to a methodological debate about ways of researching the body. It illustrates how a qualitative approach ... can provide a rich and detailed account of women's experiences of embodiment, in contrast with 'rigorous' yet decontextualized accounts ... provided by experimental studies. (Shaw 1998: 23)

It can of course be argued that the procedures for looking are also part of social life, and that finding out about them is also substantive; this would be the case if the major aim of the research was to investigate and develop research procedures per se. This was very much the case in my own thesis. In my introduction I state that I am as concerned with 'the application of ethnography' within the work of the curriculum developer as 'with the problem of the interface between the [curriculum] project and the host educational environment' (Holliday 1991: 2). Indeed, I am developing the former to help solve the latter. Thus, in my penultimate 'principles' chapter, I look closely at the ethnographic procedures I have used in order to distinguish those that could be 'eco-transferable' to other curriculum projects from those that are non-transferable. The outcome of this analysis is as follows:

> Observation before and during innovation simultaneously ... observation of eccentric classroom situations ... the use of local lecturers as co-observers, and ... keeping record of discussion with lecturers after observation, are all eco-transferable. They ... could be carried out in any local situation, barring very unusual circumstances. ... Observation of a large number of different classes, and ... observation of own classes and expatriate lecturers, on the other hand, are related to features specific to the local situation. They clearly depend on the existence of these features in the local situation. (Holiday 1991: 431)

Articulating issues

The importance of showing the workings of qualitative research is brought home to me when a student comes to see me with a question such as, 'Can I base my data collection on interviewing three people?' My response to this is, 'You can if you can articulate the justification for doing so.' Cynics might say that qualitative researchers can do whatever they want, that the research possibilities are so open and unstructured, with no inhibition about being subjective, that anything goes and that there is no rigour and accountability whatsoever. This is certainly not the case, simply because the workings have to be declared and accounted for. If a researcher wants to base her data collection on three interviews, following the principles set out in this chapter, she will have to do the following:

1   Describe very precisely in the *explanation of research procedures* who is being interviewed, in what manner, how the interviewees were therefore selected, how this relates to the research setting both in terms of appropriate relationships and representativeness – why other more 'standard' modes of data collection are not appropriate.

2   Support this in the *discussion of methodological issues* with precedents from other research, and theoretical principles within qualitative research – *or* trace it to deeper discussions in the philosophy of knowledge or science, and suggest *new theory* – in either case show how it is consonant with her conceptual framework.

3   Signal it as a prominent feature of the research in the *introduction* – especially if it is new theory – so that a reader of the study does not come upon it unexpectedly – to ensure that it is not seen as an afterthought or as response to lack of thought or planning, or of panic.

4   Evaluate its contribution in the *implications* chapter or section – its ultimate justification being that it was a major factor in achieving the particular understanding of the social phenomenon featured in the research – if it derives from theory, argue how far it is groundbreaking, making it a major procedural finding of the research.

5   Overall, make sure that the claims made are appropriate to the size of the study.

This example shows very well how the different parts of the written study are linked by the thread of a particular argument. Indeed, there will be several other arguments threading their way through the different stages of the study in this way, pulling it together and making it into a whole, coherent symphony. As the workings of the research provide the infrastructure for the whole investigatory project, their writing provides an infrastructure for the whole written study.

Summary

The following points have been made in this chapter:

- Showing the workings of the research is necessary for the accountability of qualitative research.
- The workings of the research can be found in various places throughout the written study. It can be divided into the following areas: introduction, conceptual framework, explaining procedures and significance of research strategy.
- Different studies show their workings in different ways, in different orders and to different degrees of intensity, but tend to follow a common discipline.
- Introductions generally tend to explain why and how, establish key terminology and contextualize the research.
- The conceptual framework, where it occurs, is pivotal in that it positions the ideology of the researcher with respect to current discussions and to the impact she will have on the research setting and the people in it.
- The description of procedures is condensed and factual; especially in assessed work it deals with conventions for coding and referencing, and provides a catalogue of what has been done. In some studies it is integrated with the process of data analysis and in others with the discussion of methodological issues.
- Some studies report important procedural discoveries, about how the research strategy was carried out, as well as substantive discoveries about the social phenomena they are researching.

CHAPTER FOUR

What Counts as Data

This chapter and Chapter 5 deal with the issue of data in qualitative research. Here I shall look at what data in qualitative research is like – where it comes from and what makes it valid – first of all pursuing the idea that data must be interconnected in social settings, then looking at the issues of coverage and the feasibility of very small studies, as related to the concept of thick description, and finally looking at social phenomena *as* data through making the familiar strange. In Chapter 5 I shall deal with how the researcher presents her data and what she says about it. The story of data will not however be concluded in these two chapters. In Chapter 6 I shall look at the details of language in research description, which is taken further into the issue of culturism in Chapter 8. In Chapter 7 I shall look at reflexive data – how the researcher needs to see her own presence as a potential source of data.

Overview of qualitative data

As in Chapter 1, I shall begin here by contrasting qualitative data with the more 'traditional' notion of data in quantitative research. This is because when most people, including many researchers, think about data they tend to think within the quantitative paradigm.

Bodies of experience

In Table 1.1 I listed the first activity within quantitative research as counting occurrences across large populations. Here we have the notions of 'survey' and 'statistics'. Data 'are' essentially plural – the number of Ford or Peugeot cars sold, a number of questionnaire responses, or the number of times a teacher asks a question in class. Qualitative data 'is' conceived very differently. It is what happens in a particular social setting – in a particular place or amongst a particular group of people. The uncountable singular form is in popular use but considered less correct by many qualitative as well as quantitative researchers.

Table 4.1 provides a rough catalogue of types of qualitative data which I find useful. There are also many possible overlaps – e.g. bits of talk (h) can also be present in description of behaviour (a). I have taken examples mainly, but not only, from Herrera's study of schooling because I want to show the variety that can be found in one study, but also from other sources. I have been careful to separate what sorts of things a particular type of data represents and how it is collected (columns 2 and 3). I wish to emphasize that observation notes, research diaries, interviews and questionnaires are *not* types of data, but devices for collecting it. The examples in the table, and elsewhere in this chapter are extracts of data which are cited in written studies. I shall talk about this process of moving from 'raw' field data to the presentation of extracts of data in the written study in Chapter 5.

There is not the space to look in detail at all of these examples of data; so I will focus on those which are less commonly discussed in the qualitative research literature – researcher descriptions of what they experience (a–f in the table) – and those which I feel are particularly powerful in taking the researcher into the more hidden depths of cultural reality – visual record and document (i–j). I shall leave discussion of description of research event (e) to Chapter 7, where I show how such reflections on research behaviour are a major data source for developing a methodology that is appropriate to the setting and establishing good relationships with the people in it, and discussion of personal narrative used as data (f) to Chapter 6 within the theme of researcher voice.

I shall not spend time on verbatim data – what the people in the research setting actually say (g and h in the table), because so much is written about this elsewhere and because, while it is a very important data type, I am not convinced about the higher status it is often accorded in qualitative research. Although the actual words that people say undeniably represent their views, verbatim data is as much mediated by the presence of the researcher, what she chooses to ask, the way she asks it, how she leads the conversation, how she frames the interview event, what she chooses to select from the broader corpus, how she interprets what she selects, and so on. It is certainly not the case that what people say is hard evidence of what they think. On several occasions when I have asked interviewees to confirm what they said in the past, they have told me that their words belonged only to the moment of the research event. Verbatim data has therefore to be managed for its subjectivity just as much as other data forms. Furthermore, verbatim data cannot always capture the physical aspects of what is going on; and people in the setting do not know everything about it. I see the fact that it is often hard to get qualitative research published if it is not supported by actual quotes as a political rather than a methodological matter. (See discussion of these issues in Pelto and Pelto 1970, Adler and Adler 1994, Block 2000.) It is therefore my view that all the data types in Table 4.1 have potentially equal status. This issue of how 'emic' the research is – how far it sees things from the point of view of the people in the research setting, relates as much to verbatim data as it does to descriptive data, as I shall demonstrate in Chapter 8.

Table 4.1   Types of data

Type	Characteristics	How collected	Examples
a) Description of behaviour	What people are seen or heard doing or saying	Observation notes, research diary etc.	Almost before she finished her sentence another student approached the desk, leaned forward, placing her elbow at the edge of it, and with cast down eyes began to speak. The Headmistress screamed abruptly 'Stand up straight!! Now keep your arms at your sides!' The girl flushed, continued to speak. (Herrera 1992: 8)
b) Description of event	Piece of behaviour, defined either by the people in the setting (e.g. wedding, meeting) or by the researcher (e.g. bus journey, argument)	Ditto	The Headmistress suddenly charged into the classroom to everyone's surprise. The girls looked up from their papers and slightly gasped from seeing her, while the teachers jumped up to attention. (Herrera 1992: 50)
c) Description of institution	The way the setting operates in terms of regulations, tacit rules, rituals	Ditto	[The Headmistress] presides as the head of almost every aspect of the school, from ensuring that the classrooms have proper lighting, to approving the teaching schedule, to setting limits and standards for teacher and student behaviour. (Herrera 1992: 8)
d) Description of appearance	What the setting or people in it look like (e.g. space, buildings, clothing, arrangement of people or objects, artefacts)	Ditto, drawings, diagrams	The office, cloaked in pale green paint, the floor covered by a brown Oriental carpet, had all the necessary furnishings for receiving visitors: a timeworn green vinyl couch with three matching armchairs, a coffee table and three unmatched wooden chairs positioned around the long wooden desk. The desk held an ashtray. A half-cup of tea, a thin file, and the folded hands of the Headmistress. (Herrera 1992: 7)
e) Description of research event	What people say or do in interview, focus group etc.	Observation notes, research diary etc.	I entered the class after it had begun (late finding the place) and was sat on a chair on the plinth. There was no way I could have found a seat at the back; but I found that seeing the students' faces was a big advantage. The students did not seem to notice me too much. (Holliday 1991: 257–258)

Table 4.1   Continued

Type	Characteristics	How collected	Examples
f) Personal narrative	Reconstruction of experience that aids understanding	Narrative, research diary etc.	Measuring just over seven centimetres high and standing in all its nakedness - was the most innocent little doll I had ever seen. ... I felt clumsy as the frailty of its limbs brushed against my fingers ... four thousand years after its original crafting its gentle fibres tugged at my heart strings with phenomenal strength. ... Who had cherished this little plaything so long ago? Had they felt as protective and caring as I? (Ovenden 2003: 42–43)
g) Account	What people say or write to the researcher – actual words	Interview, audio recording, questionnaire, participant's diary, transcription, verbatim notes	'When I came here I found serious disorder among the faculty and the student body. A lack of respect for the school and for all its rules predominated.' (Herrera 1992: 18, interview with headmistress)
h) Talk	What people are heard saying – actual words	Audio recording, transcription, verbatim notes	'The teachers come on time now for the classes. They are never late this year because they know the Headmistress will shout at them and replace them with another teacher.' (Herrera 1992: 21, student comment)
i) Visual record	What is actually seen	Film, video recording	See Figures 4.1 and 4.2
j) Document	Piece of writing belonging or pertaining to the setting	Photocopy, scan	'The school principal or director assumes full responsibility for taking decisions concerning his (her) own school. The Ministry and the Directorate of Education cannot interfere with his (her) work except with regard to checking the correct implementation of laws and regulations undertaken during school visitations.' (Herrera 1992: 18, citing the National Centre for Educational Research)

The content of description

There are important things to notice about the content of researcher descriptions. There is always the question of the neutrality of language used. An example of this can be seen in Table 4.1, where, for example, Herrera writes 'with cast down eyes began to speak' (row a). 'Cast down eyes' in this context seems to me to imply deference. I do not know whether the researcher (a) knows that the student is lowering her eyes out of deference and intends to communicate this, or (b) does not know and is therefore allowing her own language to run away with itself. A more neutral description would seem to me to be 'with eyes looking down'. This is a difficult issue which raises the discussion of whether description needs to be or should be neutral anyway, and how far it can be neutral. This area will be looked at in detail in Chapter 8, but in this chapter I invite the reader to look out for and consider such examples throughout the fragments of data cited. It is worth thinking about the use of 'charged' (b in Table 4.1), 'presides' (c), and 'cloaked' (d).

There is also the issue of what the researcher chooses to describe. Some novice researchers have difficulty in *finding* things to describe or knowing what is important to describe. This relates to what appears interesting and significant, which in turn relates to the sense of argument which takes place throughout the whole research process (see Chapter 5). It is significant that Herrera has chosen to note, for example, the positioning of the girl's elbow on the headmistress's desk (a in Table 4.1), the noise the girls make when the headmistress enters the class (b), and, in the headmistress's office (d) the colour of the paint, carpet and furniture, the age and material of the couch, the fact that the chairs around the desk are not matched, the shape and material of the desk, and some specific items on the desk including a 'half' cup of tea, a 'thin' file and the headmistress's own hands. All of these details not only give colour and depth, but represent aspects of people or the institution to which Herrera wishes to draw attention. They also demonstrate the rigour with which the researcher has noticed what is going on. The elbows on the desk, the sighs of the girls and the folded hands of the headmistress all seem to me to indicate a stream of warmth and intimacy which runs through an otherwise formal, authoritarian relationship. When I have shown this particular description to my students they have often overlooked the intimacy and seen only the authoritarian side. The fact that Herrera was actually there and saw broader aspects of the culture makes a huge difference. Nevertheless, this detail of observation adds to the credibility of her overall argument and also illustrates an aspect of social reality which can be revealed only in descriptive data of this type. Where readers may not agree with her interpretation, at least the researcher has the level of detail to enable her to make her point as strongly as she can. Many of the data fragments cited in this chapter display detail of this nature. I shall stop and comment on this from time to time; but, again, I invite the reader to be aware throughout.

It is important to note that in the description of behaviour (a in the table), speech is also reported. This is not verbatim data and does not pretend to be so, but a description rather than a recording of what people say as part of the broader behavioural event. Honarbin-Holliday, in her study of Iranian university art departments, takes this possibility to the extent of describing rather than recording interviews in cases where she feels the presence of a voice recorder would be intrusive and politically inappropriate. It was only when 'the participants and myself got used to the idea of photos, [that] I introduced a tape recorder to my methodological tools' – and this had to be 'in the open and in a public area at the universities'. Even then she saw the audio recording as richer than just the recording of what people said – 'Recording in public spaces has projected some additional sounds such as the muezzin's call to prayer ... and the roar of the traffic. These are of particular interest to me personally, reminding me of the moments of interaction' (Honarbin-Holliday 2005: 50). An example of described rather than recorded speech is as follows:

> The young student, in her pale colour 'roopoosh' overalls and head scarf, says that the drawings presented are her work during the summer which she has spent mostly at home with her young children. She talks about her love of drawing the human form in motion. (Honarbin-Holliday 2005: 68)

I think it is significant that, here again, what this student is seen to be saying, especially with regard to 'the human form', is in the same breath as a comment on her physical appearance – which is a major factor in Honarbin-Holliday's developing thesis. I shall look at the importance of this sort of interconnection in thick description later in the chapter.

Visual data

Honarbin-Holliday's note that she found taking photographs less intrusive than using a voice recorder brings me to the often overlooked value of visual data (in Table 4.1). Visual data is commonly categorized as photographs and film. I would also like to include cultural artefacts that carry an obvious visual message in the media and on signs, billboards, displays. In the eyes study in Example 1.6, people in the research setting are asked to show photographs of family and friends. These photographs, not taken by the researcher, but significant within the culture in question, are also important data. I shall look at photographs as data co-constructed by the researcher and the people in the setting in Chapter 5.

I do not see visual data as so distinct from the descriptive data discussed above in that both are ways of representing what the researcher *sees*. Whereas description is very clearly the researcher's own interpretation of what she sees in her own words, photographs and film are also dependent on the researcher's interpretive act of where to point her camera. Signs, billboards, displays, extracts from the media and other people's photographs, when collected as data, are also dependent on the interpretive act of which ones to choose. However, visual data has often been treated as something different and marginal within the largely word-oriented disciplines of anthropology, ethnography and qualitative research (Ball and Smith 1999: 7), or when used, photographic images remain secondary extras to the written text (Harper 2005: 749). However, the issues of discipline, ideology, sensationalism, representation, and the ethical issues surrounding images of people, which characterize discussions about how far visual data is valid (Becker 1997; Kress et al. 1997: 257; Ball and Smith 2001; Rose 2001; Holliday 2006; Harper 2005: 760) are really no different to the issues surrounding all qualitative data once the inevitability of subjectivity has been addressed. Photographs, for example, 'do *not* unambiguously and transparently record reality'. On the one hand, each one is just one of many possible views of the same thing. On the other, what is seen is mediated by the viewer's cultural and personal knowledge and 'visual literacy' (Ball and Smith 2001: 305, my emphasis).

Harper (2000) provides a detailed account of the technical issues of taking ethnographic photographs, noting the difference between what the eye and the camera actually see, and that we should not be seduced by the apparent reality they portray. The same can be said about descriptive or verbatim data, where 'what is seen' can be replaced by 'what is read'. The need to manage subjectivity applies equally to both visual and non-visual data. Nevertheless, the visual image's place on the edge of established method presents some researchers with a particularly creative break from postpositivism which contributes to a new 'way of seeing' (Pink 2001: 13). This can be seen in the use of photographs to access identity construction and counter narratives (Meinhof and Galasinski 2000; Harrison 2002). My own research on hidden and counter cultures has been very much influenced by Collier's (1979) speeded-up silent film revealing the otherwise hidden rhythms of Alaskan classrooms.

Photographs are used in my study of Egyptian classrooms. The way in which they complement lesson descriptions and also video sequences is seen in example B in Figure 3.3. The photograph in Figure 4.1 of students in a crowded Egyptian classroom is one of two which accompany a description of how the students were able to work in self-selected groups, along with a video sequence:

> The film shows about 50% of the lesson taken up with informal group work (obs.35, site 13, BE). The two photographs (6.6–7) from the same lesson show the front rows involved in group work; and in my notes from the lesson I recorded that, despite the presence of the camera: 'There was little evidence that the students were behaving differently to what they would normally do'. (Holliday 1991: 186)

This reference to whether or not the people in the research were 'behaving differently' raises the issue of researcher interference which, though relevant to all aspects of data collection, is often a particular concern when researchers bring cameras into the research setting. Despite Honarbin-Holliday's comment above, this practice is often believed to be more intrusive than voice recorders. It is important to note here, however, that whereas verbal descriptions of social behaviour, once made, leave behind the actual physicality of what was seen at the time for ever, photographs and film retain aspects of this physicality for future scrutiny – where the people in the picture are looking, the expressions on their faces, their physical demeanour, how they are dressed, the nature of their proximity to each other, and, indeed, what they may be thinking about the camera. The photograph in Figure 4.1 has taken on a life of its own which continues to remind me of what was going on at the time of taking it, and leads me to new interpretations again and again. Observers of the visual image, more than the readers of descriptions, who were not there at the time, will also continue to have their own insights. The same of course

Figure 4.1   Egyptian university students

also applies to verbatim data. Following my discussion above, this does not mean that visual and verbatim data hold more validity – simply that they contain more to seduce the onlooker. They are all images which create subjective meanings and shape-shift in our heads.

Another example of visual data in my corpus of written studies is Scholl's floor plan showing how the tourists move between spaces in his study of tourist behaviour in cathedrals (1999). I shall say more about Honarbin-Holliday's extensive use of photographs in Chapter 5. Amongst studies by recent and current students in Canterbury (Colson, Mahendru, Armellini, Moore, Carlson, Herrera Diaz, Grounds, Palfreyman, Kullman and Grimshaw) there are photographs and drawings of building exteriors and interiors which show the architectural influence on aspects of university life in Mexico, Turkey and China, stills from computer screens in studies of how people use the internet, photographs and video sequences of student, time-share seller and tourist, and mother and midwife behaviour, plus clips from the media to background aspects of cultural life.

Goulimaris (in process), in his study of Greek television news, makes a close analysis of television stills and sequences. Figure 4.2 shows an Iranian general being interviewed about the 2005 Iranian earthquake. Goulimaris notes that whereas a general from a 'more powerful', 'Western' country would be named and labelled as 'a general', the lower-status labelling of him as 'an official' at the top of the screen, without actually naming him or his specific occupation, indicates his relatively lower status of coming from a 'less powerful', 'non-Western' country, and indeed possessing less individuality, in the eyes of the Greek media. He makes the overall comment that 'since we are talking about professional people doing a job that reflects a lot of

Figure 4.2   Greek news still

ideology, there is always something to be said about the background [of the news image], about whatever people would be wearing, how they would be standing' (Goulimaris, interview).

Artefacts revealing the unfamiliar

Herrera Diaz, Grounds, Palfreyman, Grimshaw, Sharpe and Goulimaris (op. cit.) all use visual images which depict *artefacts* of cultural life – as distinct from snapshots and sequences of behaviour such as those used in my study of Egyptian classrooms (Figure 4.1). This depiction of artefacts involves an important aspect of researcher discipline in data collection. It is not sufficient for the researcher simply to collect examples and describe what she sees in the setting she is investigating. It is also necessary for her to make sure that she *sees* in a particular way. This is connected with my comments at the beginning of the chapter about trying to describe neutrally. It is also to do with taking on the role of researcher as stranger and thus seeing the familiar as strange, as introduced in Chapter 1.

The way in which artefacts can be used as data illustrates this particular way of seeing the social world, which underlies all the other data sources. Artefacts are part of the physical representation of culture – things that are made, worn, said, displayed, shown, exchanged and so on. In description (d) in Table 4.1 we see how the green paint, the Oriental carpet and the half cup of tea characterize the lived-in intimacy of the headmistress's office, and help us to see the human side of her apparent authoritarianism; and the 'clean, dark polished shoes, which should be low-heeled and should have slip-resistant soles' tell us much about the institutional regime of McDonald's in Celik's description cited earlier in this chapter. It is seeing such objects as cultural representations rather than as information that is important. We all sometimes see objects as cultural representations in this way when we think critically or creatively about our surroundings – noticing how styles of clothing, turns of phrase, types of decoration etc. represent social trends of which we approve or disapprove. However, this sort of noticing does require stepping outside the 'thinking-as-usual' about familiar objects in terms of their everyday functions. The qualitative researcher needs to get into this type of noticing all the time, as an essential element of the discipline.

An example of making the familiar strange by looking at artefacts in this way can be seen in the way Goulimaris looks at the still of a news item in Figure 4.2. The same applies to the different ways we can look at everyday documents such as a university prospectus. *In the 'thinking-as-usual' mode*, prospective students read it to find what they need to know, perhaps to decide whether or not to apply to the institution. They take from it information about what the university is like – fees, academic successes, facilities, extra-curricular activities.

When we look at it as an artefact – as *a physical representation of the university as a culture*, we see it as an artefact of how the university wants to present itself in terms of image, values, ideology in the way in which topics are selected, displayed, framed and ordered. The researcher is concerned with what the document *does* and *projects* rather than the information it provides. To see the document in this way, the researcher must step out of her normal role as user and consumer. She must attain a critical awareness, so that she can stand aside from, suspend and 'bracket' her normal view of the world. This does not mean that she stops behaving naturally, but that she behaves as she does when she encounters something so new that 'thinking as normal' is replaced by 'asking ethnographic questions', as discussed in Chapter 2. Such questions are suggested by Wallace, to address the 'taken-for-grantedness' of texts, within a framework of 'critical literacy awareness' – what is the topic, why is it being written about, how is it being written about, what other ways of writing about the topic are there, and who is writing to whom? – (Wallace 1992: 71, adapting from Kress).

In this book I am dealing with my corpus of written studies in this way – looking at them as documentary artefacts of the culture of writing in qualitative research, rather than as specific contributions to bodies of knowledge in social science. I am looking at practices in writing which may be taken for granted by their authors as internalized knowledge of how to do things. However, because I am not concerned so much with *what* they are saying about the people and settings they study, as with *how* they say it, I am not going so far as to be critical of the topics they choose and how they present these topics. In the last three chapters I shall nevertheless address some of the ideologies implicit in the way in which qualitative research is written.

Revealing ideology

Fairclough demonstrates how the values and ideology of a 1993 Lancaster University prospectus can be seen in this way:

> The promotional function is primary; it is designed to 'sell' the university and its courses. ... The content and form ... are informed by market research – evidence of what applicants most want to know ... an understanding of the literacy culture of young people (e.g. the salience of 'glossy' printed material of various sorts), and understanding of the conditions of reading documents of this sort (they are likely to be flicked through rather than carefully read), and so forth. (Fairclough 1995: 156–157)

He goes on to demonstrate, by drawing attention to details of layout, colour, graphics and language, how it uses a 'quasi-advertising genre' to fulfil an entrepreneurial ideology:

> [It] uses a brochure-style page size and layout with three print columns per page, colour (the first page of the entry uses five colours), tabular layout and a photograph. ... The personalization of the institution (as *we*), which occurs heavily in this part of the entry, is part of this. (Fairclough 1995: 157)

Sharpe similarly sees documents as data in the following observation of the front cover of a French primary school textbook, where he comments on the layout and font:

> The greatest emphasis is given to the single word 'cours' which is written in letters whose relative size implicitly proclaims the book's purpose: to give lessons in spelling to pupils at CE and CM levels. The whole impression created is one devoid of any intrinsic appeal to young children. Books more recently published have in many cases some sort of design, but this does little to alleviate the 'dryness' of the image created, one not intended to evoke interest or excitement in the child's imagination. (Sharpe 1994)

Talbot, in her study of teenage magazines, notes how an extract from *Jackie* creates a sense of characters in 'a community of lipstick wearers':

> The testimonials section provides the most explicit cues to characters in the beauty feature; namely, four snapshots captioned with names and ages and four texts marked off with speech marks. Four individuals are quoted by the editorial-as-interviewer. ... Whether or not actual interviews did take place, the interviewees have been constructed both as interactants (with the interviewer) and as characters – they are set up textually for the reader. (Talbot 1992: 182)

As with the visual data discussed earlier, with these examples of textual analysis, the actual image of the text is appended so that it can be seen by the reader. This means that there is no description of the text in the way that there might be a description of behaviour or event (Table 4.1) which cannot be seen by the reader. The actual data therefore is the document itself – the front cover of the book in the case of Sharpe, and the extract from the magazine in the case of Talbot. The above examples therefore show the researcher's commentary on the data rather than the data itself. In the next chapter I deal with how researchers use this type of commentary when they write about the data. In Chapter 6 I shall return to the example from Talbot's work to demonstrate how material such as documents is appended and then 'pointed' to by the researcher.

Revealing an underlife

Cultural artefacts like documents can reveal deeper, more tacit aspects of cultural life. It is indeed debatable just how far the designers of the teenage magazine are aware of the way in which they construct femininity for teenage girls by building a virtual community of characters who share specific values. Talbot claims in her study to be '"making strange" conventions which usually seem perfectly natural to people who use them' (1992: 174); in Fairclough's terms, 'making visible the interconnectedness of things' about which 'people are standardly unaware' (1995: 37). Documents can also reveal secret, hidden worlds which are difficult to fathom through observed behaviour and events or accounts of people in the research setting. Canagarajah uses documents and what people write on them in his attempt to reveal the 'vibrant *underlife*' of Tamil secondary school students which teachers and researchers rarely see (1999: 92). He looks at the 'glosses' or margin notes and other embellishments which students write on their textbooks, and sees that:

> Many of the glosses consist of symbols and motifs inspired by the ongoing nationalist struggle. ... Refrains from popular Tamil resistance songs are penned all over the textbooks. ... Fletcher [a character in one of the texts], seated in a prison cell in the first unit, has been given the honorific mark of *tikalam* on his forehead, a mustachio and spectacles. ... Tamil proverbs, aphorisms and riddles also fill the margins of the books. (Canagarajah 1999: 89)

He interprets these as representation of the 'counter-discourses the students use to detach themselves from the ideologies of the textbooks' (1999: 91). Different from the examples above, from Fairclough, Sharpe and Talbot, this researcher does not append examples of the documents. His descriptions are integrated into a wider description of the culture.

Arising from social settings

It can be difficult to handle the element of unpredictability which qualitative research intentionally invites (see Table 1.1). Strategies for collecting qualitative data have to develop in dialogue with the unfolding nature of social settings, and with opportunity and developing relations between the researcher and other people in the research process. You cannot decide exactly what sort of data you are going to collect before you begin. As part of their research training, some of my students have to write an assignment in which they plan a particular investigation. They often successfully state research questions and choice of setting. But they meet problems when stating their data collection strategy. When they say that first they will observe so many classes for such and such a period, and then interview so many teachers and students, I have to dampen their enthusiasm and write in the margin, '*Why? How do you know?*' Then I have to remind them that any decisions they make about data must *depend* on what they know and discover about the research setting, and that they must *explain* this – show their workings from the very outset (see Chapter 3). A 'correct' assignment would therefore read something like:

EXAMPLE 4.1   ASSIGNMENT EXTRACT

I hope to begin by observing three different classes through February and March. This will depend on the school principal giving permission, and three teachers with whom I have a good relationship letting me into their classes. The timing corresponds with the start and finish of a course in communication skills for airport personnel. I intend that the first two weeks of observation will be exploratory. What emerges will help me decide what other types of data to collect.

One would not always expect the degree of complexity faced by Herrera in her relations with educational bureaucracy and the teachers she wanted to observe; but a true dialogue with the setting must be anticipated, as we shall see in Chapter 7.

Qualitative data therefore *arises*, or emerges, from social settings. As discussed in Chapter 2, much of the effort of qualitative research is getting yourself into settings that are sufficiently rich for data to emerge.

Systems of data

Once in a rich setting, the way is open for collecting some if not all of the types of data listed above. Imagine you have gained access to a rich setting, with the full variety of behaviour, events, rules and routines, physical environment, talk, documents and artefacts. Imagine that your research question is very expansive, rather like Herrera's '*What is going on in this school?*' In these circumstances you could simply record everything you come across. In effect *everything is data* – behaviour, talk, documents, artefacts – from the school timetable being inaccurate to not being allowed into classes, to the way in which the researcher is received – from what is said, to what is done, to the placing of the furniture and the way in which materials are presented. It is not however advisable to record *all* the data you come across. On the one hand, you might end up with an unmanageably large quantity of data. One of my students made this mistake and ended up with a room full of audio recordings of every minute of talk she was exposed to. On the other hand, random collection could result in a mish-mash of unconnected data – an observation here, two interviews there, a photograph of something over there. Although the setting provides boundaries within which data can be connected, the researcher has to *do* the connecting. The social world does not have a ready-made sense which the researcher simply needs to record; the researcher must make sense of it.

Ethnographers advise that the researcher should begin by taking a broad focus by surveying the setting before deciding where to focus more closely. This is a time when she can begin to see where the connections lie and plan strategies for following such connections.

Diverse pathways

Herrera, in her ethnography of schooling, maintains a broader focus throughout. She begins with a broader research question *'What is going on in this school?'* The setting, the school, is a natural consequence of this. Reading through her dissertation, it seems that she makes sense of the rich setting of the school by pursuing a number of pathways. Some of these pathways can be seen in the emerging themes listed in the contents to her dissertation (Herrera 1992: iii–iv): (a) the reaction of the school and staff to the researcher; (b) how newcomers are oriented and initiated; (c) the headmistress, her work, how staff and students see her, her work on the school building, how she rose through the ranks; (d) the school's promotion system, the school as a 'vehicle for raising and educating children', its uniform and appearance, discipline, the home education programme, teaching values and knowledge, parents' expectations, the examination system; and (e) living on a teacher's salary, what teachers save, their expectations and dissatisfactions about teaching, their support system, the impact on the school of private lessons.

This is not an unusual list, all of the areas being those one might expect from an ethnography of schooling, except perhaps that it begins with the way in which the school responds to her own presence as a researcher, which I cover in Chapter 7. Altogether, they weave a story – 'The lives, attitudes, struggles, relationships, confrontations, aspirations of ordinary teachers, students, and administrators, create a scene; a scene of schooling in a changing society' (Herrera 1992: 79). One particular pathway that runs through the list of themes follows the headmistress, whose life, struggles etc. are revealed in a variety of types of data exemplified in the final column of Table 4.1. Herrera states in her introduction that she follows the headmistress because of her great significance. Her data in Table 4.1 only provides a sample of all the aspects which Herrera pursues, but it shows how the picture is built from different data sources. I have tried to depict this further in Figure 4.3. (The letters in each bubble refer to the data types in Table 4.1.)

Seeing research as a pursuance of pathways in this way illustrates how, no matter how extensive the research, different researchers will always pursue and see very different things in the same setting. They will collect different data; and even if they did not, they would interpret the same data in different ways.

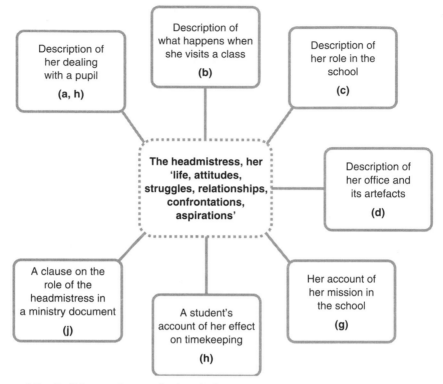

Figure 4.3   Building a picture of a headmistress

Thick description

The above examples illustrate well that quantity and coverage are not the major, nor sufficient criteria for making data valid. Even where extensive description is the aim, as in a large study like Herrera's, the most important factor is that Herrera works the data appropriately. A key to this is the notion of thick description – developed by Geertz (1973) and taken up by many qualitative researchers since. Although she does not herself use the term, the picture built by Herrera (Figure 4.3) is a thick description because it shows the different and complex facets of particular phenomena.

Interconnected meanings

Geertz (1993: 6) takes 'thick description' from the philosopher Gilbert Ryle, who talks about 'two boys rapidly contracting the eyelids of their right eyes'. A 'thin description' does no more than report the event in these limited terms. A thick description goes deeper to analyse the cultural meaning of the act, to explore whether it is an involuntary 'twitch' or a socially charged 'wink'. If one of the boys is winking, what is its social purpose? Is it to parody the other boy's twitch, '"to give malicious amusement to his cronies"' (1993: 6, citing Ryle)? Thus, 'a thin description simply reports facts, independent of intentions or circumstances' and 'a thick description, in contrast, gives the context of an experience, states the intentions and meanings that organized the experience, and reveals the experience as a process' (Denzin 1994: 505).

The knowledge that one of the boys is winking in parody of the other's twitch is the final outcome of the thick description. In order to arrive at this, the right data has to be collected – to reveal the winking boy's relationship with both the other boy and his 'cronies', the culture's protocols and formulas governing parody, and so on. Thus, the researcher must delve into the depths of the culture which give significance to these acts in which 'a stratified hierarchy of meaningful structures of which twitches, winks, fake-winks, parodies, rehearsals of parodies are produced, perceived and interpreted, and without which they would not ... in fact exist' (Geertz 1993: 7). To arrive at a thick description of, for example, a concert programme, the researcher will consider many facets which make up its full social complexity, including:

> the staffing, recent programme changes, the charisma of the choral director, the working relationship with a church organist, faculty interests in a critical vote of the school board, and the lack of student interest in taking up the clarinet. In these particularities lie the vitality, trauma, and uniqueness of the case. (Stake 2005: 457)

Data must therefore be collected to reveal all of these aspects. Indeed, this is the *purpose* of data collection.

Geertz asserts that 'the locus of study is not the object of study. Anthropologists don't study villages (tribes, towns, neighbourhoods); they study *in* villages' (1993: 22, his emphasis). The social setting within which the research takes place takes on a critical function here. Bounded social settings provide an important *means* for thick description. The facets of Stake's music programme are interconnected within the social setting of the church–school community within which it takes place. Similarly, a thick description of the winking boy might be easier to achieve if it were located within the setting of the friendship group of which he and the twitching boy are members. It is by recognizing how connections between people, beliefs, images, traditions etc. operate within a small social setting, that the 'collective representations' that thick description aims to reveal (Atkinson and Coffey 1995: 52) can be seen. According to Stenhouse (1985a, 1985b), thick description belongs comfortably with the small case study, as a sharp alternative to 'sample based' research.

Verisimilitude

What makes the thick description of a social phenomenon possible is not its exhaustiveness of coverage, but the way in which it scans the different facets of the social matrix or culture within which it is found, and comes up with good analysis. This is very different from the concept of triangulation, in which the aim is to gain a quantity of different viewpoints of the same phenomenon from different angles by checking it out – which is in effect more consonant with a postpositivist image of validity as described in Chapter 1 (Janesick 2000: 392; Richardson and St Pierre 2005: 963). (See also Atkinson and Delamont's 2005: 832 discussion of different interpretations of triangulation.) Although others also see thick description as indicative of naïve naturalism (e.g. Gubrium and Holstein 1997: vii), I see it as central to postmodern qualitative research in that it generates a richness of perception while 'reflecting and exploring data records', 'discovering patterns and constructing and exploring impressions, summaries, pen portraits', enabling a 'working "up" from data' towards theory construction (Richards and Richards 1994: 446). The important point here is that this can also be achieved in small studies. Geertz suggests that what makes a study convincing – whether it is a field journal squib or a Malinowski-sized monograph – is whether it sorts winks from twitches and real winks from mimicked ones (1993: 16).

This can be illustrated by looking not at a written study, but at a short, 90-minute television documentary, *Divorce Iranian Style*, in which Longinotto and Mir-Hosseini (1998) take the viewer into a slice of life of a downtown Iranian divorce court. Through descriptions of what people are doing, who they are, the film throws up many complex substantive issues to do with women, the management of justice, face-to-face negotiation and accessibility. This is what the various people, members of an interested public, with whom I discussed the film were interested in talking about. Although the film makers made no claim to scientific truth, there did not seem to be any question in the viewers' minds about how 'true' the film was. In their eyes it possessed *verisimilitude* – the qualities that satisfy the audience that it is true (Denzin 1994: 505) – in that it 'draws the reader so closely into subjects' worlds that these can be palpably felt' (Adler and Adler 1994: 381). In Geertz's words, 'a good interpretation of anything – a poem, a person, a history, a ritual, an institution, a society – takes us into the heart of that of which it is the interpretation' (1993: 18). *Divorce Iranian Style* does this through thick description in that it not only records what the judge and the plaintiffs and defendants say to one another, but places this within a rich milieu of interconnected social life. Thus, the film follows plaintiffs and defendants into their homes, the judge into the mosque, the court clerks into their private time when the judge is not there, where the daughter of one play-acts her version of court cases when she comes home from school, and, very significantly, the subtext side comments made by various people in the research setting to the researcher.

Another principle is that the social phenomenon which is being researched does not exist in a limited way within a confined world. Hammersley and Atkinson (1995: 54) state that '"Staffroom behaviour" may also occur in other parts of the school ... or even in the bar of a public house'. Thus, a thick description of staffroom behaviour cannot be confined to the staffroom. Looking at it within a wider social setting enables traces of the phenomenon to be seen elsewhere, allowing richer explanation. In *Divorce Iranian Style*, a great deal is learned about courtroom behaviour from the way in which the infant daughter of the clerk play-acts it, and from the way an extension of its ethos is present in the formalized family arbitration, which is written into legal documentation as a 'visit by the elders'. I have already described in Chapter 2 how Honarbin-Holliday (2005) connects conversations with taxi drivers with her observation of university art department behaviour in this way. She also connects the university lecturers' private atelier system, a private life-drawing class in a woman student's home, the way women address the government imposition of 'Islamic dress' in the university secretaries' offices, and photographs of people, buildings and events in the university.

Researcher intent

It is not, however, simply interconnected data that provides thick description. 'Sorting' winks from twitches and illuminating the deeper meanings beneath them requires that the researcher has to do something with the data and make a case for how winks are different to twitches. Although there is little overt analysis in Longinotto and Mir-Hosseini's film, it is in the way in which it organizes and presents data that verisimilitude is achieved. Geertz suggests that it is the researcher's intent that makes it all work, in that 'it is not ... techniques and received procedures, that define the enterprise. What defines it is the kind of *intellectual effort* it is: an elaborate venture' (1993: 6, my emphasis). This stress on the way the researcher presents her case is represented in Hammersley and Atkinson's comment on Zerubavel's study of 'only one aspect of hospital life, namely, its temporal structure' (1995: 47, citing Zerubavel). They say that, while this is an 'unusually sparse ethnography ... the single-mindedness of his observations and his formal analyses enable him to reveal the complex patternings of temporal orders within the organization of daily life in the hospital' (1995: 47). Thus:

> Validity is an integral element which: 'becomes largely a quality of the knower ... and forms of knowing'. ... Validity in a qualitative sense is a *personal strategy* by which the researcher can manage the analytical movement between fieldwork and theory. (Bailey et al. 1999: 172, their emphasis, citing Marshall, then Wainwright)

It also becomes clear that data alone is not enough. Collecting the right interconnected data is necessary; but it is what is made of the data that completes the thick description. Herrera is *approaching* thick description as she collects data that demonstrates the different sides and therefore social complexity of what she is looking at. It is however what she says about the data that completes the thick description. I shall deal with this in Chapter 5.

Approaching thick description

In this part of the chapter I shall look at the ways in which a variety of data provides the potential for thick description both in extensive and very small studies in my corpus of examples, even though in most cases the authors of the studies do not specify the term. It is important to note here that I shall cite only examples of the data provided in each study, very often only scratching the surface of the richness of the whole study. My aim is to illustrate diversity and not extent. To avoid over-complication I do not deal with all aspects of data at the same time. In each case I shall relate the data types to the categories in Table 4.1.

Different angles

Although Celik's study of the work culture in McDonald's is a short, 2,000-word under-graduate assignment, and does not allow for the number of pathways seen in Herrera's study, she manages to approach thick description. I have already shown in Chapter 2 how she links description of dress code with the manager's account of the work ethic (g in Table 4.1). She thus illuminates various facets of her own position in the world in which she finds herself through different types of data. There are descriptions of the physical appearance of employees, which also indicate the nature of the institution (d and c in the table) – 'We have to wear clean, dark polished shoes, which should be low-heeled and should have slip-resistant soles. ... Hairstyles should be tidy and neat as well. Hair must be kept under the hat, away from the face and styled or tied back' (Celik 1999). These are juxtaposed with descriptions of behaviour of customers (a in the table):

> The customer approached the point at the till, where there are fewer people in the line. He stayed a few paces back from the till and looked up at the big board menu. His chin was up, thinking, and then he dropped his head, taking a step towards the till. It results from his typical customer's behaviour that the customer does not step to the till at once. ... Most of the customers in McDonald's did this. ... For others there was a kind of invisible line. ... At slower times it was just two or three paces back from the counter. At busy times, especially in the rush hour, it was seven or nine paces back. ... Sometimes their legs crossed or went stiff in front of me. And then I asked the well-known server's greeting slot 'May I help you?' or 'What would you like?' With a grinning face. After a certain period, you did this as a matter of routine. Sometimes I felt really tired of this superficial game, so that I just said 'Yes please' with a forced smile. (Celik 1999)

This also illuminates aspects of tacit rules (c in the Table 4.1) – 'Allowing a previous customer to pass with his meal, he made a little "dance-shift". The customer turned his tray a bit to one side. They went around each other's backs and the ordering unit proceeded. Then he put his hands on the counter.'

Detail of space and movement

As with the examples from Herrera above, what makes these descriptions data is the meticulous detail of observation. Here Celik has been sufficiently observant to note, in the second extract, the positioning of the customer on whom she focuses in relation to other customers and the space within the environment, his detailed body movements, and then how his behaviour relates as an example to the way in which customers generally move. This is not gratuitous detail, as it serves to build the picture of the culture of the restaurant which is essentially a small space with people moving around it in special relation to one another.

Scholl (1999), in an equally short study, builds his picture of tourist behaviour in churches with a description of his brief conversation with a tourist about smoking, which reveals tacit rules (a, c, h), description of institutional behaviour – 'Small steps are taken, big strides hardly ever occur. Some women walk on their toe tips avoiding to let their high-heels touch the ground' (c) – and a drawing of the plan of one church to support his description of where people walk (d in Table 4.1). Again, this shows great attention to detail. There is a strong sense in his short piece of how he stood and watched and followed. He states near the beginning of his study that:

> The biggest part has been observing people and plotting their behaviour. This has been achieved by sitting in benches and merely observing, wandering around or joining the stream of tourists through the churches. Another good means was to follow a person from the very beginning he or she entered and paid the cashier, till the end of the round when he or she left the church. That comprised the churchyard as well. ... Another means ... were drawings. They showed where people were likely to gather and how they were distributed in the church. The interior outlay of churches has a significant impact on how visitors act on the spot. Indispensable therefore to take into account the arrangement of chairs, rows, aisles, souvenir desks, postcard racks, barriers and entrances. (Scholl 1999)

Not everyone is in the position to stay with a broad social setting such as a school or a restaurant for an extended period; and those who do cannot always find exactly what they want. Herrera was not able to choose which school she could research. After an arduous year spent gaining access to *any* school, the one she was finally given afforded her different, but equally enticing priorities (1992: 4). As mentioned in Chapter 1, the choice of social setting is determined very much by opportunity, by what the researcher is able to gain access to. It is too simplistic to say that this is a constraint. As qualitative research proceeds, it becomes clear that finding what one can, where one can, is part of the *condition* for qualitative research. The question is rarely one of choice between opportunities, but how far available opportunities fulfil valid qualitative research criteria. For example, although Celik had a matter of weeks, from the time in which she was set the assignment to the hand-in date, to collect her data, she was able to make her existing part-time job experience at McDonald's into something better than she imagined. Although Scholl had to piece together what he had seen over a brief period of watching people in Canterbury Cathedral with what he could then gain in locations while on vacation at home, this also became a collection of valuable perceptions. In this sense, therefore, the researcher is led to research whatever is there; and it is the subsequent surprise of discovery that makes the experience all the more poignant.

Reflecting the wider world

There are two ways of looking at this. In the more extensive ethnography, the setting itself provides much of the reason for carrying out the study. Although Herrera (1992) and Celik (1999) are interested, respectively, in broader issues concerning the resourcing of education in Egypt, and the ideological and economic position of McDonald's in the world, the culture of the school and the restaurant themselves become their driving concern. There is the temptation to take the naturalist stance and begin to reify it as a closed physical space. However, in other types of qualitative study, the setting is there to *reflect* aspects of the broader social issues in which the researcher is interested, as indicated in the relationship between core and peripheral data, and the subsequent achievement of a greater sociological imagination, in Chapter 2.

Maguire and Mansfield (1998) see their setting of the aerobics class as a 'microcosm' of the broader social issue of the body image of women. One of the authors states that 'clearly while I was studying what they [the women] were doing in a specific exercise context, that has to be located in a wider social view because they bring to the class all of their social cultural baggage, and that had an impact on who they are' (interview). She is thus not simply interested in 'exercise per se' and 'that pursuit of the social body' characteristic of 'the 1990s ... preoccupation with health and fitness and a specific look, with the rise of things like men's health magazines and so on and so forth'. That Maguire and Mansfield expected their data to refer to the world outside the aerobics class is illustrated in their use of interviews as their major data source. One of the authors states:

> I decided to use interviews as well as my observations to see how they [the women] verbalized their experiences – so that when I talked about images of body and image and body maintenance practices, those were shaped by issues of time and wider social issues. We talked about physical activity in childhood and their experiences of education and sport, which is a key issue because in education at key times like adolescence girls get turned off sport because they become much more aware of their bodies, not only their physical bodies but what their bodies mean symbolically. Those issues are things that come out when you talk. (Interview)

The extensiveness of their research in terms of time – six months – is intended not so much to achieve exhaustiveness, as to see a substantial working out of the relationships involved:

> You have to do long-term study. Doing a snapshot is no good because you don't get those processual ideas. Certainly it is a process of identity construction, negotiation, resistance and reflection of dominant ideologies; and for me the whole concept of ideologies is not static, is not fixed and unchallenged; but it happens over time and within space. (Interview)

Also to see the change taking place:

> There were one or two people who I could see were adapting and changing in terms of where they positioned themselves, who they spoke to, what they wore, as they became more and more confident, as they internalized markers of status and distinction in the class, as they became fitter, as they lost weight – one of the markers [of the colonization of the mind being successful]. (Interview)

Moreover, one thing can lead to another in an unpredictable manner:

> Every time I do an interview something gets thrown up that I think hey I've never thought about that, or that's interesting because that's not how I might have seen it. The important thing then is to adopt a very flexible approach to what you're doing and to what you're hearing. (Interview)

In order to get a thick description of the relationships they discover, Maguire and Mansfield collected several types of data other than interviews. The following extracts illustrate how this revealed various facets of one particular group of women who were perceived by the researchers as 'established' 'insiders' within the 'power hierarchies' that marked the setting (1998: 121). They describe their membership (c in Table 4.1):

> The established women formed a relatively stable unit showing little diversity in composition. The women in question were predominantly 'white', and the established unit consisted entirely of 'white' women. (1998: 120)

their dress and physical appearance (d in Table 4.1):

> 'Established' bodies revealed their skin surface in the clothing that was worn and drew attention to themselves by adorning themselves with jewelry and make up. At the front of the class, a 'chorus line' of tanned, toned breasts, bottoms, legs and backs. (1998: 121)

and the artefacts that distinguished them:

> Their unique, personal body space ... was reserved and protected by exercise equipment (hand weights, exercise bands, 'steps' and mats), a bag, towel, or water bottle. (1998: 120)

From their interviews, they use personal accounts to show how the group are seen by other women (g in the table):

> 'I always notice what other people look like. They look better than me.... There is one lady we call Miss Superfit .... She is really thin with long dark hair. I think "if only". It would be nice to be like that ... toned and that.' (1998: 122)

An example of interview data connecting with the world outside the aerobics class is:

> 'We used to go to the cinema, and I'd go and get sweets, and he'd say, "you don't need them"', and stop me buying them, and that made me annoyed and upset with him, because I want to do what I want.' (1998: 126)

Exploring a wider world

Another study from the sociology of sport is especially interesting because, rather than choosing a confined physical setting as a location for seeing wider social forces, Albert looks at risk-taking as a particular characteristic of 'the social world of the serious recreational and racing' cyclist in North America (1999: 159). The setting is perceived as a 'subculture' (1999: 157); and the sense of boundedness comes from identifiable manifestations of this culture across a whole continent. The data sources are documents produced by the culture, by observation, and oral and written accounts of its members. Although the observation and oral accounts come from only one corner of the wider culture – a road cycling club in New York, with which the researcher was able to 'socialize' – and the documents from the entire culture (1999: 159), they are sufficiently interconnected to allow thick description. This interconnection is further informed by Albert's own 'store of insider knowledge' (1999: 160). (The role of insider knowledge will be explored in Chapter 8.)

Thus, a rich picture is built from accounts of accidents in cycling publications (g in Table 4.1):

> 'the car that hit her ... had passed a rider who had dropped from the group. The car's occupants screamed at the cyclist and threw stuff at him. So it was presumably a deliberate act when the car ... swerved into the bike lane.' (Albert 1999: 162, citing *VeloNews*)

These are set against accounts on the internet such as 'My helmet is cracked, so I guess I hit pretty hard, but I sacrificed my body to save the bike (ha, ha)' and 'They x-rayed my neck, ribs and kneecap, and said I was extremely lucky. Scrub the wounds, take pain killers, more head checks, *and I'm ready to hit the road*' (1999: 164, citing Cycling Accident Database, original emphasis). There is also a description of cycling club attitudes (a in Table 4.1): 'James ... would frequently appear, following a weekend race, with a case of "road rash". There was talk of staying away from him for safety's sake. This reputation as a "squirrelly" rider stayed with James for years' (1999: 166). These are set against a club member account – 'Later, in private, one of these riders expressed the "serious" unease he felt riding with his friend Bob, whom he characterized as a "bad bike handler"' (1999: 166) – and description of cycling club behaviour:

> A rider at the front of the group will point to such things as holes, sticks, rocks, sewer grates, glass, or other obstacles on the ground that might impede riders directly behind. When deemed necessary, the gesture will cascade down the

line, with each rider in turn pointing the warning to the one following. Novices frequently vocalize these warnings by yelling 'hole' or 'rock!', learning by imitation – or eventually being told – that pointing to hazard is sufficient with no need to 'call out'. (Albert 1999: 160)

It is from this network of data that Albert is able to demonstrate an overall feature of the culture – that 'physical risk and injury' are 'constructed as everyday expected elements' and 'as part of the terrain' of the sport (1999: 157).

Interestingly, although accounts of cycling club members are part of the data source, there is little verbatim reporting. As with the account of his friend's bad bike handling (above), fragments of talk are built into description of behaviour.

Institutional interaction

Pierson's study of how nursing assistants cope with the feeding of demented residents in a long-term care facility in Hawaii is smaller scale in that it covers only '12 weekday mealtimes ... in the congregate dining room of one licensed long term care facility' (1999: 127). It is a good example of opportunity governing method. It is ethnomethodology, as Pierson claims, in that it looks at how the nursing assistants construct their social world. It does not however use the conversational data that many would expect of ethnomethodology because, in this particular setting, 'most of the "feeders" [i.e. residents at mealtimes] did not talk because of their severe dementia' (1999: 128). Her data instead comprises observations of behavioural interaction and the nurses' oral comment.

Pierson nevertheless manages to illuminate enough facets of the situation to approach thick description and demonstrate 'self-organizing activities and the unspoken language that nursing assistants employ ... to make sense of their interactions' with residents (1999: 127). For example, she observes that tacit rules develop to deal with a situation where there are no 'written or verbal orders' to tell the nursing assistants what to do (c in Table 4.1):

It was impossible to tell if the resident was finished, satisfied, unhappy with the flavour, unable to chew the large pieces of food, or simply being fed too fast. ... Although there were no posted time limits for the length of meals and no instructions to feed residents for one hour only, most feeding I observed did not last for more than one hour. (Pierson 1999: 129)

This is also seen in what the nursing assistants say (h in Table 4.1) – 'You just use your common sense ... You can tell who needs it ... No one assigns you. It's just if you walk in and no one is there and it looks like ... someone needs to feed them so you just do it' (1999: 128) – and observation of sequence of action (a in the table):

Finally C notices Mrs P's fingers in her mouth and sees the unchewed bun coming back out onto the plate. 'Oh, you pau [finished] already?' There is more than half of the food, all soft or liquids, remaining on the tray. But C stops feeding Mrs P. (Pierson 1999: 129; brackets in original)

Illuminating instances

Not only is Pierson's study small in scale, it is also *unfinished* in the sense that, with more time and access, more data could be collected, over a wider scope. Wider aspects of the care facility could be explored over a larger number of events and over a longer period. Indeed, it could be said that the study is merely scratching the surface. However, especially with research that informs professional practice, in this case long-term care, this is not a problem. For example, in education, Hoyle explains how 'unfinished' research is adequate for the needs of curriculum planning. He distinguishes between 'verified but useless knowledge' and 'unverified but relevant knowledge' (1970: 18). He says that the latter is of higher priority where our understanding of the total complexity of what we are looking at can never be complete anyway (1970: 16).

Because in many professional settings, we are primarily concerned with pragmatic decision-making, it is possible to operate at relatively lower levels of probability (MacDonald 1971: 167n). Carrying out extensive research for the sake of it is like 'employing a sledgehammer to crack a nut', whereas 'time and effort should be tailored' according to the importance of the task in question (Elley 1989: 271). This is very much the case with action research, in which the progressively spiralling dialogue between fragments of investigation informs action, the outcome of action informs the focus of the next piece of investigation, and so on. On a more general note, regardless of whether research is a basis of action, Geertz reminds us that 'cultural analysis is intrinsically incomplete. And, worse than that, the more deeply it goes, the less complete it is' and that 'there are no conclusions to be reported; there is merely discussion to be sustained' (1993: 29).

Above, I note that Pierson 'illuminates' facets of nursing behaviour, and Celik 'illuminates' facets of her own position in the world. Very small amounts of data are instances of social behaviour, which, if taken in isolation, may not seem to relate. However, within a holistic view of a social setting they become pieces of a huge jigsaw puzzle, which, when put together, take on meaning. It was because I related my singular experience to others within the setting that a knowledge of the whole began to take shape. Thus, a very small qualitative study can be just one piece of a very large jigsaw puzzle, illuminating one instance of social behaviour, which, when put alongside other instances from other studies, begins to build the larger picture.

The following are single instances which changed my entire perception of international education. The first is a description of an aspect of physical environment (d in Table 4.1):

> The pigeon-holes indicate the existence of channels of communication unheard of and alien to those at the University, since members of staff at other institutions at the University normally communicate only verbally. ... The keyboard, too, marks a cultural difference from other parts of the University since all the keys to the seminar rooms and the language laboratory are kept there to be used by the teachers when needed. (Barmada 1994: 204–205)

The second is an oral account from an interview with a teacher (g in Table 4.1):

> 'But sometimes I feel as if I represent the West in the classroom and as if I were telling my students that our methods of learning and thinking are not good and should be replaced by those of the West. We are unpaid soldiers of the West. This made me very nervous. I should pay attention to what I say in the classroom.' (Barmada 1994: 174–175)

Both come from a doctoral thesis about the curriculum project at Damascus University, Syria, with which I was involved as one of two expatriate consultants between 1980 and 1985. The thesis is written by my Syrian colleague and evaluates the project. Despite my five years there, which were characterized by my extensive observation of the institution and the people in it, and wariness of the dangers of 'Western intervention', these are two particular aspects of 'foreign influence' of which I was totally unaware. These fragments alone are sufficient to change my whole perception of the situation. Furthermore, it does not matter that they are written almost ten years after the period of my stay. A significant part of their impact is that they 'ring true', even though they constitute completely new information. I shall deal with this aspect of 'truth' in Chapter 5.

Illuminative instances can be single fragments of data or small case studies. Stake thus notes that 'how we learn from a singular case is related to how the case is like or unlike other cases we do know' (2005: 445). It only takes one instance of the unexpected to discredit generalization. Stenhouse uses the example of the novel to illustrate the contrast between illuminative research and 'calculative' sample-based quantitative, or indeed naturalistic research:

> The contrast is between the breakdown of questionnaire responses of 472 married women respondents who have had affairs with men other than their husbands and the novel, *Madame Bovary*. The novel relies heavily on that appeal to judgement which is appraisal of credibility in the light of the reader's experience. You cannot base much appeal to judgement on the statistics of survey. (Stenhouse 1985a: 31)

It is not the size of the study nor the quantity of data that necessarily makes the difference.

The example of Pierson's study shows that thick description is still possible with small studies. It is also possible with single data sources. Berman's study of children growing up in violence is interesting in that it creates a setting out of two separate populations, '16 refugee children of war and 16 children of battered women' (1999: 57), the first group from a range of countries – Somalia, Liberia, Burundi and Bosnia; the second group Canadian, all 13–15 years old (1999: 59). The single data source comprises accounts resulting from interviews (g in Table 4.1) – 'Participants were asked open-ended questions about the violence in their lives, their feeling about what occurred, their thoughts about the reasons for violence, and their ways of surviving and growing' (1999: 57). Berman's data approaches thick description in that it networks between these two populations, revealing a common picture of how the children 'make sense' of their experience, largely constructed around perceptions of normality. She thus includes accounts of normality before violence:

> 'My house was really big. My grandpa grew vegetables and flowers. I had many friends and I was happy like children all around the world. I couldn't tell who was Catholic, Orthodox or Muslim in my class.'

There are also accounts of normality between bouts of violence:

> 'There was always some yelling. He would yell and scream at me, and also at Mom, and sometimes Murray [her younger brother], but not as much. I thought it was normal.' (1999: 59, brackets in original)

There are accounts of change to a different normality:

> 'All of a sudden everything was changed. ... Kids could not even play any more, we hardly had any food. We could hardly wash clothes. Everyday there would be trucks coming with people that were injured'

and 'good times gone bad': '"We'd go to amusement parks, but every trip we went on was a disaster. It was kind of like the happy and the bad times were all mixed up"' (1999: 59–60).

Maximizing observation

Despite Adler and Adler's caution that verbatim data should always be present somewhere, my doctoral study of university curriculum innovation was based entirely on observation. This meant that the data did not include accounts, talk or documents. However, the observation was rich and produced a wide range of description, of behaviour, events, institution, appearance and research event, including photographs and video sequence (a–e in Table 4.1). The descriptions were of different aspects of the core setting, the classroom in 17 institutions, as well as of the periphery settings of the broader environment I was studying. Thus, as described in Chapter 4, my data includes a description of the behaviour of university lecturers as they travelled to work:

> At a certain point on the return journey, one of the lecturers went around the bus with a list of names, checking who was there and collecting money. I was impressed at the high degree of voluntary organization taking place. I believe that a different lecturer takes this role each time. There is no apparent official role taken by either the driver or anyone else. (Holliday 1991: 239)

It also includes a description of classroom and seminar events:

One student who had been sitting on a cupboard at the front of the room got up and went to ask the lecturer a question, apparently unnoticed in the general hurly-burly of the lesson. ... Students all around me were practising in groups during group work: the room was buzzing, and students who were standing were writing on anything they could – walls included. (Holliday 1991: 334)

This description is a good example of why my data did not include the transcribed talk between students and teachers, often expected of classroom research. Because the classes were very large it was impossible to catch what individuals were saying; and what they did in terms of group behaviour took on greater significance. Note how this description includes details from different parts of the room, showing how its physical environment – the cupboard at the front and the wall at the back – are important factors in the classroom event. There is also description of institutional practice, for example relating to which head of department receives visitors, where attention is drawn to the physical space and time:

It is common for such people to hold audience with several different parties at the same time. If the office is large, and a large number of parties are present, one may have to wait a considerable length of time to get attention. Often, in such cases, waiting parties, or parties that have had their turn, may hold their own separate meetings in the same room simultaneously. (Holliday 1991: 239)

There is also description of the appearance of buildings and classrooms:

All the corridors and staircases are inside the building, providing no outlet for the noise. The floors and stairs were very dusty, as though someone had lifted off the roof and poured in all the dust from the very dusty streets of the town. The classroom, like many others seen, had predominantly glass walls giving straight out onto the corridor. ... About 150 students were packed very tightly into a rectangular lecture theatre with terraced wooden benches. The acoustics were better than usual: there were no windows and little noise from outside. The room was fitted with a good blackboard and there was an overhead projector and screen positioned in the corner left of the lecturer. Many of the students had to stand in the aisles because of insufficient seats ... Some students also stood down the sides forward of the front benches. (Holliday 1991: 225)

Description too of what informants said in interviews:

S/he said that s/he sensed my wonderment at what was going on sometimes (although I seemed to have guessed accurately quite a lot) and said that, yes, s/he knew exactly what was going on and that, yes, it was culturally normal to be talking and listening at the same time. (Holliday 1991: 242)

Summary

The following points have been made in this chapter:

- There are many types of data, including the researcher's description of what she sees and hears, what people in the research setting say and write, and what they use and produce.
- Decisions about what sort of data to collect will depend on what the researcher encounters in the research setting. Which data is important will emerge during the research process.
- A criterion for good data is that the researcher sees the familiar as strange and does not see things as taken for granted; she sees things as artefacts of culture rather than the information about it.
- Data is more meaningful when it is interconnected in systems or pathways.
- Another important criterion for good data is the degree to which it provides the potential for thick description by revealing different, deeper aspects of the phenomenon being studied.
- Another essential criterion is what the researcher does with the data, the sense that she makes of it, and how well she communicates this sense.
- Thick description can be achieved in both large and small studies. In the latter it may be sufficient to describe instances of social action which illuminate and add to a large picture when set beside other studies.

Writing about Data

Chapter 4 explored what can constitute data and how it can be collected. Data collection is crucial to any research project, from the smallest to the largest. However, as many novice and experienced researchers find out once they have got their data, deciding what to do with it and how to talk about it on paper can become equally crucial and even more problematic. In this chapter I shall look at how data can be organized and used in the process of writing. The major relationship I shall deal with is between data as *evidence* and writing as presentation and *discussion* of this evidence within the context of a developing *argument*. I shall begin with a brief tour of the process from initial data collection to writing. I shall then look in detail at how data can be organized thematically, and then at how it is embedded within the argument of the written study, and how thick description is finally achieved.

First it is helpful to define some terms within the two basic activities of qualitative research. The first major activity, once the setting has been defined and engaged with, is *data collection and analysis*. This involves *the data*, which is what the researcher sees or hears which is collected or recorded, the *corpus of data*, which is all the data which is used in the research, and *data analysis*, which is the process of making sense of the data and discovering what it has to say. The role that data plays in the process of writing is very different. It normally appears in the *data discussion* sections or chapters (see Figure 3.1), which is the place where the *outcome* of data analysis is articulated and discussed. My observation of the written studies in my corpus indicates that in almost every case this process involves three significant components of the writing process.

(1) *The argument*, which is the major driving force of the data discussion. It says what has been found – what the researcher now believes as a result of the data analysis. It provides the storyline which gives structure to the data discussion. It is part of the argument of the whole written study. (2) *Data extracts*, which are taken from the

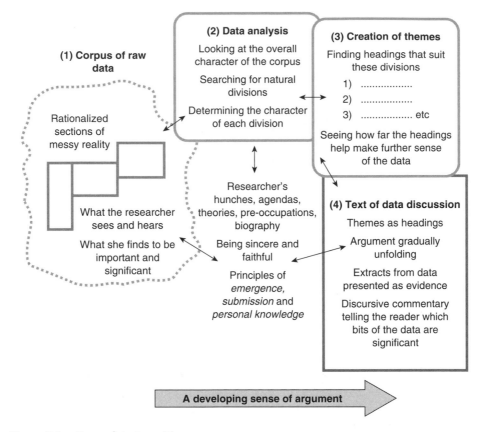

Figure 5.1 From data to writing

corpus and deployed strategically to provide evidence to support the argument. (3) *The discursive commentary* tells the reader which bits of each data extract are significant and why, showing the reader how they provide specific evidence to support the argument. Overriding these three elements is the *theme* – the basis upon which the argument, the data extracts and the discursive commentaries are organized, providing headings and stages in the argument.

While it is very important to understand the conceptual differences between data collection and analysis and writing, these two major activities need to happen at the same time and to feed off each other. While data analysis is different to writing about data in the data discussion part of the written study, they have a lot to learn from each other. The writing of drafts of the study can begin before data collection and analysis are complete, and can indeed help to provide direction in the latter. Figure 5.1 shows that the movement from the corpus of raw data to the written study is by no means a strictly linear process as each stage influences all the others.

From data to written study

The process through which the researcher gets from data collection and analysis to writing is mapped out in Figure 5.1. The grey rectangles (1) of the corpus of raw data represent rationalized sections of the original, complex, 'messy' reality of the social setting (the jagged bubble) – the mélange of social life depicted in Figure 2.4 which is beyond the scope of any social research to capture completely. Its roots and symbols may well be the product of thousands of years and lost in the mists of tradition and history. The whole story will certainly extend far beyond whatever the research can attempt. The devices used to capture the data can only therefore address aspects of this reality. Thus, the carving out of data already takes the researcher at least one step from social reality, and is the first act of interpretation. The data at this stage is nevertheless still raw and largely unworked by the researcher.

The data is then analysed and subsequently organized (2 in the figure). A common way of doing this is to take data from all parts of the corpus and arrange it under thematic headings (3). Although it hardly ever comes out as ordered as the researcher would like, it is her own organized construction, and will be different to what other researchers would do with the same data. The thematic headings then become the basis for the data discussion sections or chapters, under which the argument, extracts and discursive commentary are organized in the (hard black rectangle) written study (4).

The text of the written study is thus considerably removed from both the reality of the social setting and the data as it was initially collected. Geertz reminds us that:

> Anthropological writings are themselves interpretations, and second and third order ones to boot. ... they are thus fictions; fictions, in the sense that they are 'something made', 'something fashioned' – the original meaning of *fictio* – that that they are false, unfactual, or merely 'as if' thought experiments. (Geertz 1993: 15)

The written study itself takes on an agency of its own – its own story – the argument. However, in doing this, it also expresses a reality which distorts the social world from which the data is taken. It is 'an object' which is 'radically removed from the initial experiences and perceptions on which it is based'; the written text 'itself is an object of knowledge' (Thornton 1988: 298). It is essential that we are aware that the 'representation of reality, whether on note cards or in chapter headings' which is produced by the research should not be 'confused' with the social reality that inspires the research. We must also be aware that our data can be 'manipulated as objects in ways that culture or society cannot be' (1988: 298). Hence the concern that science can be compromised by the social constructions of scientific communities and ideology, which I shall return to in detail later in Chapters 6, 8 and 9.

One might therefore be tempted to present the data in its rawest possible state because it is closest to the reality of the setting. I have seen several students try to do this, going to the lengths of reproducing raw interview transcripts or observation notes with a minimum of commentary. They have always been astonished at the minimal to fail grades they have received. It is essential to success in writing about data to understand why raw data cannot simply be left as it is, and why the researcher must organize it and develop a strategy for writing about it. Miller et al., in their study of researchers' dilemmas in expressing their voice, remind us of this difficulty:

> The transition from reading and summarizing the research of others ... to explaining one's own ideas independently 'is, perhaps, one of the most difficult transitions budding researchers need to make'. ... making that transition to 'voice after silence ... as one struggles to express one's own voice in the midst of an enquiry designed to capture the participants' experience and represent their voices'. (Miller et al. 1998: 402, citing Clandini and Connelly)

To get over this difficulty, the researcher first needs to appreciate that her data is *already different* to the social reality it is taken from. She cannot pretend that it is a raw, true representation. Second, because this is the case, rather than leaving it alone, she must demonstrate explicitly how it has been constructed – hence the need to show the workings of the research. Third, if little more than the raw data is presented, the researcher's argument is not presented. The question which readers will always raise when being referred to data is *What is the point*? If the point is not clear, it is very difficult to assess what is being written. I will show in Chapter 6 how it is central to this particular culture of academic writing that evidence, whether from literature or data, may not be presented without argument. The coherence of all parts of the writing of the research is also based on this argument.

Dark night of the soul

Getting from data to written study can be a traumatic time for the researcher. The busy work of collecting data may largely be done; and the process of analysis, sorting and organizing has the potential to take the argument in many directions. At this point in the writing of my doctoral thesis I came up with ten possible directions which emerged from my data, each of which could have generated different arguments – (1) the value of studying classroom deep action, or (2) institutional deep action, (3) the value of doing classroom ethnography, or (4) institutional ethnography, (5) how to find culturally appropriate methodology for classroom teaching, or (6) for institutional innovation, (7–10) combinations of 1 and 2, 3 and 4, and 5 and 6 (Holliday, research notes). This extract from my supervisor's response illustrates his attempt to make sense in a way I myself could not see at the time:

> I got confused, though understood your alternatives. Yes, need to synthesize otherwise you'll continually chase your own tail. ... As I interpret it all: (Your use of 'methodology' and its ambiguity gets in the way here) your prime focus is the effort to implement educational change; your means is evaluation; for you,

synonymous with research. Your method is ethnographic. Your *ethnographic focus* is upon the interface between surface and deep action within a curriculum project within a particular socio-cultural context. Your ethnography *uses data* from classrooms, the wider institutional location of the curriculum project, and from the designing of the project. Your pedagogic *motive* is to inform future project developers of certain variables they had better watch out for. (Personal letter, his emphasis)

He then goes on to tell me that it might still be too soon to tie it all up, and to let my data speak to me:

In any case, my instinct tells me not to try to answer your question – as you suggest! The real issue, for me, at this distance, is *what your data can tell you*. Think in a data-driven way for a while. List your answers to *this* question. (Maybe how you *should* see your work will emerge.) (Personal letter, his emphasis)

This advice reminds me that, in my struggle to make my own sense, I must remember the data and to achieve a true dialogue between the data and my own argument. Although Figure 5.1 may appear an authorial take-over, it must in effect achieve a balance between data as the major resource and what the researcher has seen. I shall look at how this balance can be achieved at the micro level in the details of language in Chapter 6. Here it is important to appreciate the need for a balanced relationship at a more macro level, as represented in the centre of Figure 5.1, which shows on the one hand the researcher's personal influence and on the other a principled desire to be as faithful and sincere as possible to what was found in the research setting. These areas of researcher discipline will be looked at in Chapter 8.

Organizing and presenting data

I shall now look at how researchers in my corpus organize and present their data in the data analysis section or chapter. Although I have advocated, and personally favour, a thematic analysis as a means of organizing the data, this needs to be interpreted broadly. There are various ways to manage the transition from raw data to text. However, there are important principles that need to be met within a postmodern paradigm.

While it is understood that the postmodern researcher is still the arch designer of data collection, she must *submit* herself to *emerging* patterns of data and be free to engage strategically and creatively with the complexities of realities that go beyond her initial design. The bottom centre of Figure 5.1 places these two principles of emergence and submission at the centre of the whole process of moving from data to writing. There is a very common postpositivist procedure which does not fulfil these principles – where researcher-designed interview questions drive the whole research from beginning to end, culminating in the 'reporting' of the responses to each question as 'results'. This inhibits the emergence of independent realities which may be counter to or hidden by the dominant preoccupations of the researcher.

Taking a purely thematic approach, in which all the data is taken holistically and rearranged under themes which emerge as running through its totality, is the classic way to maintain these principles. This is the procedure, with some variation, which is demonstrated throughout my corpus of written studies, and which I shall spend time on here.

Submitting to emergent, holistic themes

Berman (1999), in her study of children growing up in violence, takes the data from two distinct populations of people, international war victims and Canadian children of battered women, and groups the interview data she collects under common themes. I have already demonstrated how she uses the rich theme of normality to create a common picture for these two populations (see Chapter 4). She presents her argument under the following headings and subheadings:

> Growing up: two different kinds of normal
> > A sudden end to everything we knew and loved
> > The subtleties of everyday violence
> Uncertain enemies
> Public wars on the battlefield and private wars at home
> Finding unexpected resources in seemingly empty places

The emergent nature of these themes is evident in their wording. Once she has collected all her data, following the hunch, which has driven her research, that the two groups have something in common, she sought a common storyline which grows out of the data itself and represents the character of the data as a whole. The phrasing of the thematic headings thus struggles to be comprehensive yet succinct. The corpus of data is like a text for which headings are sought after the event. Moreover, these themes are not just the figment of the researcher, as 'emerging themes were shared and revised with the children, thus involving them actively in the co-construction of meaning' (1999: 59).

The formation of themes thus represents the necessary dialogue between data and researcher, as represented in Figure 5.1, which emerges from and then helps to further make sense of the data, and then to provide a structure for writing. The figure also shows that arriving at the themes can be the result of formal data analysis, but can also be born from what was seen during data collection. Often the themes have been growing within the researcher's mind through the whole research process. Researchers often know the character of their data regardless of any formal analysis. It is after all largely a product of their own thinking during the process of collecting and recording. Furthermore, the way in which the researcher sees the data will be influenced by her 'own background and latent theory', which means that 'the construction that emerges through this practice is but one of many possible constructions of reality' and that 'no other scholar would discover the same categories' (Erlandson et al. 1993: 118, citing Lincoln and Guba). Figure 5.1 attempts to show that the argument that is central to the final written product is implicit in and developing throughout the whole process. It is difficult to say at what point the argument really emerges. Different research projects are driven in different ways, with different intensities of argument; but it has to be recognized that the development of themes and the organization of data are intercon-nected with the development of an argument. The whole purpose of organizing the data is to serve and structure the argument in the written study. At the same time, as emergent headings will help make further sense of the data itself, they will also help to form, adjust or even re-form the argument.

Similar emergent theme headings can be seen in Albert's study of danger in cycling (1999). A range of data sources, from documents and observation, are brought together under these headings and subheadings:

> Producing and managing the orderly character of risk
>> Rules of the ride
>> Pointing to hazards on the road
>> Calling out hazard at rider level
> Anticipating the inevitable
> When risks turn to injury
>> 'How's the bike?' as a demonstration of commitment
>> 'Ready to hit the road'
> Managing causal attribution in accidents and injuries
>> Ironic reconstructions of self-esteem
>> Reaction accounts as warranting the unattributable
>> The group caused it as self-exemption

One can see here how the reading is made easier as the headings create the sense and stages of the story through the data.

Moving from chronology to themes

It is easy after the event to see the sense and indeed simplicity of a thematic treat-ment. However, for many researchers, the process of arriving at a thematic structure is very difficult if not painful. This is because the thematic structure is very different to the structure which governed data collection, which they may well have been working with for a considerable time. This was the case in my own doctoral research on foreign influence in a curriculum project. I had spent three years cataloguing my data according to *when* I collected it – *chronologically*. I rationalize the change towards a thematic treatment in my explanation of research procedures:

> To understand the reasons for moving from a chronology to a thematic treat-ment it is necessary to distinguish between two uses of the data. On the one hand there is the collection and practical use of data within the day-to-day work of a curriculum project. Here, the gradual accumulation of data is motivated

first by the professional requirements of the curriculum project and secondly by the sequence in which opportunities for observation emerge. This accumulated data informs various aspects of the project in a piecemeal way ... and the process is, as I have argued above essentially ongoing, beginning when the project begins, and not finishing until the project finishes ...

On the other hand there is the situation which would arise when the data is used retrospectively for the purpose of writing an academic study. Here the data collected over a specific period needs to be taken as a consolidated whole and reorganized according to how the meanings of that whole can best be managed. This type of analysis is what will be described in the next two chapters. (Holliday 1991: 214)

A comment in a footnote to the thesis makes the point that:

The only alternative to a thematic treatment for this type of analysis would be a day-to-day account of the insights which were formed during data collection. This would be lengthy and tedious – in fact a three-year long train of thought of a curriculum developer, which would indeed be of interest in a phenomenological study of her or his psychological interaction with the project process, but beyond the scope of this thesis. (Holliday 1991: 214n)

The result was four themes, each containing several smaller 'points of focus', arranged into two chapters in the data analysis part of the thesis:

Chapter 5: Non-pedagogic classroom culture
Theme 1: Classroom conditions (Physical conditions, Institutional conditions)
Theme 2: Non-pedagogic interaction (Students and teachers, Interaction with outsiders, Formality and casualness)
Chapter 6: Pedagogic classroom culture
Theme 3: Pedagogic interaction (Responsibility for learning, Perceptions of 'lecturer')
Theme 4: Innovation (Student adaptability, Expectations regarding lesson structure, Immunity of expatriate lecturers, Immutability of classroom conditions, Local lecturer perceptions of the curriculum project).

As well as providing a means for organizing the data, this thematic structure greatly facilitated writing, as it became the basic plan for 45,000 words – almost half the entire thesis. Furthermore, as the headings clearly show, instead of being an administrative, blow-by-blow account of 'findings', the data analysis chapters became a coherent, thick description of the classroom culture. The emergent nature of the themes is explained as follows:

Following basic interpretive procedures ... the labelling of these themes was done *after* data collection. They were adjusted several times during the process of analysis, depending on how effective they proved as descriptive tools. They are therefore by no means prescriptive: they are instead a means to organize the issues thrown out by the data. (Holliday 1991: 217–218)

From before and after

Researchers need to be aware and honest about the influence they bring to their thematic analysis from their original preoccupations, where the themes themselves, although emergent, are also influenced by questions or issues that the researcher brought to the research. It is also important that the researcher should acknowledge this influence. In Shaw's study of how the female body is represented in the media, interview data is 'organized according to the main research questions *and* emerging themes' (1998: 11, my emphasis). Her major headings – *The female body in the media*; *Media images and women's body images*; *Media images and women's body-related behaviour* – correspond with parts of her interview, while within each part, themes emerge:

> The first part of the interviews explored the women's perceptions of media images of the female body. Three main themes emerged: the dominant image of the female body portrayed by the media; the media's construction of an 'ideal' female body type; and media images versus the 'reality' of women's bodies. (Shaw 1998: 12)

With regard to the third part of the interviews: 'When the women talked about their dieting or fitness activities and what shaped their behaviour, three main themes emerged: reasons for dieting or participating in fitness activities; trying to achieve a particular body size or shape; and influences of the media on their body-related behaviour' (1998: 18). Similarly, in searching for categories to organize the discussion of her action research data in her master's dissertation, Linehan uses a mixture of the categories that derive from her original research aims and those that emerge from both the data and the research process. The data comprises diary observation and video of students doing writing activities during open learning sessions. In the part of her dissertation which sets out the research procedures, she describes her 'prime aims' as:

> (1) To observe how the students' involvement 'shaped' the sessions; (2) To observe the interaction and motivation of the students; (3) To see how the students responded to the materials; (4) To gather information from the students' observations on their own writing; (5) To assess the value of writing sessions as a context for enhancing the learning process. (Linehan 1996: 25)

In her analysis of the data, she uses the following headings:

> (1) Student motivation, interaction and involvement in 'shaping' the sessions;
> (2) Student response to the materials and observations on their own writing;
> (3) An assessment of the value of the writing sessions as a context for enhancing the learning process; (4) My role in the proceedings. (Linehan 1996: 29)

Numbers 1–4 in the first list are conflated into 1–2 in the second list, which implies an overall continuity between the research aims and the data that was produced. She confirms this as follows:

> Many of the headings actually stayed. When I was carrying out the procedure for the research I had these headings in mind because this is what I wanted to find out about. Although I ended up slightly altering them, I was lucky that for the things I looked for originally, I felt I found material in the data. I got answers. I didn't know at the beginning what data I actually would get, or what the answers would be. Therefore, it was interesting because I found out what the answers were. It was as if I had asked questions and found material for answers. (Interview)

Her justification for conflating some of the original categories was that:

> Each question involved a whole load of the other things. I cut them down because it's actually quite difficult to get clear pictures for each one. I didn't get enough information in them singly. I felt they fed off each other. So, when I actually did the data analysis, I combined them. (Interview)

Another difference between the first and second list is the addition in the second list of *My role in the proceedings*. Linehan explains how she discovered that her role was an important factor during the process of data collection:

> The one I added was *My role in the proceedings* because I found out from the video data of myself managing the self-access session, that my role completely changed. Instead of being an instigator of the writing sessions, monitoring, keeping my role very quiet, I became a very bossy, dominant teacher, telling people what to do when they already knew what to do. I observed this in myself. It was the video data that brought that forward. I included my role as one of my headings because it surprised me. (Interview)

She also noted that the original list of research aims 'was very student focused' and ignored the factor of teacher role. This last point is very significant because it illustrates well the researcher's recognition and use of her own participation in the research process as data.

Embedding data in the argument

Determining the headings under which to organize the data provides a structure within which the researcher can now use *discursive commentary* to talk about the *data* within the context of her *argument*. I shall show how this is done through a skilful interplay of these three elements as introduced at the beginning of this chapter. Throughout, I shall also be concerned with the way in which they complete thick description. In the last chapter I made the point that the data alone is not sufficient for thick description. It provides the potential, which can be fulfilled only when the researcher shows, in her discussion, *how* the data interconnects and represents the richness of the social setting from which it has been taken.

Herrera's ethnography of a girls' school is the least explicit of the texts in my corpus in demarcating argument, discursive commentary and data as evidence. This may be because it is the 'purest' of the studies, with the intrinsic objective of finding out what is going on per se. The pressure of argument is thus low; and discussion is very much integrated with description of behaviour, event, institution and appearance. However, lines of argument are there and do constitute the binding for the dissertation. An example of this can be seen in her chapter 3 which deals with the major theme of socialization – 'The gift of being a girl: the school's role in socializing future women'. Although she begins the chapter with a long oral account from the headmistress, this piece of data is used to introduce the argument. Thus, the headmistress says: 'My most important priority is to raise the level of the girls scientifically, intellectually, morally: the whole being of the girls. To implant values and morals in them. To teach them to follow the correct rules of society' (Herrera 1992: 28). The argument is then carried through a series of subthemes concerning school uniform, information about boys, classroom discipline, home economics (in greater detail), and teaching values with knowledge. The following extract shows how the last of these subthemes also begins by continuing the argument. Her point, that the syllabus is used to carry values about women in society, is quickly supported by evidence (underlined) in the form of a description of classroom behaviour and teacher talk. Each extract of data is thus brought into the text to work for the argument. Furthermore, to ensure that the reader understands what each piece of data is intended to demonstrate, it is preceded by a small amount of discursive commentary (broken underlining).

Teaching values with knowledge

The basic academic subjects, uniform for both boys and girls, are sometimes reinterpreted to suit the needs of gender. While the girls may have educational advancement and professional objectives on their minds, the teachers let their own biases or values regarding the role of women in society mix with their teaching.

Art, for example ... takes on a feminine framework when being introduced to girls. In their second art lesson of the term, a class of Third Year students dutifully yet disinterestedly opened sketch books and began mechanically copying a picture. ... The teacher, a graceful young woman ... watched for a few moments and then stood up, commanding the students to stop working. She began an impassioned speech in the form of a theatrical monologue, about the importance of art for them as girls. ...

Food served as a major and drawn out example: 'Food must always be nicely presented, delighting the eye' she emphasized. 'Even for something as simple as a fruit bowl. You must know how to put the colours of the fruit together in a pleasing way. ... Drawing and art will help you with knowing what to do.' (Herrera 1992: 40, my underlining)

The transition from argument to comment to data is marked by change in tense. In Herrera's dissertation, the argument is in the present to denote a state of affairs; the data (except for verbatim quotation) is in the past to denote what she saw or heard; the comment can be either, denoting the link between the other two.

This style of incorporating data seamlessly within the main text is common in ethnographic writing. However, longer stretches of verbatim quotation from people in the research setting accounts are usually separated from the main text by indenting, in exactly the same way as long quotations from literature would be indented. Thus, Herrera continues:

> Male teachers may lack the female experience with a woman's duties, but have their own convictions regarding their responsibilities as teachers of girls. One of the more experienced and respected math teachers at the school put forward his overall ideas about women in society in this way:
>
> > Most girls will grow up, get married and have children. Some will work, but it's best for the woman to stay at home. ...
>
> (Herrera 1992: 40, my underlining)

The quotation continues in this way for six lines. I have once again marked the discursive commentary leading up to the data extract with broken underlining.

Figure 5.1 illustrates how the discursive commentary has the key role of telling the reader in what way the extracted data provides evidence to support the argument. It is significant that the data is not simply *shown* and then left to speak for itself. The researcher must then *tell* the reader what she believes the data extract to be saying – what she believes it contributes to the argument (Golden-Biddle and Locke 1997: 58, citing Booth). The researcher continues to show the workings of her research through the data analysis part of the written study. These authors talk about this relationship in writing about organizations, explaining that 'we both show data and tell their significance. We theorize the fragments of life we show. Consequently, in our manuscripts, we couple the fragments of organizational life with our theoretical points and commentaries' (1997: 58). It can be counter-productive to show the reader too long stretches of data without telling her its significance. One of my students learnt this lesson the hard way when he presented data in his thesis without telling the reader in detail what was important about it. His examiners entirely missed the point he was trying to make and made him re-submit. Herrera does not leave the reader alone for too long with description or participant account (underlined), without her argument and commentary to tell the reader how she as the researcher is making sense of it. Golden-Biddle and Locke provide some good examples from published studies of how researchers sequence this relationship between argument, commentary and data (1997: 58, 62).

Within each subtheme Herrera takes data extracts from whatever different data sources she has at her disposal as she needs them to support her argument. In the example above she cites description of classroom behaviour, teacher talk and a teacher's oral account.

Completing thick description

I demonstrated in Chapter 4 how researchers approach thick description by collecting networks of data which show the different facets of the social phenomena they investigate, but that thick description cannot be fully achieved until the interconnections are fully articulated in the written study. The example from Herrera before shows how she completes a thick description, within her chapter 3, of the way in which girls are socialized at school. It is her argument and discussion which bind together the data she presents and *demonstrate* the connections, thus showing the workings of thick description.

Pierson, in her study of the interaction of nursing assistants and demented health care residents, completes a thick description in a similar way. Her first thematic heading is *Member's knowledge – 'it's just my common sense'* (1999: 128). This already provides a strong sense of the substance of her argument about the way in which knowledge of how to behave is constructed between the people in the research setting via non-verbal signals. The thematic section begins with a preamble about how mealtimes are heralded by 'the arrival of kitchen carts containing food' and 'the appearance of food and bibs', which, together with knowledge of 'the time of day', provides sufficient evidence for the first main point in the argument that 'any "competent member"' would realize without oral or written instructions 'that this is the beginning of the meal service'. The scene thus set, a skilful combination of argument, discussion and data follows. I have extracted the entire first half of this thematic section below. First there are extracts from four different oral accounts (underlined), already cited in part in Chapter 5, which are explained for the reader by discursive commentary (broken underlining):

> Feeding residents was something that the NAs [nursing assistants] did out of their own understanding of the situation as the following comments by NAs indicate:
>
>> 'Well, you just use your common sense, ... You can tell who needs it.' ... 'No one assigns you. It's just if you walk in and one is there and it looks like ... someone needs you to feed them so you just do it. You use your common sense and get behind the feeding table.' ... 'It makes sense. I have to feed all these people so I get behind the feeding table.'
>
> (Pierson 1999: 128, my underlining)

This is followed immediately with further discursive comment (broken underlining) which tells us exactly what Pierson wishes to point out about the data extract. She baldly states that *she* interprets the data in such and such a way. This is followed, in the same paragraph, by the continuation of the argument, which moves gradually from the reported past to the abstract present:

> I interpreted these comments to mean that NAs were constantly assessing the situation and reacting accordingly. When a resident was not actively engaged in feeding or was known as a 'feeder', any competent NA would recognize what was needed to be done and do it. Feeding a helpless resident does not happen until the NA makes that assessment and begins the feeding. Feeding, like all other interactions is 'indexical' and 'reflexive'. Its practices are 'embodied', 'circumstantially contingent', and 'unwittingly' performed (Garfinkel 1967; Lynch, Livingston, and Garfinkel 1983). (Pierson 1999: 128, my underlining)

The argument is also characterized by a statement of theory (to do with indexicality and reflexivity in ethnomethodology), which is supported by reference to literature to complement the data extracts as further evidence. There is certainly no reason why reference to literature should be restricted to the 'discussion of issues' part of the study (see Figure 3.1); it is a source of evidence which in many ways behaves like data.

Her next paragraph continues the argument, and contains another data extract. There is no substantial commentary here, except in the last phrase (broken underlining) before the data extract (underlined) which links it directly, as an example, to the argument.

> Once an NA recognizes the need to feed a resident a variety of embodied, cir-
> cumstantially contingent, and unwittingly performed practices are revealed,..as.
> described in the following field note:
>
>> R., a large male NA, is standing behind the feeding table this morning
>> attempting to feed the three most difficult feeders. I ask him what special
>> things he does to get these residents to eat. 'Like Mr [H], you have to push
>> his tongue down.'
>
> (Herrera 1999: 128, my underlining)

As with the Herrera teacher's oral account, Pierson indents the long stretch from her field notes, which goes on for four more lines.

Pierson's argument is thus developed in complex dialogue with data extracts and discursive commentary. The way in which this demonstrates and brings out the thick description already implicit in the data is illustrated in Figure 5.2. One of the necessary ingredients is the system of interconnected data (on the left). The other necessary ingredient is the argument and discussion (on the right). I have listed there in detail (a–f) what this comprises – in effect bringing out the way in which the data works – with examples of how this list is realized in the specific language of Pierson's text (taken from the above extracts). There is also, in the case of (c), reference to the way in which the themes imply the interconnectedness of the data.

Degrees of explicitness

Different researchers demonstrate the way in which their data works towards thick description in different ways with different degrees of explicitness. The variation will depend partly on the different requirements of assessment, for assignments and dissertations, of editorial policy in different publications, or of tradition in different disciplines or professions. Pierson, for example, unlike Shaw (cited above), does not *say* that her section headings comprise themes that emerge from the data. However, she is more explicit than Herrera in the way she separates data from the rest of her text,

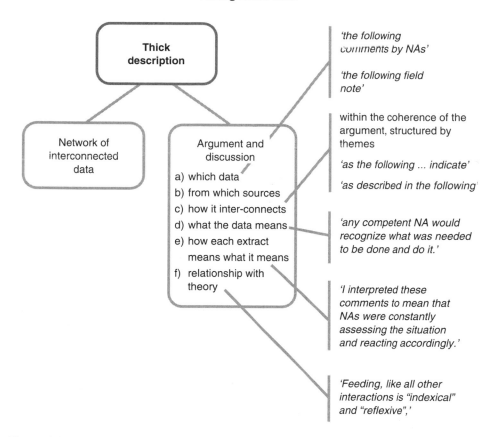

Figure 5.2   Constituents of thick description

for example by indenting the material from her field notes. On the other hand, in the paragraph following these field notes, Pierson includes the following description of behaviour, undemarcated, within her main text: 'Often, the NAs faced the residents and closely observed the natural eating movements of their mouths. By timing the insertion of the spoon with the relaxation of the jaw or the protruding of the tongue, they usually encountered little resistance' (1999: 128). This implies a distinction between her field notes, which she does demarcate, perhaps as more 'formal' data, and more general, perhaps ongoing observation, presumably not written down in such a formal way.

Yet more explicit is the way in which Hayagoshi, in her study of Japanese student quietness, specifies her data sources by including bracketed reference to type and number of data source in the following extract (i.e. whether it is a lesson observation or discussion with a student, and which lesson and which discussion):

The quietness of these seven Japanese definitely dominated the atmosphere of the classroom. There was nobody to throw a stone into this quietness.

> They were very slow to react and rarely express their opinions. ... The teacher went out for a while ... I felt that the tense (hard) atmosphere ... suddenly changed dramatically to a mild gentle one. Actually, I heard one Japanese student sigh with relief. However, this mood vanished when the teacher returned. They were quiet, tense and stressed, again. (Lesson observation 1)

> After the class, these quiet Japanese became *normal* students ... friendly and, of course, quite talkative! ... I asked some Japanese students why they were quiet in the classroom. One student answered that 'there are some *invisible walls* around me which prevent me from speaking in the class' (discussion with a student, lesson 1). (Hayagoshi 1996, her emphasis)

I have already discussed the importance of cataloguing and coding data, as part of the explanation of research procedure, to enable this degree of specification in Chapter 3. This enables the reader to ascertain which parts of the data have been used in the argument and discussion. In this extract, the decision whether or not to indent the citation from data follows the literature citation rule.

Another example of explicitness can be seen in Shaw's study of women's identities and the media:

> There was consensus among all of the women in each group that the media fail to reflect what the majority of women's bodies are 'really' like: 'I don't think they really reflect what women are like at all' (Alternative Identity, 1). The underlying reason for this failure was the narrowness of the representations of women's bodies ... They only present perfection, ignoring the 'imperfections' of real women's bodies: the media emphasize people like Claudia Schiffer and most women aren't that size, aren't that shape, so it's totally illogical (Alternative Identity, 3); women are all different shapes and sizes ... there's very few people like that [supermodel], six foot and seven stone ... it's not the way we are at all (Diet 2). (Shaw 1998: 13)

Here, Shaw shows the reader where her interview data comes from in terms of which group of women, according to its name ('Diet', 'Fitness' or 'Alternative Identity'), and which woman in each group. She explains the group names in her explanation of procedure, as cited in Chapter 3.

Selecting rich data

As it becomes clear that the data cited in the data discussion section or chapter is *selected* from the corpus of raw data to act as *evidence* for the argument of the written study, the question remains – how does the researcher decide which data she should select? Below is a typical extract from the *raw data* collected during my doctoral research. The underlined parts were extracted to be used in my thesis on the pages marked in square brackets.

> There was an awful crush as students coming out met students trying to get in [p. 227]. Several students were carrying flowers. One of the men gives a flower to AH, which s/he takes and keeps during part of the lesson – evidence of a profound integration with their culture – s/he holds it as they do. [p. 359] It took ten minutes for the class to settle down [p. 227]. I sat on the left amongst the standing men. Some of the students did not have notes; however, those who did seemed to have useful data in their hands which helped them cope with the poor mike [p. 334]. There were many serious students sitting at the back. … Some of the men standing at the front seemed a little flippant, though the majority seemed to be concentrating, interested and learning. When students went to the front to write something on the blackboard, even those who hadn't seemed to be concentrating showed that they had been all the time (cf. obs. 28) [p. 242]. (Holliday 1991: 532)

There are several consequences of this use of data. On the one hand, the data is broken up to be used as evidence in different parts of the data analysis chapters under different thematic headings (two extracts to p. 227, *Classroom conditions*, subtheme *physical conditions*; one to p. 359, *Innovation, immunity of expatriate lecturers*; one to p. 334, *Innovation, student adaptability*; one to p. 242, *Non-pedagogic interaction, students and teachers*). Moreover, some of the data is not used at all. Hence, the coherence of the raw data is lost. On the other hand, the data is marshalled anew to create a new coherence within the argument of the thesis. This can be seen in this extract from page 242 of the thesis, where three fragments of data, all underlined, are interconnected to support the argument that classroom communication is not what it seems:

> S/he said that … it was culturally normal to be talking and listening at the same time … and that although some students were talking a lot, perhaps only 60% about the lesson, they were very much in touch. (Obs. 28, site 6, LK)

> Although both observations 28 and 25 contain much which is due to individual lecturers' idiosyncratic teaching styles, both are examples of the existence of implicit communication rules which are shared by their local lecturers, but which are *hidden* from the outsider. … This could also be seen in an expatriate's class: 'When students went to the front to write something on the blackboard, even those who hadn't seemed to be concentrating showed that they had been all the time' (obs. 39, site 9, AH). (Holliday 1991: 242, original italics, underlining added)

This new formulation is in fact richer, as thick description, than the 'untouched' text of raw data shown earlier – because it is placed, interconnected and given meaning within the argument of the thesis. Therefore, although something is lost in the break-up of the raw corpus, more is gained through embedding in argument. It must be remembered that the raw data was only my own construction anyway, and removed from the 'original reality' of the research setting. It would be researcher vanity to wish to preserve it.

In this example, like Shaw (1998), I make specific reference to the origin of the data fragments by placing in brackets the observation, site and lecturer. This shows the reader the workings of *how* and *from where* I have selected the fragments to help her assess as far as possible the extent of my evidence. These references can be followed up in the catalogue of data in my explanation of research procedures – which parallels the way in which reference to literature can be referred back to the bibliography, as mentioned above.

The criteria for determining which fragments of data are selected will always be as subjective as all the other aspects of qualitative research. The major driving motive will be that selected fragments contain the elements that have been recognized during analysis, which generate the thematic organization. Another factor is that the fragments that are chosen are likely to be the ones which are *rich* in the sense of containing as many of the key elements as possible within a short space. They are therefore efficient for the job in hand. This can be seen throughout this book, where extracts from my corpus of written studies are chosen for this very reason. For example, the extract from Pierson (see above) is particularly rich because it contains multiple features in a short space. Similarly, I spent considerable time hunting through my own raw data, looking for a short extract which displayed a maximum of fragments used in different parts of the thesis, before I came up with the one used above. Despite all the technical procedures employed in data analysis, the act of selecting examples will always be as creative as any other aspect of the writing process.

Keeping things separate

A major theme in this chapter so far has been the separation of data, discursive commentary and argument. By making this separation apparent in the text, the researcher shows the workings of what she has done, as far as possible making it transparent to the reader where and what she has described or recorded during data collection, and what she now wishes to make of this data. This display of clarity adds to the validity of the written study by revealing to a large extent how subjectivity has been managed. It also indicates that, during the process of data collection and analysis, the researcher has exercised a degree of discipline within her own mind, as she has tried to manage her own perception of the difference between (a) noting physically what can be seen and heard and (b) noting what this means and why it is significant. I have tried to diagrammatize this difference in Figure 5.3. It represents a notebook where field notes are written. On the left is the straight description, written as neutrally as possible. On the right is an entirely separate note of what this might mean. It helps to discipline the mind if one tries to keep these notes physically separate in this way. The figure then shows how these separate activities become the data fragments and discussion and argument in the written study. Of course, at a later date there could be further layers of comment to the original comments taken at the time; and these will develop into the separate voices which I shall describe in Chapter 6.

DATA: what can be seen and heard	**COMMENT:** what this means, why it is significant
The women tended to sit down the right of the room while the men tended to sit down the left of the room. Down the centre of the room there were many instances where the division was not precise, as men and women sit shoulder to shoulder and talk to each other	This might connect with gender segregation seen in other parts of the society – e.g. on buses. But the men and women sitting together in the centre seem comfortable. Other factors might therefore easily override the segregation principle. This connects with observation of men and women working together in small groups
Used as an extract to provide evidence	Contributes to the argument

Figure 5.3   Managing perception

Preserving original richness

Throughout this chapter I have argued for interspersing relatively short, but interconnected data extracts with short bursts of argument and commentary. As argued earlier, it is essential not to leave the reader alone with the data without guidance as to what the researcher, who was there when it was collected, thinks it signifies; indeed, this is a good way to achieve thick description. However, because of the linear nature of the written text, such short extracts may fail to represent the coherence and richness of larger chunks of data. One way of escaping the confines of linearity might be by means of electronic texts, where argument is hyperlinked to parts of the data which are still embedded in the original part of the raw corpus. Harper (2005: 751) describes how video footage can be seen in full alongside commentaries about them 'in different parcels of time'; but here I am going to explore some creative ways in which this dilemma of presentation can be addressed within the written paper text.

In Chapter 1 I referred to anthropological ethnographers beginning to be critical of the subjectivity implicit in the lengthy reconstructed renderings of what they have observed. Nevertheless, some qualitative researchers have revisited reconstructions as a means, when skilfully created, for maintaining thick description through interconnection between pieces of data, while at the same time preserving the internal coherence of the original experience (Holliday 2006).

Using reconstructions

My first example of how this can be done is in Wu's study of English language teacher discourses in a Chinese university. To represent his experience of a network of conversations between the teachers, Wu constructs a series of what he refers to as 'stories' from a range of data sources including 'records made in the research field, for example, video/audio tapes, classroom notes, meeting minutes, teachers' diaries, casual conversation, curriculum documents, letters, and etc.' (2002: 58). To address the issue of faithfulness to the original data, these reconstructions 'were not invented, but constructed collaboratively' by inviting the people in his study to verify them through 'stimulated recall discussions' (2002: 58).

Cognizant of the need to show his workings, the further Wu departs from the expected routine of presenting his data, the more he has to explain. It is necessary to know *how* the 'stories' are constructed through submission to emergent themes:

> The data for constructing this story are constituted of Yinsa's diaries (File 4) from the 3rd of November to the 5th of November, meeting minutes (File 51, see sample at Appendix 12), our recalling conversation about these diaries (Tape 145/6/7,150), Yinsa's response to Haifen's stories and my field notes. The story was subsequently discussed with Yinsa, and modified accordingly. (Wu 2002: 65)

Wu's ability to do this is strengthened by his insider status as a colleague of his informants, which in turn increased complexity in his relationship with them. It was also therefore important for him to show in detail how he dealt with this:

> As a participant my ways of living and telling stories of curriculum change are similar to the ones our teacher participants lived and told. We were absorbed in the same events with a similar type of curiosity and motives, and as a result we underwent a sharing of experiences. But as a researcher I had a task to retell these stories, which were not necessarily shared by all the participants. ... This means that some of my own stories might be told from a third person's point of view (e.g. *An Incidental Gain*). Whereas some of our teacher participants' stories may be told from the first person's point of view (e.g. *it was buzzing with activity*). The stories about my research experiences will be always told from the first point of view. In whatever case, I will make the points of view explicit. (Wu 2002: 59–60)

Honarbin-Holliday similarly writes about how she reconstructs her interviews with Iranian art students and tutors:

> I highlighted, condensed, summarised, and presented these in short forms as texts in Chapter Four. Though 'fragments', these have each been read, and re-read again and again to make sure the specific terminology used by the participants, and the tone and direction of the 'whole' were preserved. This is as much to do with my integrity, as is to do with theirs. The nature and extent of the data collected have simply been too great to present fully. Repetitions, and forms of direct questioning by myself, have not been included in these texts. (Honarbin-Holliday 2005: 38)

The strategic value of personal knowledge

It can be seen from Wu's account of how he made his reconstruction that not only is his personal knowledge of the research setting a crucial factor in enabling him to understand what is going on amongst colleagues whose own experiences are intermingled with his own, but he uses this knowledge in a specifically strategic way to construct his 'stories'.

The role of personal knowledge, the third principle at the centre of the process illustrated in Figure 5.1, in reconstructing data is very evident in my second major example. Ovenden's (2003) study of the experiential meanings of primary school children's encounters with ancient Egyptian objects in a museum context draws upon her own prior experience of teaching to help her build a fictional account of a teacher taking children to the museum. She feels that this 'literary text' helps 'illuminate the meanings' embedded in her data and 'to access the pre-reflective sphere of the experience through the richness of the description'. The fiction is grounded in the data, which comprises observations of the children's behaviour during their visits to the museum at which she is the curator, and their written and verbal statements:

> In the process of trying to convey the complexity and spontaneity of the experience, I adopt the voice of a teacher using a narrative format. In addition, I use six children's voices which comprise composite statements from my research data. ... The description covers the preparation for the visit; travel to and arrival at the museum; the three activities (sketching, the treasure hunt and the handling session); departing from the museum, and finally, returning to school. (Ovenden 2003: 207)

This fictional account enables Ovenden to 'unfold' the experience of the children visiting the museum, which gives her the insights which enable her to write a second data chapter which comprises a more traditional thematic discussion of the data (2003: 168).

However, Ovenden's fictional account becomes more than a useful means of presenting data in the written text. It goes deeper into her need to get closer to an understanding of the children's experiences of touching objects in the museum as part of their 'being-in-the-world', by means of a hermeneutic phenomenological methodology inspired by Husserl and Heidegger. She thus seeks to demonstrate how 'the children's experience in the museum, like waking up, washing, dressing, breakfasting and travelling to school and then to the museum that morning was an integral part of their *being* as children' (2003: 143). In the fictional account she makes use of a passage in C.S. Lewis's *The Lion, the Witch and the Wardrobe* where Lucy 'finds a mysterious winter wonderland concealed within a wardrobe' to illustrate how some of the children in her data said that 'they felt "scared" and "spooked out" in the darkened galleries amongst the weird and wonderful exhibits, they also felt a compelling curiosity to explore' (2003: 165–166). Personal knowledge does not therefore need to be specific to the particular setting being investigated, as 'insider knowledge', but to settings or experiences within one's own biography which help provide insight into the setting.

Ovenden's aim in constructing her fictional account is to express what she terms, citing the work of van Manen, 'a poetizing activity' which results in 'a primal telling … that authentically speaks the world rather than abstractly speaking of it' and enables the reader to be 'grasped intuitively or epiphanically … and think differently about themselves' (2003: 166–167).

'The good story, and valid research'

West, in his discussion of how he conducted his study of the identities of inner-city doctors, says several things which support the value of the reconstructions. He follows the postmodern critique of postpositivism and naturalism introduced in Chapter 1 by decrying the artificial sense of truth and the unnatural 'detachment and distance' which presents a 'closed text to which readers have a "take it or leave it" relationship only' – 'a "fetish", a "God trick … that pretends to offer a vision that is from everywhere and nowhere, equally and fully"' (West 2001: 34, citing Stanley and Harraway). Instead, he presents a notion of 'auto/biography' in which 'research is always and inevitably a work of fiction, a *representation* of experience rather than in some way constituting the experience itself' (2001: 39), and maintains that:

> The good story, and valid research, is a product of making connections across disparate, often disconnected parts of life, and seeking this with new eyes, and from diverse perspectives and creating more of a whole in the process. Such 'wholes' can speak to others in similar conditions, and may empower them to reenvisage their experience too in more diverse and challenging ways. (West 2001: 40)

This resonates with the discussion of verisimilitude in Chapter 5. By interconnecting and then projecting in coherent forms what we see around us, we are not simply making things up. We are not simply falling short of the positivist intention to make an objective, uncontaminated record. Arundhati Roy puts aside the positivist notion that writers 'cull stories from the world':

> I am beginning to believe that vanity makes them think so – that it's actually the other way around. Stories cull writers from the world. Stories reveal themselves to us. The public narrative, the private narrative – they colonize us, they commission us, they insist on being told. … There can never be a single story: there are only ways of seeing. (Roy 2002, track 3)

There is a subtle turn from what might be expected here. Whereas the positivists may think a more subjective researcher is vain in imagining she can produce something worthwhile by integrating herself messily with the research site, and that what she ends up with is more ideological than objective, in Roy's statement, the researcher submits herself to complexity, thinking that it is vain to imagine she can rise above it. What makes the work of Wu, Ovenden and Honarbin-Holliday significant is that they apply scientific rigour to the immense complexity in which they find themselves in order to communicate its messages as faithfully as they can.

The rigour which is required to produce successful reconstructions or fictions is great; they are by no means easy options. I have already referred above to the preparatory 'stranger' observation which Duan carried out in his daughter's unfamiliar primary school. Another exercise to help researchers tune their abilities to see things freshly could indeed be to create fictional accounts of the events they know to be there but cannot quite marshal the data for. These accounts may or may not become data in the written study, but they will serve to interrogate diverse entry points into the research.

Photographs as co-constructed text

This context of data reconstruction throws a particular light on Honarbin-Holliday's use of photographic data as *co-construction* in her study of art students in Tehran (Holliday 2006). The photograph in Figure 5.4 is one of 300 which she uses as a major data source (see Chapter 4). What is noticeable about this picture of an art student standing with her painting is that it is quite obviously posed. Asking the young woman to stand with her paintings in this way for the camera is not however an artificial imposition of the researcher's fantasy on the people in the research setting. Honarbin-Holliday felt that this pose best represented what she had already observed, and discussed with the art students, as a significant feature of their perceptions, and of this particular student's expression of self-image expressed in interviews with her elsewhere in the thesis. 'This photograph was furthermore taken to represent seen phenomena and to demystify the perceptions that people outside Iran might have about an art student and her paintings.' Although the art student had never before stood beside her paintings for a photograph in this way, she, and other students who were asked to pose with their paintings, by no means thought it was an unusual act and seemed to think it made eminent sense (Honarbin-Holliday interview). As in the reconstructed 'stories' in Wu's (2002) thesis, it is co-constructed by the researcher as photographer and the student, 'both of whom carry their social positions and interests to the photographic act' (Pink 2001: 10, citing Harper). This breaks open the postpositivist, naturalist illusion of the virgin, untouched culture.

Indeed, in the case of this particular student, when Honarbin-Holliday asked her to hold her arm in a similar position to the bathroom pipe in the painting, the student agreed that it helped emphasize the relationship between the pipe which is 'fluid' but truncated and her feeling about the position of women. This is in turn contrasted with the position of the man's hand at rest on his lap in the top right of the painting. The photograph thus takes on a new compositional life as the student holding her painting becomes a further expression of the painting itself. Honarbin-Holliday being herself an academic artist, able to understand and discuss with the

Figure 5.4   Posing

student the messages she wished to project, was of course instrumental in being able to join with the student as co-constructor.

Caution

In this chapter I have demonstrated a complex process, of getting from data to writing, which is at the centre of qualitative research. Its complexity lies partly in the way in which themes are determined and fragments of data are selected and redeployed, and also in the way in which the final written text is constructed. Both are highly creative and rely very much on the ingenuity of the researcher as an architect of meaning.

Caution is necessary, however. On the one hand, it is the presentation and organization of data and its analysis which bring credibility:

> When such written accounts contain a high degree of internal coherence, plausibility, and correspondence to what readers recognize from their own experiences and from other realistic and factual texts, they accord the work (and the research on which it is based) a sense of 'authenticity'. (Adler and Adler 1994: 381, citing Atkinson)

There are also considerable dangers in the way in which the neatness and artfulness of the final production can overcome the integrity of research. We must not be seduced by this coherence:

> Coherence cannot be the major test of validity for a cultural description. ... There is nothing so coherent as a paranoid's delusion or a swindler's story. The

force of our interpretations cannot rest on the tightness with which they hold together, or the assurance with which they are argued. Nothing has done more, I think, to discredit cultural analysis than the impeccable depictions of formal order in whose actual existence nobody can quite believe. (Geertz 1993: 17–18)

This will be addressed in Chapter 8.

Summary

The following points have been made in this chapter:

- Moving from data collection and analysis to the writing of the data analysis part or chapter of the written study involves organizing the data into themes which then act as headings in the written study.
- This process involves several stages of removal from the 'original reality' of the social setting. The data analysis section or chapter thus takes on an agency of its own, with an argument for which extracts of data act as evidence.
- Thematic headings can emerge entirely from the corpus of raw data, or may sometimes relate to the stages in data collection, or can be both.
- A thematic organization may require a complete break from the chronology of how the data was collected. Principles of *emergence* and *submission* need to be applied to enable the data to take on a life unexpected by the researcher.
- Extracts from the corpus of raw data are embedded within the argument of the data analysis section or chapter with different degrees of explicitness.
- Each embedded extract of data is usually preceded and sometimes followed by a discursive commentary which guides the reader to the specific meaning the researcher sees in it, and links it to the argument.
- Long extracts of data can be indented separate to the main text, following the rule used for citing from literature.
- Thick description comprises (1) the network of interconnected data plus (2) the argument and discussion which demonstrates the way in which the data interconnects.
- The data extracts used as evidence for the argument are selected from the corpus of raw data when they display (1) key elements from data analysis and (2) maximum richness within a small space.
- Breaking up and leaving behind the corpus of raw data is not problematic because (1) it was itself a construction of the researcher and (2) the redeployment of parts of it within an argument presents a greater richness of thick description.
- Separating data, discussion and argument in the written study helps to make the research process transparent to the reader, and also represents the discipline of keeping data and comment separate in the research process itself.
- Reconstructions and fictionalizations may be used to help preserve the original richness of data, and should be underpinned by personal knowledge of how society works.

Writer Voice

In Chapter 3 I described how showing the workings makes a major contribution to the rigour and validity of qualitative research. At a more micro level, the rigour of qualitative research is to a large degree carried within the conventions that run throughout the discourse of academic writing. There is, however, a concern that these conventions alienate the person of the writer, and help create a distorted image of the people who are being written about. In this chapter I shall look at the first of these two issues and explore how the researcher as writer can work with the conventions and find her own voice, and use this voice as an important methodological tool. The second issue concerning the image, world and voice of the other people in the setting will be addressed in Chapter 8.

I shall first contextualize the issue of conventions within the broader issue of genre and discourse and how this relates to the social world and the individual writer. This will be followed by examples from my corpus of written studies of how the researcher can write her own agendas into these conventions. The final part of the chapter will look at how the skilful use of these conventions increases the credibility of the research.

The struggle with convention

The written study in qualitative research represents a particular genre within the discourse and broader culture of qualitative research. These terms are often disputed, but I find it useful to define them as follows. *A culture*, as discussed in Chapter 1, can be defined as a set of behaviour, for example the culture of a family, a street, a grocer's shop, international business, New York cab drivers. *A discourse* can be defined as a specific rule-governed set of language behaviour, a larger set of 'language use conceived as social practice' (Fairclough 1995: 135), or, as discussed in Chapter 1, 'domain of social practice' (Lankshear et al. 1997: 22) or a way of talking, for

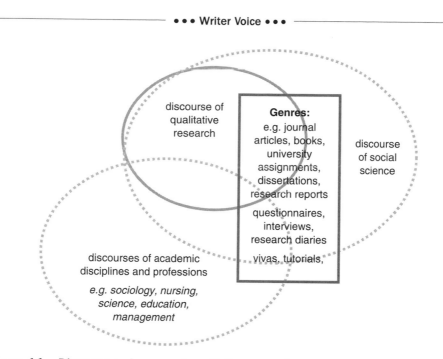

Figure 6.1   Discourse and genres of qualitative research

example the discourse of sexism, of parenting, of selling computers. *A genre* is a specific rule-governed language event or text, a smaller, perhaps more concrete entity than discourse, a 'particular social activity' (Fairclough 1995: 135), for example the genre of tax forms, of road signs, of science fiction literature, of university tutorials in the humanities, of job interviews in banking. The relationship between these entities is clearly complex, and the distinction between them often blurred, especially as they are anyway only relative, heuristic concepts for making sense of a mélange of social reality (Clark and Ivanič 1997: 15). As with 'culture', 'discourse' and 'genre' are movable concepts. Figure 6.1 therefore attempts only a rough representation of discourse and genre in the case of qualitative research.

The darker rectangular bubble in Figure 6.1 contains examples of genres that are employed generally within the discourse of social science. The discourse of qualitative research is contained within social science and makes use of these same basic genres, while imposing its own variations on them, as do various discourses of academic disciplines and professions. The focus of this book is on the cluster of written 'genres' at the top of the darker bubble, which I am taking as having common features. I exclude research reports, which involve a very different type of activity. It should be remembered that because what constitutes 'a genre' is relative, another drawing of this figure could indicate separate genres of, for example, 'qualitative' and 'quantitative' research journal articles. Whether these are separate genres, or variations within a broader genre of social science journal articles, is to me a purely academic question, depending on viewpoint and level of generality. In a sense, as one zooms in out of the picture represented by Figure 6.1, one will get, respectively, more smaller, or fewer larger genres. One could also conceive of separate genres, say of introductions and conclusions within journal articles. There are also perceptible generic divisions between the various discourses of academic disciplines and professions operating within and through the different academic discourses (bottom left of the figure). It should also be noted that in the detail of each chapter, I present variations between say articles and assignments, between differences connected with discipline and profession, with the style of individual writers, and also with discoursal differences between ethnography, grounded theory and so on (see Chapter 1) – which could have been included in the figure as yet another circle.

Figure 6.1 demonstrates that the overall genre of the qualitative research written study derives generally from the social sciences, and is not, as some students think, imposed by the people who assess their assignments. Nevertheless, in simple terms, what and how the researcher writes is very largely decided by others within academic and professional communities (bottom left of the figure). With reference to organizational studies, Golden-Biddle and Locke make the point that 'our professional community sets the topical boundaries for our writing, broadly delimiting the phenomena that fall within the domain of organizational studies', and that 'our audience also broadly sets out the manuscript's structure and progression: the movement from literature reviews to methods, results and concluding discussion' (1997: 9). This is largely to do with being accepted as members – 'those disciplinary writing conventions allow readers to consider our work as coming from one who is a member of the scientific community' (1997: 9). Miller et al. (1998) demonstrate this very well in their study of how researchers are constrained in the way in which they are allowed to write by research committees and supervisors in university departments. They talk about a deep conflict within qualitative research itself, between postpositivist naturalist and what I have described in Chapter 1 as postmodern paradigms connected to the degree to which researchers can express their own voice.

Reducing personal power

The ideological nature of qualitative research, both in its impact on the research setting and the people in it, and in the way it constructs its own realities, makes its writing a highly sensitive task. This is the case even for researchers who are fully versed and at ease with the conventions. For others, who criticize the conventions for representing current hegemonies of class and gender, of who can write and who is always written about, there is the added, political dimension. For them, 'texts become "an arena for struggle"' (Clark and Ivanič 1997: 174, citing Hall) over 'whose meaning prevails' (1997: 173, citing Vološinov) and how the world is thought to be organized as a 'sociohistorical construction' (Richardson and St Pierre 2005: 960). The situation is even more problematic for many novice researchers, such as undergraduate and master's students, who find the discourse itself as difficult to conceptualize as the principles of qualitative research themselves.

For novice researchers, difficulty with academic writing is indicative not necessarily of weaknesses in basic literacy, but of becoming autonomous within a new, strange discourse. A personal anecdote demonstrates the problem:

EXAMPLE 6.1   NOT SWITCHING DISCOURSE

Mark had a first class bachelor's degree in English literature from a well-known university in England. He then became a language teacher and, after accruing a considerable amount of professional experience, he enrolled on a master's programme in language education. As a master's student he displayed considerable ability as a critical thinker, with a sophisticated awareness of the politics and ideology of education. However, he 'failed' as an academic writer. His assignments were articulate and elegantly written, and succeeded in communicating a profoundly critical argument; but they were in the wrong genre. Mark wrote competently in the polemic style of his undergraduate literature days, not in the technical genre of the social sciences. He found the latter impossible to work with and eventually left the programme.

This is a rather extreme case; but many students have problems of this type, especially when they consider English their own language, and feel it an affront to have to conform to conventions which they consider lacking in creativity and 'style'. Thus, the student who has difficulty with academic writing does not have to be a 'non-native speaker' of the language, or one who has difficulty in writing per se. In particular, students who are also experienced professionals, such as nurses, sports-people, businesspeople or teachers, who are returning to education to get a higher degree or professional qualification, will experience discomfort if not anger when their accounts of professional experience are not accepted by their tutors and assessors unless presented to them according to 'unnecessary' academic conventions. They begin to realize that, as writers, they cease to wield power over what they say (Clark et al. 1990: 85, citing Hall). They find themselves newly constructed, not as experienced professionals, but as 'junior member[s] of an academic discourse community' which decides for them what they are allowed to say, how they are allowed to say it and who they are allowed to be as writers. They have to 'conform to the standards' required by this community (1990: 91) and can feel cornered:

> From the perspective of the student who disagrees with the orthodoxy, the options appear to be: conform to it, appear to conform to it, challenge it tactfully, challenge it openly, change the topic of the essay altogether. … [They believe] that they will be marked down if they disagree with or challenge their tutor or that the argument can be more persuasive if they follow the books … playing a safe game. (Clark et al. 1990: 94–95)

Ivanič and Roach make a useful distinction here. As a mature student, Roach is struggling with the discourse:

> '*Privilege power*' is what people acquire from joining the club: from conforming to the discourse conventions in order to gain qualifications, status and credibility. '*Personal power*' is the result of gaining control over our own lives, being in a position to exercise choice and know the consequences. Where academic writing is concerned, this means being able to write for our own purposes in our own way, choosing among the available conventions and at times flouting them in order to make a stand. (Ivanič and Roach 1990: 103, my emphasis)

These two types of power can also be aligned with two types of voice suggested by Clark and Ivanič. 'Voice as *form*' is not personal in that it operates conformity with convention as given. 'Voice as *content*' is personal in that the writer uses the content of language to express her 'own ideas and beliefs'. It is the second type which 'authoritative writers' use in 'establishing an authorial presence in their texts' (1997: 151–152, their emphasis).

Mixed messages

A major factor which makes the conventions of academic writing in English problematic for the novice is that there are conflicting signals. At first sight, a major criterion for 'acceptable' writing seems to be that there should be a huge amount of reference to other people, leaving very little room for the ideas and experience of the writer. This apparent negation of the person of the writer is compounded by the fact that what other people say in the literature, their ideas, findings and research methods, are not 'free goods': the writer must constantly acknowledge that she does not 'own' them, and say where she got them from (Bloor and Bloor 1991: 4, citing Goffman). This leads to what appears to be an overwhelming barrage of citing, referencing and bibliographical detail.

What puzzles the writer about this is that when she thinks she is 'succeeding' in citing chapter and verse of what other people have said, and gets all the referencing conventions correct, her work is still not accepted. There is a final subtle twist. Showing what you have read *is* important, but not for the purpose of showing you know the 'facts' which reside there. The crucial thing is to show what you *think* about what you have read (Bloor and Bloor 1991: 2). Indeed, points are given for criticizing respected authority. Here again, though, the person of the author seems to be negated, because this should be done *through* literature sources which tend to disprove rather than support authority (Richards and Skelton 1991: 24). Therefore, 'good writing' becomes a complex balancing act between showing what you have read, being critical of it, but doing this by still more citing of other people. The writer is discouraged from coming out and saying openly 'I criticize this literature because…'. The use of the passive pushes the person of the author into the background with 'this literature is criticized by X and Y, who say that …'.

At this point the humanities and social science split in that the former uses a referencing convention which minimizes the intrusion of references to literature in the main text by placing them all in footnotes or endnotes, as in this example:

> Lane's purpose was to deliver Egypt and the Egyptians to his readers, 'to keep nothing hidden, to deliver the Egyptians without depth, in swollen detail'.[29] Lane wished to achieve the 'imposition of a scholarly will upon an untidy reality',[30] to appear only in the reserved persona of annotator and translator and lexicographer.[31] The humanity of Lane's narrative undertaking was sacrificed. (Kabbani 1986: 44, citing Said)

Although to a certain extent this makes more of the author's voice, as she is encouraged to be creative in manipulating her own and other's words eloquently, yet the writer speaks entirely through reference to others.

In contrast with this, the social sciences have traditionally maintained the passive, but without the eloquence, by adopting 'a "windowpane" model of language' in which 'discovered phenomena' are thought to be so clear to be seen that 'all associations, emotional colouring, and implications of attitude and judgement' can be avoided (Golden-Biddle and Locke 1997: 3, citing Brooks and Warren). Researchers must '"deliberately strive" to avoid all literary tropes in their writing so as to "tie scientific communication to observable phenomena by way of direct reference' (Golden-Biddle and Locke 1997: 4, citing Pinder and Bourgeois). The result is an 'anonymous disciplinary code in which "it is concluded that" and only "the data", not researchers, "suggest" anything'. The researcher must 'write herself out of her texts and let "the findings speak for themselves"' (1997: 4). Talking specifically about ethnography, Richardson explains that:

> Needful to distinguish their work from travellers' and missionaries' reports as well as from imaginative writing, ethnographers adopted an impersonal, third person voice to explain an 'observed phenomenon' and trumpet the authenticity of their representations. ... The author as an 'I' is mostly absent from the text, which talks about the people studied, the author exists only in the preface, establishing 'I was there' and 'I'm a researcher' credentials. (Richardson 1994: 520, citing Van Maanen)

The 'windowpane' model is thus transformed into 'realist tale' (1994: 520) which adheres to a naïve naturalism in which a hands-off researcher describes a self-evident world.

Here, the loss of researcher voice is compounded by a much more explicit form of referencing characterized by such 'technical' devices as subheadings, numeration and diagrams, and by putting citations in the main text in brackets. To someone brought up in the 'higher' literary humanities (e.g. Example 6.1), the established genre of social science academic writing, with the same restrictions on the use of the first person, but the creative notion of 'rhetoric' removed, indeed seems dull, mechanical and impersonal.

New thinking

I wish to emphasize, however, that this picture of impersonal social science writing does not have to be so, and that there is a place for powerful, personal authorship. There is a new thinking which comes from the postmodern, critical break with the naturalist, post-positivist tradition (see Chapter 1). This involves an acknowledgement that it is the agency of the researcher as writer that makes the research, which is associated with a post-structuralist realization of a *'continual cocreation of Self and social science'* which 'are known through each other' (Richardson 1994: 518, her emphasis) and an acceptance of creative rhetoric, which plays an important part in thick description (Richardson and St Pierre 2005; Atkinson and Coffey 1995: 46; Bailey et al. 1999: 169). This creativity is demonstrated in Chapter 5 in the way in which themes, fragments of data and argument are woven to make a coherent whole, and in Chapter 4 in the way in which descriptive data is composed. The agency of the researcher is also being acknowledged more and more as an ideological force which impacts on relations with people in the research setting and the way in which they are perceived. This has been discussed at length in Chapter 3, where I demonstrate the importance of a strong statement by the researcher about her own ideological and conceptual position. Moreover the researcher, by using 'I', can create 'a different, more transparent relationship with her readers. ... She tries to make it very clear what her own opinions are. In other words, she tries not to disguise 'opinion' as 'fact' by using impersonal so-called objective language' (Clark and Ivanič 1997: 169).

Consequently, especially in professional applications of social science, the use of the first person has for some time been acceptable, and is becoming more so (e.g. Golden-Biddle and Locke 1997). There is a growing feeling among qualitative researchers that more attention should be given to the researcher as writer – to rectify the irony that 'we neither teach writing nor talk much about it' despite the fact that 'it is a practice that consumes much of our professional efforts' (1997: x). This might be seen as a '"coming out" to colleagues and students' about a 'secret displeasure with much of qualitative writing, only to find a community full of like-minded discontents' (Richardson 1994: 517). Miller et al. see the move towards a liberation of researcher voice in writing as a major battle between 'the more participatory interpretive voice' and 'the more detached positivist voice' still very evident in what I have referred to as postpositivist, naturalist qualitative research (1998: 401). A researcher in their study remarks that 'the problem of speaking voice is more than just using the first person. It also includes how you see things. ... Your perspective and your voice are integrated'. Miller et al. pursue this notion that postmodern qualitative research *requires* a liberation of voice. They note that in studies of dissertations it was found that a more '"restricted" ... traditional reporting structure was often incompatible with researchers' "felt sense" ... of the research experience' (1998: 401, citing Meloy), and that 'the problem with interpretist researchers trying to use traditional research textual patterns [is that] "Qualitative analysis will only appear as bad quantitative research"' (1998: 401, citing Athanasas and Heath, and Nielsen).

The outcome is a reformed genre which keeps some of the more traditional social science conventions and changes or opens a discussion with regard to others. Even at the more radical end of this reform, there seems to be an adherence to explicit referencing conventions. This can be seen in this extract from an article which critiques traditional convention:

> We also struggle with *representation*, working hard to figure out how to represent and contextualize our narrators, ourselves, and the people about whom they are ranting. Under the tutelage of historians Scott (1992) and Katz (1995) and psychologist Cross (1991), we try to understand how and why these categories of analysis, these 'others', and these accusations are being cast at this moment in history, and who is being protected by this 'scope of blame' (Opotow 1990). (Fine and Weis 1998: 28, their emphasis)

What is new here is the way in which the writers liberate their own authorial voice by using the first person ('we', 'ourselves'), non-formal, opinionated and self-revealing language ('figure out', 'ranting', 'try'), and personalized labelling ('these'). At the same time they rigorously cite all literary sources in the conventional way. This 'we', which is the plural 'I' of both authors, is significantly different from the impersonal 'we' often used in more traditional writing to reduce the presence of the author by referring to the broad community of readers and writer or to create a sense of 'usness' with the reader (Clark and Ivanič 1997: 165). The outcome is a far more explicit distinction between the voice of the researcher as writer and those of others than in the more traditional social science text or the ritually eloquent humanities text. They produce particularly bald-on-record statements about their identity and ideological preoccupations:

> We are two Jewish white women academics, trained well in the rigours of social psychology (Michelle) and sociology (Lois), experienced in the complexities of critical ethnography ... eager to traverse the borders of research, policy, activism, and theory ... This article may be conceptualized as an early 'coming out' about some of the methodological, theoretical, and ethical issues that percolate from our fieldwork. (Fine and Weis 1998: 14)

(This can, though, get a bit too hyperbolic and over-indulged – as when they go on to talk about high email bills, long nights and discussions with friends and colleagues.) They also use, throughout their text, headings and subheadings to explicitly mark the structure and progression of their discussion – *Echoes (and aches) in our head*, with subsections. As with themes in data analysis, using headings also helps the researcher to place her creative stamp on the text.

Writing as investigation

A key part of this new thinking is the realization that writing is itself part of the process of qualitative investigation. Part of the positivist vision of research has been the view that data is collected until the research is 'finished', at which point 'writing up begins'. Post-positivist, naturalist qualitative research continues this tradition with the idea that there comes a point at which social exploration is exhausted and data complete and self-evident, and the writing-up stage is simply a matter of reporting. This is established in the British university system, where doctoral students are given a 'writing-up year' after the end of their registration, during which they do not get supervision. Golden-Biddle and Locke confirm that 'this "it's as plain as the nose on your face"' assumption does not square with the experience:

> When we sit in front of our terminals with our piles of field notes, transcripts, analytic memos, expecting to 'just write up' ... we discover all too clearly that it is not that simple. ... Contrary to the windowpane assumptions of findings as self-evident, we never yet have had a piece of data tell us its significance. (Golden-Biddle and Locke 1997: 6)

Golden-Biddle reports that 'she has not yet been able to figure out how to tell in journal article form what, to her, is the central story of her fieldwork' (1997: 9). Thus, contrary to the traditional view, Richardson presents writing as itself:

> a *method of inquiry*, a way of finding out about yourself and your topic. Although we usually think about writing as a mode of 'telling' about the social world, writing is not just a mopping-up activity at the end of a research project. Writing is also a way of 'knowing' – a method of discovery and analysis. By writing in different ways, we discover new aspects of our topic and our relationship to it. (Richardson 1994: 516, her emphasis)

This can be seen in the way in which the sense of argument develops throughout the whole process of data collection, analysis and organization.

This makes qualitative writing in essence very different from quantitative writing. Qualitative writing becomes very much an unfolding story in which the writer gradually makes sense, not only of her data, but of the total experience of which it is an artefact. This is an interactive process in which she tries to untangle and make reflexive sense of her own presence and role in the research. The written study thus becomes a complex train of thought within which her voice and her image of others are interwoven. Therefore, 'unlike quantitative work that can carry its meaning in its tables and summaries, qualitative work carries its meaning in its entire text ... its meaning is in the reading' (Richardson and St Pierre 2005: 959–60). The voice and person of the researcher as writer not only become a major ingredient of the written study, but have to be evident for the meaning to become clear.

Genre as gateway and social exploration

Another contribution to this new thinking comes from an understanding of how conventions, genres and discourses are part and parcel of the fabric of complex society which all individuals need to understand and navigate. Recent work in literacy studies suggests that learning or confronting academic genres might have the intrinsic value of learning or confronting how society works. These genres thus play the role of 'secondary discourses', which, like 'schools, clubs, churches, government departments etc.', are 'encountered through participation in social institutions beyond the primary group' (Lankshear et al. 1997: 26). This means that even those students of qualitative research who are only 'passing through' the peripheries of social science, for the purpose of getting qualifications or a general education, can benefit from this experience. This experience helps instil 'critical literacy' as they learn how social 'truths' are constructed differently within different discourse communities and their genres. Thus, struggling to achieve personal power involves coming to terms with how discourses and genres help construct the wider politics of their world. People need to know through this kind of experience that where one 'biological and medical' discourse 'renders the statement "the tubercle bacillus causes tuberculosis" obviously true', another 'socio-political' discourse 'renders it problematic' (Gee 1997: xviii).

Understanding how dealing with discourse and genre is social initiation in the general sense leads to an appreciation of its specific importance in professional and academic socialization. For students and novice writers who wish to join the discourse community of qualitative researchers, the genre of academic writing behaves as a *gateway* through which they must pass, first to be allowed membership, and then to participate creatively within the community, whether from within academic departments or from within their own professional communities (bottom left of Figure 6.1).

Hence, despite the critique of conventions as ideology, these must be learned before they can be manipulated. Throughout this book I show how the conventions of academic discourse are necessary to maintain the rigour of qualitative research. Here I wish to demonstrate that this does not mean that the writer has to minimize her presence. The discussion on the preceding pages has shown that there is indeed room in the genre to allow her to use the conventions while at the same time being creative and achieving personal power. I think that the degree of variety seen in Chapter 5 already illustrates this potential. Moreover, the verisimilitude of qualitative research is very much created by the way in which a representation is accepted within the culture of the discourse community within which it works. So it is partly that the audience is *used* to this particular genre of television documentary, and has become party to its verisimilitude, that gives it credibility. One could cynically say that we have been 'conditioned' into believing whatever we see in television documentaries; but I doubt if we are that stupid, because genres do change and revitalize themselves as audiences demand more. It is nevertheless necessary at least to begin by working from within the conventions of that community.

The author writes back

Given that these openings do exist within the qualitative research genre, it is necessary to identify exactly where they are – where the researcher can express her voice to claim personal power in writing. One such place has already been dealt with in Chapter 5, where I demonstrated how the whole written study is driven by the researcher's argument, marked by personal phrases such as Pierson's use of 'I interpreted these comments to mean' in his discursive commentary on nursing assistants' accounts (see Chapter 5). All the way through there is a dialogue between 'your argument and agenda' and 'evidence', selected and organized by 'you', which is driven firmly by the former. This is illustrated by many of the statements on the right of Figure 3.1, which show how this argument and agenda are placed throughout the whole written study. In the written study, literature is collected, organized under headings, selected from, and embedded in the fabric of the argument in a very similar way to data. I have already given examples of common conventions in Chapters 3 and 5. Hence, *your* evidence includes literature as well as data; and in both cases this is set against *your* experience.

There are various ways in which the researcher can create and assert her own space. The following are examples, this time taken from all parts of the written studies in my corpus.

Asserting agenda

Albert, in his study of risk in cycling, declares his own research and agenda clearly within his discussion of issues, where he looks at literature:

> For a number of years I have been examining the process of reality construction in the subculture of serious recreational road cycling and racing (Albert, 1990, 1991, 1997). As I understand that subculture, it is a unified one, more accurately described as a 'social world' in the sense that Crosset and Beal (1997) use the term. (Albert 1999: 159, my underlining)

It is clear from the underlined phrases what *he* has been doing and what *he* thinks. This is done primarily by using the first person. Moreover, he skilfully takes ownership of the literature he cites. He takes the term 'social world' from Crosset and Beal, acknowledges that it belongs to them by placing it in inverted commas, but uses it as a resource to strengthen *his* argument. He thus places himself and his quest within a wider discussion, within which he becomes the focus. He also shows that he has his own credentials and stake in this discussion as he cites his own work – not just one but three published pieces.

Maguire and Mansfield make a similar personal statement in the first paragraph of their study of aerobics classes, again taking terminology from the literature to support their cause – 'We locate the exercise discourse within a wider network of interdependencies defined as the "exercise-body beautiful complex"' (1998: 109, my underlining).

The novice reader might think that these writers can 'get away' with this because they are published researchers. After all, Albert cites his own work. However, Hayagoshi, in her first major piece of writing, her master's dissertation, writes in her introduction:

> I took a general English course for about six months ... This has <u>given me</u> a good basis for comparing the learning habits of the Japanese and those of others ... <u>I had</u> several opportunities to talk with many Japanese students ... <u>To my surprise</u>, it seemed that many teachers still have stereotypical ideas. (Hayagoshi 1996: 2, my underlining)

This shows her own presence in the work; later in the introduction she continues, but sets an open, honest mood. She shows 'where she comes from', sets the whole tone of the work and creates the impression of the sorts of claims she can make. It may seem inappropriate for a researcher to show that she is 'surprised' – but why not? After all, she is only a person like the rest of us, trying, like the rest of us, to make sense of the world. She continues to state what she intends and aims:

> In this dissertation, <u>I intend</u> to contrast British teachers' perceptions of Japanese students ... with Japanese students' own perceptions ... The goal of <u>my dissertation</u> is to find out if there is a gap ... If there is a gap <u>I aim</u> to determine its nature. (Hayagoshi 1996: 2)

This is very clearly *her* dissertation. She puts forward herself and her own experience and agenda very strongly from the outset.

It is not only the use of the first person that gives the writer voice, as can be seen in this extract from the discussion of issues section of Emami and Ekman's study of elderly Iranian immigrants in Sweden:

> A knowledge of cultural factors <u>plays</u> a very important role within the health care field. ... If cultural differences <u>are not</u> given appropriate consideration, conflicts and problems are sure to arise, which <u>will</u> potentially prevent a healthy sense of well-being, and/or delay illness recovery (Leninger 1978; Lipson and Meleis 1989; Lipson 1992; Meleis et al. 1992; Ekman et al. 1993). (Emami and Ekman 1998: 184, my underlining)

The underlined words show that the authors use a series of active sentences – x plays, y are not, z will – to state their view of the way things *are*. Indeed, the second two underlined phrases mark a conditional sentence which sets *their* conditions – if x, then y. Once again, literature is brought in at the end, not simply to show that they have read, but to reinforce their point of view. Literature is thus their evidence, used as a resource to support their argument. Note the technique of listing references to literature to provide maximum strength of support within a short space. Albert also uses this technique in his statement that 'in sport, the propagation of these dominant values is especially prevalent in hierarchical environments like high-school and college-level athletics (Curry and Strauss 1994; Messner 1992; Nixon 1994, 1996; Young and White 1995)' (Albert 1999: 158). The reader might remember that Pierson also uses literature in this way to support the argument in her data analysis section.

Making personal contact

Another way of establishing the self of the researcher is by speaking as a person to the person of the reader. This is done explicitly by Pierson in her study of feeding demented care residents. She begins in her introduction by creating a sense of common experience with her readers:

> Excluding infants, the actual work of feeding is an activity you normally perform by and for yourself. You decide about the bite size and the mix of foods. When you are fed, someone else makes those decisions for you. You are then expected to accept what the feeder gives you and how he or she delivers it. (Pierson 1999: 127)

The use of 'you' distinguishes this as personal experience from what follows, which refers to 'observations in long-term care ... facilities' and the 'many studies' which catalogue them. Similar examples occur in Linehan's account of growing up in Greece and Herrera's account of hearing the noises of the school from her student hostel, both of which set the scene for their written studies and include strong personal phrases – 'I learnt', 'I wondered' (see Chapter 2).

In the example above, Albert might be thought cautious because his exposure of self does not occur until the third page of this study. However, he has already set a personal tone by starting with an anecdote of how a sports commentator talks about danger – 'British sports commentator Phil Liggett articulates features of the wider sport of cycling' (Albert 1999: 157). By referring to Phil Liggett by name, he draws on a sports cultural reference which he shares with his readers.

Shaw, in her study of women's body image, uses a less personal tone throughout. However, in her introduction she makes contact with her reader's experience of 'everyday life' by referring to advertising, the press, and to personal contact with a psychiatrist, all of which are centred around a topical public concern with anorexia:

> The 'Omega' watch company withdrew its advertisements from *Vogue* magazine in protest at the use of 'distasteful' pictures of a model of 'anorexic proportions', which could influence its audience of 'young and impressionable females' (*The Times*, 31 May 1996). Following this incident, a psychiatrist working with young women with eating disorders commented:
>
> > I do feel that there is a strong relationship ... virtually all of our patients report having been influenced by the media in some way (personal correspondence, June 1996).
>
> (Shaw 1998: 7)

Note that even though this is anecdote, Shaw still makes use of academic referencing conventions – being careful to place quoted phrases in inverted commas, indenting the longer quote from the psychiatrist as though it were literature or data, placing details of the newspaper article in brackets, and using the accepted convention of 'personal ...', properly dated, for impromptu encounters.

Generally, making personal contact in this way emphasizes the close connection between qualitative research and everyday experience. Qualitative researchers arc just people, going about their daily lives and trying to make sense, just like everyone else. The difference is that, like Shaw, they take care to catalogue and make clear reference to their evidence. Thus, Herrera's whole dissertation is simply an extension of her initial 'I wondered'.

Experience as evidence

The researcher's own experience of life, which technically stands outside the realm of 'data', in that it has not been systematically collected within the research setting, can also be used as evidence. In the above examples, it provides evidence for the importance of the research. It can also provide valuable evidence once the major argument is well under way in either the discussion of issues or data analysis chapters or sections. This can be seen in these two extracts from my study of international curriculum innovation. The first is part of my chapter on methodological issues. A statement from my own experience about gaining access to research settings is sandwiched between a general, theoretical statement (broken underlining) and support for this in the form of reference to literature (underlined):

> One of the most crucial aspects of gaining access to a situation for both curriculum developers and ethnographers is finding local personalities who are both accurate informants and who will lead them into the *informal order*. It is common, in my experience, to spend a considerable amount of time, on first arriving in a new host situation, working through false leads, and discovering that personalities first met are not *key* personalities at all. Hammersley and Atkinson, citing a range of ethnographic studies, refer to key local personalities as 'gatekeepers' (1983: 63–68). (Holliday 1991: 141, original emphasis; underlining added)

In one sense, this statement of experience is redundant in that the rest of the extract is sufficient to carry the point. However, adding the statement of experience brings personal presence and ownership to the discussion, which may indeed strike a chord with readers who have had similar experiences, also reminding them that this a 'real world' issue. The phrase with which I begin my personal statement, 'it is common', tones down the claim I make to suit experience of this type. Thus, a statement of experience *adds* to the overall argument, but is not sufficiently interconnected with other data to stand by itself in any significant way.

Once again the conventions are used to preserve personal voice by demarcating the three types of statement in the extract. The phrase, 'in my experience', marks one. The reference to literature is marked at the beginning by the names of the authors, and at the end by the reference in brackets. The reference to literature is also strengthened by 'citing a range of authors' – giving yet further validity to my personal experience. If these explicit markers were not there, the text would look like this:

> One of the most crucial aspects of gaining access to a situation for both curriculum developers and ethnographers is finding local personalities who are both accurate informants and who will lead them into the *informal order*. It is common to spend a considerable amount of time, on first arriving in a new host situation, working through false leads, and discovering that personalities first met are not *key* personalities at all. Key local personalities can be referred to as '*gatekeepers*'. (Hammersley and Atkinson 1983: 63–68, their emphasis) (Reconstruction)

The result would be an appearance that the whole thing is attributed to the literature – which would in fact be inaccurate – and the loss of my personal statement and the overall personalization of the text.

The second extract is from a data analysis chapter. It also shows a personal statement embedded, this time, between references to data:

> When we arrived LL was not there. Another [local] lecturer, LT was there instead. ... LT said that s/he had last seen LL several weeks ago, and that s/he believed that s/he was not feeling very well at that time. (Obs. 69, site 9, LT, LL)
>
> It is not clear whether or not this type of communication problem was beneath other examples of miscommunication, or whether it was simply due to misunderstandings, which were a common occurrence in project business (personal experience). For example, on one occasion I had understood that I had been invited to give a demonstration lesson and instead found that I was expected to give a public lecture (obs. 9, site 10). (Holliday 1991: 246, my underlining)

Once again, conventions are used for explicit demarcation. The indentation marks the long fragment of data at the beginning. The underlined statement is marked as a paraphrase of data by 'for example' at one end and the bracketed reference at the other. 'This type of communication problem' marks the broken underlined statement as discursive commentary on the indented data fragment; but then, the bracketed reference to 'personal experience' shows that what remains is from my own experience. Again, this adds valuable personal voice to the discussion. Note also how the phrase 'a common occurrence' once again reduces the claim to one that is appropriate for a personal observation of this nature.

The conventions of explicitness in social science writing can thus be used to *preserve* the voice of the researcher by demarcating her presence from those of others. The use of the first person and personal statement shows where the researcher is speaking for herself; the use of bracketed reference shows where she is using other sources. Unlike the more traditional humanities genre, in which the rhetoric creates a sense of seamless continuity between hidden author and an ongoing texture of literature, the social science genre provides explicit segments within which the writer can carve out a personal territory.

Creating coherence

Once the researcher has asserted her presence, she also has to make her presence worthwhile and meaningful. Within the academic discourse community to whom she is writing, she must make herself a credible presence. Once again, the conventions of the writing genre can be used to achieve this. Just as a teacher in a classroom, a technical demonstrator or a person in the street depends on devices such as whiteboards, wall displays, maps, pointers or simply arm movements to *show* other people what she knows or what they should do, the researcher has devices at her disposal within the conventions of writing. In several places I have drawn attention to the way in which researchers refer to various sources of evidence that exist elsewhere – literature, data, the press, and personal encounter sources – often with the use of brackets.

Referencing of this sort is not simply a tedious mechanical insertion into the flow of the text, it is a very useful means of *pointing*. This is not an esoteric process. There are parallels with, for example, the genre of oral presentations, which is used extensively throughout the professional world. In *oral presentations*, the presenter supports, demonstrates and enriches what she *says* (a) with extra information, diagrams, tables etc., on transparencies, wall displays and handouts, (b) by referring to other work, writings, examples etc., and (c) by linking different parts of the presentation. This is facilitated by pointing – often using body language, changes in intonation etc. In *social science writing*, the researcher writer supports, demonstrates and enriches what she *writes* (a) with extra information, diagrams, tables etc., embedded near the main text or appended, (b) by referring to other literature, data etc., and (c) by linking different parts of the text. This is facilitated by reference to which date, page, part of the table or figure – often using brackets, indentation etc. In the same way, there are parallels with teaching and lecturing. The conventions of academic writing are thus no more than specialist representations of much broader forms of communication, using alternative means to compensate for the lack of face-to-face contact.

The following examples show how researchers *point* in this way to information elsewhere within the text in figures and tables, and longer pieces of supportive information appended at the end of the text.

Pointing to further detail

Byrd, in her study of maternal care giving in the United States, refers to a table in which she lists different types of consequences of how nurses ask questions during home visits. Placing this detail elsewhere in the text frees her to get on with her argument in the main text. However, she needs to *point* to where this information resides by stating that 'the potentially possible negative consequences are shown in Table 1 under headings that emerged from an earlier literature analysis (Byrd 1997b)'

(Byrd 1999: 30). Furthermore, she skilfully links the information with what she has done elsewhere in the literature.

Emami and Ekman (1998), in their study of immigrants in Sweden, use a figure to show the stages of selecting informants. This enables them to pinpoint aspects of this detail within their main text, while directing the reader to where the rest of the detail resides: 'Within the list received, 123 individuals fulfilled the selection criteria and were contacted by letter to request their participation in the study (Figure 1). Only 90 people received the communication; 33 letters were returned due to outdated addresses' (Emami and Ekman 1998: 186). The statements following the bracketed reference to the figure, though not explicitly connected, clearly also refer to aspects of the figure once the figure has been seen. The underlined phrases in the next example show how Linehan, in her study of open learning, is more explicit in guiding the reader to different parts of the table:

> Although the receptive skills such as reading and listening are catered for, the productive skills of speaking and writing are rather neglected. This point is illustrated in Table 2. <u>The section on the left describes</u> the nature of the self-access materials in the centre. ... <u>The right hand column illustrates</u> the nature of the productive skills. (Linehan 1996: 12, my underlining)

The reader will have noted how my own writing throughout this book makes full use of tables and figures in this way. Elsewhere, Linehan refers the reader to information that is placed in appendices because it is too extensive to include in the main text. She carefully indicates which appendix in the bracketed references:

> This is particularly true of the vocabulary listed in the letter of complaint (see Appendix 6D). They [the students] also seem to enjoy the postcard writing possibly because they are provided with postcards on Canterbury at the end of the pack to send to friends (see Appendix 7C). (Linehan 1996: 39)

Talbot, in her study of how gender is constructed in a teenage magazine, places her major data source in the appendix. As with Linehan's table, she guides the reader around what she considers the important features of the appended material. She has just introduced the idea that the magazines promote the idea of sisterliness:

> I will look for evidence of this sisterliness in the sample of data in the Appendix for this chapter (pp. 197–9). The sample I have chosen is a consumer feature. ... The two page feature contains various elements: a column of text covering an assortment of topics relating to lipstick (reproduced on p. 197 and the first paragraph of p. 198, and referred to below as 'the column'). (Talbot 1992: 181)

She is careful to make very specific reference to the pages on which the appended material appears; and in the last line she sets up a form of language with which she will continue referring to the appendix.

Especially in short articles and chapters like this, the researcher is not normally expected to append data. This is an exception because she is doing discourse analysis of the written text, which therefore needs to be seen by her reader. Furthermore, the data is small and *can* be appended in two pages. Nevertheless, she is unable to reproduce its full pictorial quality, presumably because of lack of space and publishing cost. Talbot also explains this to the reader – 'The article is reproduced ... without photographs and the proliferation of "kissprints" which adorned the segments of the written text' (1992: 181). This is a good example of how material outside the main text still needs comment within the main text. Many novice writers fail to do this, appending material and inserting figures and diagrams without making any explicit reference to them, and are then surprised when their readers do not know how to make use of them, or even ignore them.

Pointing to other parts

Another example of providing commentary is from my thesis, where I include, as a figure, two sketches of how students sit in the classroom. As well as explaining how the sketches relate to specific fragments of observation data, I also summarize what they show (underlined), in one case enriching this with an extract from the data:

> The sketches, in Figure 5.4, made during observation, of the seating arrangements in two classes, show a tendency for blocks of seating according to gender. <u>Sketch A shows</u> the local lecturer's class in observation 30 in which: 'The men were mainly at the back of the room and the women at the front, with two small colonies of women in the men's section' (obs. 30, site 11, LN). ... <u>Sketch B shows</u> the expatriate lecturer's crowded class of 450 in observation 39 in which the division corresponded with the central aisle of the room. (Holliday 1991: 276, added underlining)

In longer pieces of writing, it is also sometimes necessary to refer to different parts of the text itself. This extract is from the implications chapter of my thesis where I draw together the major points from my data analysis chapters. The bracketed page references show where the discussion of these points can be found:

> That standards were falling was partly due to the increasing numbers of students per lecturer in university English departments, created by increased enrolment, a relaxation of entry standards, and local staff working abroad (pp. 185–6, 283). This resulted in class sizes of up to 450, with the majority between 100 and 200, which was compounded by ill-designed rooms with poor acoustics and difficult institutional conditions (pp. 186, 223–8). These conditions both underlined the need for change and for innovation specially tailored to the local situation, as expressed in hypothesis 1 (p. 235): *Hypothesis 1: Difficult and unchangeable classroom conditions require the adaptation of imported curriculum innovation.* (Holliday 1991: 400)

The extract also shows how I took the decision to reproduce the hypothesis from page 235, thinking that it was too much to expect the reader to keep referring back to something which I was also going to make use of in this part of the text. One can also see the concentrated quality of a piece of writing designed to collect points from other places. The first sentence thus contains a list of points; and each bracketed reference contains a list of page numbers. (See my earlier comments on listing literature references.)

Personal orientation, history and narrative

In this last part of the chapter I am going to look at how the researcher's voice can also make a major contribution to the data itself and how it is understood. I have already referred in Chapter 2 to the contribution of the researcher's personal history in the overall orientation of the research. There are a variety of other ways in which it can contribute.

Personal narrative

Personal narrative can be defined as any form of narrative which recalls past experience. In a research setting, this past experience can often help to give a greater insight and a fresh perspective to the data. By seeing this as a form of data which can be embedded, like other types of data, within a broader discussion, I am taking a different line to one where an entire ethnography may take the self as the subject (e.g. Ellis and Bochner 2000; Holman Jones 2005). Personal narrative at first seems problematic, especially in postpositivist terms, because it is so subjectively personal that it cannot be validated. Because of its autobiographical nature, it will inevitably comprise one's own images, interpretations and indeed imaginations of past events, which may be so far in the past that there is no way they can be attested to by anyone else. It can appear to do no more than tell a novelistic story which has no scientific value. Nevertheless, in a more liberated postmodern mode, Ovenden, in her (2003) study of children's perceptions of touching museum objects, recalled her own experience, as a museum curator, of touching an ancient Egyptian doll for the first time, and produced the text in Table 4.1 (f). In recalling this experience, she was better able to understand how the children in her study felt, and to see more deeply the interviews and descriptions of behaviour in her data. The ability to reconstruct, as discussed at the end of Chapter 5, is an important skill here too.

In my own study of cultural chauvinism, or culturism, in international English language education, I found personal narrative very useful to enable me to excavate aspects of this chauvinism in my own professional past. The following recollection of an event early in my career demonstrates this in the way I perceived one of my students as in need of cultural improvement:

> I was 24 years old and beginning my career as a teacher at the British Council in Tehran. In the middle of one of my lessons, an Iranian man who must have been in his 40s or 50s stood up at the back of the classroom, apologized for

interrupting in this way and asked me if I could explain the grammar underlying the language structure I was asking him to repeat. I put him down rather abruptly by saying that in '*these* classes' he did not need to think about grammar and that to do so would get in the way of his learning. I thought the request was unscientific and unnecessary, and showed the lack of understanding of 'how to learn' that I expected from Iranian students. More than this, but connected, I though his whole manner was ridiculous because he translated directly from a Farsi expression of politeness and had not even realized that this was inappropriate in English. (Holliday 2005a: 64)

The value of this description becomes evident as I connect it with other forms of data and begin to see residues from this earlier time in current practice. Learning about my own narrative also enabled me to understand the voice I was able to project in the study as a whole. Much of my other data came from the accounts of colleagues and students who might be constructed as recipients of this chauvinism. My own privileged position on the 'other side' made it inappropriate for me to presume in any way to represent or 'speak for them'. I could therefore only speak *for myself*, as someone who has worked with and learnt from them – turning the entire study into a larger personal narrative which incorporates the voices of others as I have interpreted them (Holliday 2005b).

Coffey contrasts this emphasis on the 'autobiographical practices of the researcher-self' with the more 'conventional' view, which I would attribute to postpositivism, that 'has emphasized the *other* lives that are being observed, analysed and produced' with the researcher 'as a biographer of others' (1999: 7, her emphasis). I would like to argue that in the written form of research, the *only* narrative is that of the researcher. The accounts and talk produced by the people in the research setting are done so in response to the elicitations of the researcher and then incorporated into her own narrative.

A complex of voices

I find it useful to articulate the role of personal narrative as one of a collection of interconnected voices in the written text of the research (Holliday 2005b). The *first voice* is the personal narrative because this is about what happened to stimulate the research or to help the researcher get into the data. The *second voice* comprises the data (descriptions, artefacts, transcripts, recordings, documents etc., as depicted on the left of Figure 5.3). In this sense separated pieces of personal narrative, such as the one presented above, are also data about the self and take on the same status as an interview transcript. The *third voice* comments on the data at the time of collection (as depicted on the right of Figure 5.3). At the time of writing, this can also act as data – about how the researcher felt when she was collecting the data – and can in itself appear as another personal narrative about the experience of doing the research. The *fourth voice* comments on the first three voices at the time of writing. This voice has the critical role of directing the reader to the specific aspects of the data which is extracted from the corpus into the written study. The *fifth voice* is the final overarching argument which connects and pulls together all the others, and which speaks about the whole research process and takes the final responsibility. Voices 1–3, voice 4 and then voice 5 thus correspond to the distinction between *data*, *commentary* and *argument*, as described in Chapter 5.

It is not easy to be too specific about these voices, which can overlap and swirl around each other. It is easy however for writers of research to become stuck in any one of them. Studies that become rambling, formless personal statements are stuck in the first voice; while those that find it difficult to stand back and give interpretive space to their data may be stuck in the second voice. Written studies which are not clear in how they are dealing with the research and the data have not succeeded in getting into the fifth voice. *Thick description* is built from all the data in voices 1 through 3; and it is the fourth voice which speaks the description. Although the claims which can be made are largely subjective, because they are based on fragments of interview, artefact, experience and so on, it is the rigorous way in which these fragments are interconnected as thick description which will provide the validity for these claims. This picture of a researcher-led text which includes a complexity of other texts can be expressed as follows:

> By incorporating, fragmenting and mingling these texts, and by reinforcing the intertextuality of ethnography, the claims to authenticity may be strengthened rather than weakened. Writing the self into ethnography can be viewed as part of a movement toward greater authenticity, and as part of a biographical project. (Coffey 1999: 118, citing Atkinson)

Reconstructing other through understanding self

Honarbin-Holliday uses her own art as a means for both understanding and interacting with the Iranian art students in her study. The exhibition of her ceramic sculptures and video at a major venue in the location of her study is at the same time: a series of texts informed simultaneously by the students and her own struggles as an artist; a means whereby she can simultaneously communicate with the students about how she is an artist like them and how she has understood them; and an integration of the life histories of the students and herself. She explains that:

> The sculptures, individually and collectively, deconstruct my engagement with clay, speculating, projecting, and reflecting on aspects of my multi-cultural visual identity in my particular spatio-temporal context in Canterbury. Simultaneously, they have been my tools for understanding myself, and the participants' rigour and strife for expression and articulation of aspects of their identities through their art. They thus externalise the chain of my inner thoughts as the participant researching-artist, and the way I perceive the female participants in Tehran. (Honarbin-Holliday 2005: 53–54)

Rooted in the fine art academic tradition, and inspired by Derrida's notion of *différance*, she decides to present the multimedia thesis as 'a constructed space' in which her art work and oral, descriptive and photographic data are 'positioned next to one another and in dialogue', as a series of 'texts and spaces' which represent 'an installation of ideas ... possessing traces of ideologies, histories and sensibilities of the participants' (Honarbin-Holliday 2005). Within this context, the way in which she presents her oral and descriptive data mirrors the way in which she construct her art. As her ceramic sculptures are worked and crafted deconstructions of her dialogue with herself, her data is presented 'as worked and crafted reconstructions' in which she remains as faithful as she can to the students' accounts and generally to 'the tone and the spirit' (2005) of the data, in a similar fashion to her written reconstructions of interviews, cited in Chapter 5. Exhibiting her own work for the art students and faculty is also a means whereby the researcher opens herself up to being observed and thus resetting the balance of scrutiny, especially where they interpret her work in parallel to her interpreting them.

A layering of voices can also be seen in the way she becomes present in her descriptive data. The following extract from a description of a drawing class in someone's home shows how she interacts with the setting, using an unexpected artefact to draw out more data:

> I am sitting behind the group and really wish that I had a video camera. I notice a book near the model's chair, Toktam placed it there a few moments ago. I leave my post and take a few steps and pick it up. Everyone is drawing. I look at the book, it is 'Fra Angelico, Phaidon 1992' with a stamp from Honar University Library. ...Toktam and I speak about Fra Angelico. I ask her what she might say to people who believe Western art must be understood in a certain way. She laughs and says 'People can say what they wish. But look at it' she shows me 'The Virgin and Child Enthroned with Four Angels' and says 'I look at the similarities of the organization, the content, it is not dissimilar to some Persian paintings'. (Honarbin-Holliday 2005: 129)

Achieving credibility

In this chapter I have demonstrated how the researcher as writer can be firmly in control of the genre of writing qualitative research. Although it is very technical in the way in which multifaceted aspects of evidence and arguments are pulled together, she can take a central position in guiding the reader to the places where *she* wishes. I have shown how one aspect of the genre, that of referring as *pointing*, has parallels in other professional areas. The same parallels can be found for all aspects of the genre referred to in this book, across several aspects of social life. Therefore, learning academic writing should contribute to developing broader skills in precise communication. The proponents and specialist users of academic discourses need to be aware of and communicate their own position within the wider world of culture, discourse, genre and ideology – to achieve the sociological imagination I refer to at the end of Chapter 1. They must not, however, take themselves too seriously, nor exude an image of privilege power in what they do.

Summary

The following points have been made in this chapter:

- The conventions of writing qualitative research are placed within the larger genres and discourses of social science academic writing.
- Academic writing is an 'arena for struggle' in which students and researchers can find it hard to achieve personal power and voice.
- There is however new thinking, especially within postmodern qualitative research, which provides scope for researchers as writers to use the conventions to establish a strong personal presence in the genre.
- This is centred around realizations that writing is itself part of social investigation in which researchers impose their thinking on the realities they wish to present.
- The mastery of the academic genre is also part of an overall acquiring of cultural competence in late modern society, which involves a critical awareness of the politics of discourses.
- The use of the first person is a major device for separating the researcher's agenda from the other voices in the text, thus increasing transparency and accountability.
- Personalized forms of discussion also enable the researcher to make contact with the reader and emphasize the 'everyday' nature of qualitative research.
- Explicit, personalized referencing enables the researcher to take control of the bringing together of interconnected elements, and to show the reader where she wishes her to go.

CHAPTER SEVEN

Writing about Relations

In this chapter I am going to pursue the theme of the personal position of the researcher into the very complex area of how she writes about her relations with the other people in the research setting. Because it is in the essential nature of qualitative research to explore the deeper elements of social action, and because qualitative research is itself social action, the relationship between the researcher and the participant is an issue which inevitably pervades all aspects. I have already provided some examples of the complexity of these relations in earlier chapters. In Chapter 1 an Egyptian academic tells an American interviewer things that are 'untrue' in order to provide him with 'the information he is looking for'. In Chapter 3, Herrera describes how 'personal interest and political pragmatism' influenced which school she was allowed to visit; and Anderson talks about how being an insider influenced the course of his research. In these cases things are not what they at first seem, and the presence of the researcher is entangled with the politics of the research setting. In Chapter 2, Scholl turns this entanglement into an explicit research strategy and finds out how a tourist in a cathedral reacts to a non-smoking rule by asking him for a light. What he finds out is in direct response to his own presence.

Any form of researcher presence is considered contamination by positivistic quantitative researchers, whose emphasis is on eliminating, reducing and controlling variables. This desire to remove researcher presence persists into postpositivist, naturalistic qualitative research, where the aim is to see the research setting as though the researcher were not there – untouched by the researcher's fly-on-the-wall presence. Within a postmodern qualitative research paradigm, however, there is a very different attitude. Here, it is recognized that the presence and influence of the researcher are unavoidable, and indeed a *resource*, which must be capitalized upon.

I shall begin this chapter with the principle of reflexivity, which rationalizes the relationship between the researcher and the research setting, how the setting looks with an acknowledged researcher presence, and why it is important for this to be addressed within the written study. I shall then go on to demonstrate, from my corpus of written studies, how researchers write positively about the presence of the researcher, and how, in some cases, they use this presence as a data source. On the way, the central ethical issue will be discussed, of the feasibility of open, collaborative relations in which the researcher 'comes clean'. This will lead into the final chapter, where I shall deal with the issue of preserving the voice and identity of the people in the research setting.

Reflexivity

There are various uses of the term 'reflexivity' in qualitative research. It is an ambivalent term, both 'an immense area of comment and interest' and also 'used to stand for as-yet unrealized alternative possibility' (Marcus 1994: 568). It responds to the realization that researchers and their methods are entangled with the politics of the social world they study (Hammersley and Atkinson 1995: 16; Gubrium and Holstein 1997: 9; Smyth and Shacklock 1998: 1). Different people see it as 'self critical', 'dead-end indulgence, narcissism, and solipsism' and committed to objectivity (Marcus 1994: 569). It is to do with the 'politics of location' of the subject matter and voice of research (1994: 570). It relates to both how researchers think and act, and to social phenomena themselves. I see it most helpfully as the way in which researchers come to terms with and indeed capitalize on the complexities of their presence within the research setting, in a methodical way.

Although the naturalist adherence to a non-intrusive, fly-on-the-wall methodology may be naïve, 'research must be carried out in ways that are sensitive to the nature of the setting' (Hammersley and Atkinson 1983: 6). Reflexivity provides the solution. Thus, 'rather than engaging in futile attempts to eliminate the effects of the researcher, we should set about understanding them' (1983: 17). The researcher acknowledges the unavoidability of interacting with, and perhaps changing the culture she is investigating, but opens all channels of perception to capitalize on what is revealed about the culture during this process. The researcher thus uses her presence as a catalyst which effects revealing change and becomes:

> the research instrument *par excellence*. The fact that behaviour and attitudes are often not stable across contexts and that the researcher may play an important part in shaping the context becomes central to the analysis. Indeed, it is exploited for all it's worth. (Hammersley and Atkinson 1983: 18)

To do this, the researcher employs her natural human propensity for learning culture, which, if allowed to operate, involves a natural scientific method, much like that used by children – in effect a reflexive methodology. The following perception from visual anthropology expresses well how the social setting might be more fluid and resilient than the naturalists think:

Digging necessarily disturbs the successive strata through which one passes to reach one's goal. But there is a significant difference between this human archaeology and its material counterpart: culture is pervasive and expresses itself in all acts of human beings, whether they are responding to customary or extraordinary stimuli. The values of a society lie as much in its dreams as in the reality it has built. Often it is only by introducing new stimuli that the investigator can peel back the layers of culture and reveal its fundamental assumptions. (MacDougall 1975: 121)

Here, 'the filmmaker acknowledges [her or] his entry upon the world of [her or] his subjects and yet asks them to imprint directly upon film their own culture' (1975: 119).

As I have argued previously, the significance for writing here is that the researcher does not pretend to escape subjectivity, and must therefore account for that subjectivity wherever possible.

The small culture of dealing

Before going into my corpus of written studies, I would like to deconstruct what is likely to happen when the researcher enters the setting. A comparison I have found useful is with the relations between tourists and local people, as in this example:

EXAMPLE 7.1   TOURISTS AND BUSINESS

A group of European tourists arrive in a rural area in Asian country X to look at some ancient ruins. People from a nearby village have established stalls to sell souvenirs near the ruins. Despite diverse countries of origin, the tourists form their own *small tourist culture* which has its own marked characteristics. The villagers similarly form a *small business culture* around the stalls which is also different from the parent village culture. Between these small cultures a *small culture of dealing* forms, within which the tourists and the local people interact. Two of the women tourists have casual sex relations with two of the village men. This behaviour is very specifically located within the tourist and business cultures coming together within the culture of dealing, and would be unusual within the cultural background of either the village or the European settings from which the women come. The women would only have casual sex in very specific circumstances while on holiday; and the men would only have casual sex with foreign tourists outside the village. Nevertheless, the people on each side generalized the behaviour to the extent that the villagers thought all European women were 'loose' and the tourists thought all Asian men were 'gigolos'.

The example demonstrates several aspects of what can happen when two groups of people from different backgrounds come together – such as researchers and people in a research setting, where the researcher is like the tourist and the research setting is like the tourist business set up by the villagers (Holliday and Hoose 1996). This translation into research relations is demonstrated in Figure 7.1. The two unbroken grey circles represent the small cultures of the researcher and the research setting. As in Example 7.1, a new culture of dealing (the broken dark grey bubble) is set up between the two sides as a place where they interact. The multiplicity of cultural influences behind each of the researcher and research setting cultures (the broken grey circles) show that the interaction between them is bound to be a complex affair. Furthermore, the research setting culture is not the untouched place imagined by naturalists in which an 'active' researcher tramples on a 'passive' virgin culture. The people in the research setting can be as adept as the researcher at entering into new cultural relations. Where they care to do so, they will watch and build strategies for interacting with strangers as much as the researcher. In this sense, the people involved are certainly not 'passive "cultural dopes"; they are active, often skilled users of culture' (Crane 1994: 11). The people in the research setting are as culturally skilled as the researcher, and have the potential, if they wish, to be as much involved as the researcher in negotiating the research event. Interaction with the researcher is likely to be just one of many other interactions they encounter. Indeed, both the researcher and the people in the research setting enter into a relationship of culture making as they construct the culture of dealing. It is therefore evident the researcher culture has significant influence on the research setting, making qualitative research an interactive process. On the other hand, the research process is less an invasion by the researcher than a relationship of dealing.

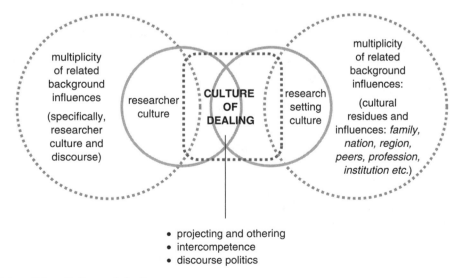

Fgiure 7.1   Culture of dealing

Looking at research relations in this way also shows the dangers of overgeneralization. What the researcher observes while interacting with the people in the research setting may be more to do with the specific nature of the culture of dealing than with the culture of the research setting. In other words, the people in the research setting may behave in an uncharacteristic way because they are interacting with a researcher. Behaviour within the culture of dealing will say something about the two small cultures it derives from; but this relationship will be complex and require considerable excavation; and it will be entirely inappropriate to generalize from any of these small cultures to large regional cultures. Such generalization contains the seeds of othering or reducing whole swathes of people to deterministic description, an issue which I shall deal with in Chapter 8. It is important to note that the cultures of dealing, of the researcher and of the research setting, are not 'subcultures' which are hierarchically subordinate to or deviant from their respective 'parent' cultures. Instead, these 'small cultures' have a multiplicity of relationships both with and transcending larger entities (Holliday 1999: 239).

The politics of dealing

To demonstrate the complex politics created by the cultural baggage brought by the two parties, which is brought into the culture of dealing, consider this conversation which I recently had with an Iranian carpet shopkeeper in my own town:

EXAMPLE 7.2   SHOPKEEPER INTERVIEW

A: How would you react to somebody coming to your shop to ask you questions?
B: Depends what for.
A: She says she wants to present your case to a wider audience.
B: I would tell her something harmless and wait to see what she did next.

This immediately demonstrates an element of dealing on the part of the shopkeeper. Let us imagine what happens when the researcher returns to interview him in depth. Table 7.1 provides details of the conflicting perceptions held by the two parties. This is my own fictional extension of the real Example 7.2, which I feel is more appropriate than 'real' data because it is a sensitive area which concerns the more private motivations of the two parties which I would not feel in a position to 'expose' in a 'real' setting. It is however reconstructed from observed instances (see my discussion reconstruction in Chapter 5). While maintaining the researcher as 'she', the shopkeeper is 'he' to facilitate the distinction between them.

Table 7.1 Shopkeeper research

	Shopkeeper Iranian, carpet shop	Researcher Management student doing an assignment on the attitudes of small shopkeepers
Background cultural influences	• a small business code of honour found in bazaars and souks throughout the East • nourished on a diaspora throughout the cosmopolitan cities of the world • linking with cognate cultures of antique dealers and gallery owners • depends on an informal network of contacts • a powerful specialist discourse connected with an esoteric technology of carpet production, quality and pricing	• student culture • department culture • university culture • instrumental, commodified education culture of late-modern society • 'caring' society, concerned with political correctness • culture and discourse of qualitative research
Projecting and othering	He sees her: • as the representative of a meddling 'caring' society • as pretending to be on 'his side', championing 'his voice', but of the same class and orientation as the local government bureaucrats who cause him so many problems • as belonging to an establishment which basically supports high-street chains and is the enemy of struggling carpet shops • as 'a student', these days only displaying a veneer of rebellion before joining the establishment	She sees him: • as belonging to an ethnic minority, therefore lacking 'voice' • as belonging to 'Iranian culture', therefore being religious and thinking women are inferior
Intercompetence	He appears lacking in 'voice' because: • he is a little intimidated by her academic expertise, which he doesn't understand • he doesn't really have time to spend with her – customers don't come in because she is there • he finds her mixed messages difficult to follow and doesn't really understand what she wants • he is angry (but too polite to show it) because she is obviously confusing him with chauvinistic, religious Iranians with whom he doesn't want to be associated	She is not herself and transmits mixed messages because: • she is determined not to let him (as a chauvinistic Iranian) dominate her (as a woman), and therefore tends to be (out of character) 'cold' and forceful • she wants to be patient and respectful of his 'Iranian culture', and to give him 'voice'

Table 7.1   (Continued)

	Shopkeeper Iranian, carpet shop	Researcher Management student doing an assignment on the attitudes of small shopkeepers
Discourse politics	In one sense he is at a disadvantage because: • his specialist discourse is not much use in this encounter – he therefore appears again lacking in 'voice' • he doesn't really understand her discourse In another sense he is immune from her discourse because: • he isn't that interested	In one sense she is at an advantage because: • she is able to use her highly technologized researcher discourse to negotiate an 'appropriate' research relation-ship with him – 'collaboration', 'co-editing texts', 'putting him at ease', 'anonymity' etc. In another sense, she is at a disadvantage because: • she is so involved in her own discourse that she doesn't see that he isn't really participating in it and therefore isn't subscribing to her research 'contracts'

The table begins by listing the background cultural influences on the two parties. Those on the researcher culture will be partly institutional and partly within the discourses described in Chapter 6. There are also other elements connected with her persona as a university student with orientations connected to her position in a late modern society (Fairclough 1995). The background of the carpet dealer is internationally oriented.

The strong sense of potential equality in this picture comes from the fact that there is a meeting of two small cultures which have the same systemic potential for making sense of and responding to the world within their own spheres of action. However, this potential will be realized to different degrees in different scenarios. The comment on the culture of dealing bubble (in the middle bottom of Figure 7.1) suggests a number of things which make it a dangerous arena. The dealing itself will inevitably involve each side projecting their own preoccupations, agendas, images of the world and insecurities on to the other. Each is bound to reduce the other according to their prejudices and the general human tendency to make complexity simple. Hence, as with the tourist scenario in Example 7.1, each side will tend to overgeneralize from the behaviour of the other. Thus, the shopkeeper lays on the researcher the problems he is having with a municipality which prefers chain stores, and a resulting overall ambivalence about society; while the researcher reduces him to a common, though inaccurate national cultural stereotype. By 'intercompetence' (row 3 in Table 7.1) I mean the clumsy anomalous behaviour characteristic of people encountering others in strange, new situations (Holliday 1992b). Table 7.1 shows how the researcher's intercompetence is precipitated by her mixed-up reaction to her mixed-up image of this Iranian male; while his results from her mixed messages and his unsureness about researchers.

To be caught amongst such misconceptions is an occupational hazard of the qualitative researcher, who is always a 'stranger'. From the viewpoint of the people in the research setting, there will often be the mystifying concept of 'qualitative researcher' itself. For those who have not been qualitative researchers, it is very difficult to understand exactly what such a person is really about. Most of us know about market researchers, who collect statistics about how we feel about the products we buy, as we know about the army of social scientists who do surveys and collect statistics about every aspect of modern life. But the qualitative researcher who claims to be 'exploring', armed only with notebooks, or even only with watchful eyes, is a very strange concept.

The final row of the table, corresponding with the third category of dangers connected with the culture of dealing in Figure 7.1, concerns discourse politics. Here can be seen even more conflict between the perceptions of the two parties. The researcher is supported by a technologized vocabulary with which she can state her position and the role she invites from the carpet dealer. In very simple terms (for I shall go into this in detail later), a 'technologized discourse' is one that has been carefully studied and tuned to meet professional criteria (Fairclough 1995: 91). It is however largely wasted on the person it is intended to reassure of his rights and probable role in the research, who finds it esoteric. On the other hand, the researcher, absorbed in getting the technicalities of the discourse right, is perhaps unable to notice that she has other agendas elsewhere.

The need for discipline

One of the major implications of this picture of the relations between the researcher and the research setting is that the researcher needs to work hard to distance herself from and thus make scientific sense of the mélange of interaction within the culture of dealing in which she herself is a major actor. This will require a similar management of perception to that involved in separating what can be seen and heard from what it might mean, as described at the end of Chapter 5. Implicated as she is in this culture of dealing, she has to distance herself from her own prejudices and easy conclusions, such as seeing the carpet dealer as a representative of 'chauvinistic' 'Iranian culture', as well as from the politics of her own professional discourse (Table 7.1).

The researcher needs to learn the lessons of Stoller, reported here by Denzin and Lincoln:

> He learned 'everyone had lied to me and ... the data I had so painstakingly collected were worthless. I learned a lesson: Informants routinely lie to their anthropologists' ... This discovery led to a second [lesson] – that he had, in following the conventions of ethnographic realism, edited himself out of his text. This led Stoller to produce a different type of text, a memoir, in which he became the central character in the story he told. This story, an account of his experiences in the Songhay world, became an analysis of the clash between his world and the world of

Songhay sorcery. Thus Stoller's journey represents an attempt to confront the crisis of representation. (Denzin and Lincoln 2005: 18, citing Stoller and Olkes)

Of course, seeing the behaviour of the people in the research setting as 'lying' is not the answer. When the carpet dealer tells the researcher something to 'keep her happy', as in the case of the Egyptian lecturer in Example 1.5, it is not so much 'lying' as defending his position. Stoller is right however in writing himself into the text in order to be able to see the position of the people in the research setting as entangled with his own – as I have argued in Chapter 6.

Writing thus, once again, becomes key to the issue. It is by *showing the workings* – the theme of Chapter 3 – of the way in which she sorts out her relationships with the people in the research setting that the research is able to communicate the validity of the whole research project. I will now therefore look at examples of how this can be done in my corpus of written studies.

Writing about researcher presence

The dynamics of the researcher's presence in the research setting, how it affects the research, and what she learns from it, must become another significant part of the written study. This discussion could appear in several places (see Figure 3.1): (a) in the discussion of issues related to research methodology, perhaps as part of a conceptual framework, where the way the research is characterized by the impact of the researcher on the setting is discussed; (b) in the explanation of research procedures, where the way in which researcher presence is managed can be described; and (c) in the data discussion sections or chapters, where data arising from the impact between the researcher and the setting is used as evidence.

The degree to which this happens in written studies is variable, dependent partly on the research interest and space, and the degree of realization of the importance of talking about researcher presence. It is 'an aspect of the research process which usually has great volume but low surface area – its substance is always high for the researcher(s), but its visibility is often low for the research (product) audience' (Smyth and Shacklock 1998: 2). It is significant that all of the examples are from unpublished master's or doctoral dissertations (except for Herrera's, which has become a monograph in its own right), thus having the room to spend on this area.

Setting up relations

I shall begin with examples of writing about how the researcher manages the initial relationship with key people in the setting. Access has already been gained, and the researcher can find herself casting around for what exactly to do to make the most of the very special opportunity of having gained access. Herrera takes some time to describe this initial predicament near the beginning of her first major chapter, entitled 'Newcomers' orientation'. For example, while waiting to see the headmistress in the girls' school in which she is doing her research:

> Occasionally, someone in the office would look over at me as if I were an odd curiosity and ask, knowing that I wasn't, 'is this a new teacher' to be answered by the Headmistress 'no she's a researcher'. A response which usually provoked a curious 'oh', or simply left the enquirer speechless. (Herrera 1992: 9)

This feeling of being alien may continue for some time, not only for American Herrera in an Egyptian institutional setting, but also for Pakistani Shamim in a group of Pakistani schools, who writes that she seemed 'the only person "hanging around" without any set role to perform' (1993: 98).

Such initial feelings should be reported, because they show the predicament of being inevitably an 'outsider', at least in the early days. It is not surprising that the researcher who goes to the carpet shop to do her assignment should initially fall back on the prejudices and stereotypes which her society uses to explain the unknown (Table 7.1). The following sections therefore show the researcher's huge effort to achieve discipline and scientific insight from this difficult psychological position.

Negotiating the right story

Herrera devotes much of her first chapter to the development of her relations with the teachers and other people in the research setting. The 'newcomer' is of course herself, and she indicates that she finds it useful, reflexively, to begin her ethnographic account with how the institution responds to her presence. She begins with how she adapts her behaviour with regard to the headmistress, who is a gatekeeper, and whose presence becomes a major pathway in her ethnography (see Chapter 4). She is in the presence of this formidable woman, who is surely going to ask her what her research is about. This makes her ask the key question which all qualitative researchers ask themselves, before being forced to say something to the headmistress – 'How and where exactly to begin this "study" I didn't know, but had to think of something quickly as the Headmistress leaned over and finally asked, "What exactly do you intend to do here at the school?"' (Herrera 1992: 9).

Herrera goes on to explain how she deals with the important question of how to explain research to the people she encounters. This is not a simply a matter of 'telling the truth' or 'coming clean'. Indeed, these people might not have the interest or the background to share her theoretical preoccupations. Also, at this stage in the research, which is designed to respond to the setting rather than to impose agendas on it (see Table 1.1), the researcher herself may not know in clear terms exactly what she is about. Thus, Herrera is worried about creating a bad impression by being 'vague'. Significantly, her answer comes to her in response to what she has already learnt about her questioner:

> Knowing very well that a vague response would not cut much ice with this very pragmatic woman, I reinterpreted my position both for her and myself, and answered in broken Arabic that I was working on a kind of history of education

in Egypt. I went on to say that the way to best understand this was to go to a school itself and study it. (Herrera 1992: 9)

This shows that Herrera's definition of her research purpose and the relationship she projects to this gatekeeper is in response to what she discovers through negotiation. The negotiation continues, eventually arriving at a position which seems to satisfy both parties:

> Not quite convinced, and even a bit suspicious she asked 'Why was this school chosen for you?' Giving out a slight laugh, recalling the long and laborious process of obtaining permission and the arbitrary way in which the school was chosen, I told her that it was chosen both because of proximity to my home and because my Ministry of Education contact knew the previous Headmaster of the school. She seemed reassured, and replied 'at your service' as if after one or two questions I would be on my way. (Herrera 1992: 9)

This final position also emerges from Herrera linking the apparent preoccupation of the headmistress, her own belief about what her research is about, the earlier negotiations in gaining access within a principled spirit of opportunism, and finding a 'polite' way in which to communicate the latter to this 'interested' party. Herrera has probably learnt by now that personal contact – i.e. knowing the previous headmaster – will be considered valid within this particular locality.

'Insider' as 'outsider'

Shamim, in her doctoral study of Pakistani secondary school classes, has a similar experience to Herrera, but makes a more explicit issue of her relations with the people in her research setting by taking it as the central theme of her research procedures chapter, which she entitles 'The process of research: a socio-cultural experience'. She begins the chapter by citing literature to support her approach to the issue:

> The fact that research is more than a matter of applying some research techniques has increasingly been noted by researchers working in the qualitative tradition. Burgess (1984) argues for the need to raise questions about the actual problems that confront researchers in the course of their investigation, and 'the ways in which techniques, theories and processes are developed by the researcher in relation to the experience of collecting, analysing and reporting data' (p. 2). The acceptance of this view is particularly noticeable in the burgeoning of autobiographical accounts, in recent years, of the social dimension of the research process, for example Margot et al. (1991), Vulliamy et al. (1990), Littlejohn and Melouk (1988), Burgess (1984) and Dingwall and Mann (1982). (Shamim 1993: 79)

(It is interesting to note that several people cited here come from a previous generation of researchers within Shamim's own department at Lancaster University. Many novice researchers overlook this resource for supportive literature.) She then goes on explain how she is going to handle the issue. The underlined phrases show how she embeds the more 'ordinary' description of what she did amongst questions of access, role and response to stakeholders:

> The following account of my research process is an attempt to discuss some issues that seemed to affect both the kind and amount of data collected during field work. I will begin by giving <u>a brief description of the research project</u>. Secondly, the <u>modes of access</u> used for gaining entrée to different sites in the field will be discussed with specific reference to the socio-cultural context of the community in which the study was undertaken. Thirdly, the <u>role of the researcher</u> will be described in terms of the <u>response of the stakeholders</u> to the presence of the researcher in their schools and classrooms. (Shamim 1993: 79, my underlining)

Using the management term 'stakeholder' to label the people in her research also demonstrates how she sees *interest* as a prime force within the relations she is about to describe. Although Shamim might be considered more an insider than Herrera, being Pakistani in a Pakistani setting, rather than a 'foreign' Western American, she has less initial success in presenting herself as a researcher:

> When I discussed my research plan with the teachers in the introductory meeting ... it proved intimidating. ... I was told by my teacher friend, the next day, that by discussing my research plan, I had inadvertently alienated myself from their culture, i.e. the culture of practising teachers. Therefore, despite reassurances to the contrary, the general feeling amongst the teachers was that here was a researcher (an academic) from the university, who wanted to observe their classes to find fault with their teaching. And of course no-one was happy to be exposed in this way. (Shamim 1993: 96)

Prescribed moves don't work

Both Herrera and Shamim thus learn quickly that they cannot present their research as an independent package, brought as a whole concept to be planted within the setting. The way in which they present it must itself be a product of negotiation with, and of what they learn about, the people concerned. This becomes especially clear when Shamim tries to 'come clean' – an accepted step within the qualitative research community in establishing ethical relations. This move becomes a basic mistake. It does not fit with the culture of the setting in which she finds herself:

> Another mistake I made ... was to put all the cards on the table at once ... as a result of my belief in the ethics of coming clean in ethnographic research. What I failed to realize at that stage was that a discussion of the research plan could be intimidating. ... My openness of attitude and willingness to share the details of the research plan with the teachers seemed to make them very uncomfortable. (Shamim 1993: 96)

Following another prescribed course of action, that of collaboration with the people she is researching, she gets herself deeper into difficulty:

> I tried to put forward the possibility of research exchange to the teachers ... This was regarded with a great deal of suspicion ... as an insincere move on my part. It seemed to be difficult for the teachers to imagine how *they* could gain from *my* research. (Shamim 1993: 96, her emphasis)

Later on, as she tries in vain to pursue the possibility of collaboration, or at least sharing her research findings to confirm her validity, 'none of the teachers showed any interest in reading or discussing my observation notes more than once' (1993: 108).

The perception of who was going to 'gain' from Shamim's research certainly did not seem to be anything that *she* could engineer. It became apparent to her that, for the people in her study, research was to get the researcher a higher degree (1993: 97). 'One teacher tried to rationalize it in terms of gain for the self, thus: "We come early to school out of duty. You come because you have to do your thesis"' (1993: 98). Thus the notion that the teachers might gain from the research itself, giving them voice or in some way 'empowering them', seemed to be totally a product, perhaps even a fiction, of the researcher's own discourse.

Technologized conversational discourses

Shamim's difficulty is connected with the discourse problem encountered by the carpet shop researcher. In the bottom right-hand row of Table 7.1 there is a note about how easily this researcher can find the words to 'put the participant at ease', or, looking at it differently, to 'read him his rights and state for him his options'. These phrases might not have the same meaning for the carpet dealer, who is not party to this discourse. Fortunately, he is sufficiently 'uninterested', and sufficiently perceptive to see the prejudices that lurk under her professional veneer. Fortunately, Shamim is also sufficiently perceptive to see quickly that the people in her research setting are also not interested.

There has been much discussion about the power of discourses in critical linguistics – about how they can create change in organizations and in society by invading several aspects of life in late modern society. What Fairclough sees as a particularly 'dominant discourse' is connected closely to the qualitative research discourse. It is a conversational discourse which is 'colonizing' 'public orders of discourse' (1995: 19). On one level it seems a common-sense, 'rational' improvement in that people such as doctors and managers can be more effective if they talk to patients and employees in a friendly manner. However, on another level it is ideological in that it results in a 'breaking down of divisions between public and private, political society and civil society' (1995: 80). Thus, covertly disciplinary practices such as counselling, appraisal and activity based pedagogy replace 'overtly disciplinary' practices (1995: 81). This creates:

> An apparent democratization of discourse which involves the reduction of *overt* markers of power asymmetry between people of unequal institutional power – teachers and pupils, academics and students, employers/managers and workers, parents and children, doctors and patients ... not as the elimination of power asymmetry but its transformation into *covert* forms. (Fairclough 1995: 79, my emphasis)

The outcome is 'a hegemonic technique for subtly drawing aspects of people's private lives into the domain of power' (1995: 81) in the sense that 'the widespread simulation of conversation and its cultural values may lead to a crisis of sincerity and a crisis of credibility and a general cynicism, where people come to be unsure about what is genuine and what is synthetic' (1995: 106). This view corresponds with the growing critical image of 'learner-centredness' in British education, which reveals 'the learner' as a technical compilation of accountable, teachable needs, skills and competences (Usher and Edwards 1994).

Central to Fairclough's argument is the way in which these discourses become 'technologized' by professional groups. As 'redesigned practices' they become the key feature of professionalism, training and quality assurance 'in a widening range of types of institution, notably within the service industries and the professions, and in increasingly systematic ways' (1995: 91). Thus, discourses of research can become highly technologized and take on a power which might easily dominate interactions with people in research settings, or create internal systems which might cloud the view of what is really happening in the very different world being studied: 'In Foucault's language, the participant observer/observed relationship can, in certain contexts, materialize as a technology of power, inscribed with messages of domination' (Jordan and Yeomans 1995: 393).

The researcher discourse that Shamim initially feels she should use falls into this category. It has its own equivalent to 'learner-', 'customer-', 'patient-' or 'citizen-centredness' in 'research-*participant*-centredness'. The original rationale for this is admirable, based on an understanding that researchers can too easily ride rough-shod over the privacy of the people they try to involve. We must however be careful that this concern to protect 'the participant' has not become simply a means for building research professionalism. I am concerned that the notion of the 'research participant' is an image constructed by researchers which may not relate to the actual people in the setting, who remain 'elsewhere'. The experience of Herrera and Shamim above shows that it is far too presumptuous to consider the people encountered in the research setting as 'participants', because they may not wish to be 'participating' at all; and if they do, it may not be in the way in which the researcher imagines.

This is expressed in Figure 7.2, which looks again at the relationship between the small cultures of the researcher, of dealing and of the research setting, introduced in Figure 7.1 (turned on its side for purposes of space). Here the researcher culture is presented very much as dominated by the characteristic of the technologized discourse of research (listed on the left), the ones that Shamim takes with her to the research

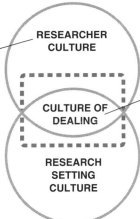

- Technologized professional research discourse: *vocabulary and procedures*
- Attempts to be 'participant-centred': *concerned with ethics, rights, voice, power, ownership*
- Sets up activities to ensure 'participant' involvement
- Professional, academic construction of 'participants'
- Researcher accountability
- THE REAL PEOPLE IN THE RESEARCH SETTING ARE ELSEWHERE

RESEARCHER CULTURE

CULTURE OF DEALING

RESEARCH SETTING CULTURE

- Meeting participants on more neutral ground
- Finding socially appropriate means for:
- Setting up relations: negotiating a meaningful research story
- Establishing relations: working out a meaningful role
- Behaving appropriately: developing strategies for behaviour and presence
- Using experience as data: understanding experience as culture
- DISCIPLINED LEARNING FROM CULTURAL EXPERIENCE

Figure 7.2   Entering into the culture of dealing

setting. As with the imagination of the person in the research setting as 'participant', this discourse can become a barrier to investigating the research setting, and can prevent the researcher from entering into the culture of dealing in any effective way. This syndrome can be called 'sociological blindness' (Holliday 1992a: 406, citing Morris) and has the effect of *de-skilling* the researcher. Professionals, whether teachers with students, doctors with patients, or researchers with people, can forget their more 'ordinary' knowledge about people when they step into professional roles. There is also a danger that the people themselves may be deceived into believing that they are being treated fairly when perhaps they are not. Jenkins provides us with a useful metaphor for this. He suggests that invitations to 'collaborate', 'share', 'edit' and find mutual benefit can take the form of 'bogus co-authorship', whereas in actuality everything is 'in the hands of the researchers' and 'for one audience' of academic papers, reports and assignments. The outcome is 'a rhetorical con-trick' (Jenkins 1986: 223–226). The presumed empowerment of 'the participant' thus becomes a myth which serves only to increase the power of the researcher.

My own view, however, is that the people in the research setting are not easily deceived and are likely to be far more worldly than researchers might believe, and that it is the unworldly researcher who needs help. On the right of Figure 7.2 are a set of strategies which are more negotiative than those prescribed by the technologized discourse or research and which allow the researcher to enter more successfully into the culture of dealing – allowing for a common ground within which both the researcher and the people in the research setting can be equal. It is in the breaking down of this barrier between the technologized discourse and the culture of dealing that allows the researcher to *submit* to the world of the research setting. It is this submission which is an essential antidote to the discourses and structures which are so inevitably the predominant overarching voice of the written research, described in Chapter 6, spinning out of control.

It is within this domain that Shamim is fortunate that the people in the school are sufficiently interested in her to 'teach' her to see through her technologized discourse into the realities of their world. They are not there to participate in the designs of the researcher. They are there anyway as people, with their own affairs; the presence of the researcher is therefore a peripheral part of their world. Because this new culture of dealing is in many ways liberated from the technologized discourse of research, it becomes possible for the researcher to recall the social knowledge and skills to which she has been 'blinded'. This is perhaps why, when both Shamim and Herrera begin to notice how the people in the schools they are visiting prefer to deal with them, they are not surprised; they *remember*. Of course, they knew this before; but their professionalism had caused them to forget.

A new accountability

A major motivation for being seduced by the technologized discourse of research might indeed be the accountability that the researcher needs to attain, to satisfy her readers, assessors or sponsors (listed on the left of Figure 7.2). Within the culture of dealing this accountability ceases to be a matter of prescribed procedure and is implicit in all the negotiated strategies of culture learning (listed on the right of the figure). This makes it all the more important for the researcher to write about what happens to her as she forms relationships in the setting – *showing the workings* of what she actually did to make her research respond to the realities of the situation and its people. Miller et al. put this well, while considering the difficulty postmodern qualitative researchers have in establishing notions of validity which are in true dialogue with the realities of their research settings:

> For qualitative research at least, standards of rigour and ethics should be merged to emphasize connections between researchers and those they research. In this case, the field might also benefit from merging these standards with the conduct of research practice to emphasize relationships between researchers and those whose work we assess. (Miller et al. 1998: 412, citing Lincoln)

This can be seen in the way Herrera and Shamim have both accounted for how they have set up relations in the research setting within the spirit of the right-hand list of Figure 7.2. Within this culture of dealing there are clear choices. Such common strategies as 'coming clean', establishing mutual research benefit, inviting the people in the research setting to collaborate, and being inconspicuous are only possibilities and may be inappropriate. However, the researcher needs to be careful here and must *search* for whatever social equivalent is appropriate for their specific setting. Herrera takes the cautious line of negotiating her position in response to initial relations; and Shamim discovers that pursuing an explicit researcher role is not appropriate, and that the people in the research setting are looking for less research-based gains.

Therefore, as these researchers move into trying to establish their relations, things are still far from clear; they are still feeling their way in their attempt to behave appropriately. I shall deal with these two areas in the following parts of the chapter.

Establishing relations

The initial ambivalent responses to Herrera and Shamim could lead one to expect that the people in the research setting might behave in ways quite different to what the research plan anticipated. Once the researcher has entered the setting and encountered initial response to her agenda, there is bound to be an extended period of dealing, in which relations are worked out.

Wife and mother

Herrera's initial working out of 'her story' in dialogue with the headmistress became integrated within the complex of protocols and interest in the cultural process of the setting. The strong sense of negotiation implied that it was not only Herrera who was manoeuvring to find a mutually appropriate positioning; the people in the research setting were also looking for appropriate ways to interact with the researcher. The researcher is thus as much an 'object' of their attentions as they are of hers.

Several pages on in the same chapter, Herrera describes how this process of mutual positioning continues. Initially, they resist her presence as 'a researcher' but accept her as 'a wife and mother'. In the following extract she has already 'tagged along' with a group of English teachers and made 'polite demands and requests to accompany them to their classes'. She has found this less than satisfactory, having got 'relatively little feedback' from them about 'their work and family life' (Herrera 1992: 13). Here, she describes the response when a senior teacher who is looking after her asks a group of teachers if she can observe them:

> 'Does anyone have a class next period?' A few teachers seemed to look up at me with what seemed a look of absolute annoyance, as if to say 'what is this snooping foreigner bothering us for'? I kept my bearings however, smiling slightly, when a man in his mid thirties said nonchalantly, 'she can come with me'. I happened to mention that I was married and had a daughter and he became immediately more attentive, treating me more seriously and formally. (Herrera 1992: 14)

She goes on to describe how she then had to tell the teachers details about her family – how many children, why although her husband was Muslim she hadn't converted. Thus, once

> the vital statistics of my life were made public knowledge to a full audience ... my reception at the school improved markedly. Identified not only as a

> researcher but as the wife of a Muslim, a mother, and an American of Arab ancestry, the hostile and suspicious glances to which I was getting accustomed changed to warmer and more friendly expressions. (Herrera 1992: 15)

Reflecting on this later, Herrera stated that as well as being considered more respectable as a 'wife and mother', her identity served to make her appear less of a threat:

> My husband's identity as a Muslim man from the East was likely an even more important factor in my gaining credibility and legitimacy among the researched community. As an American doing research among middle-class Egyptians who were very critical of America's foreign policy, its support of Israel, its anti-Muslim leanings, I had to prove, particularly to the adults, not so much the students, that my intentions in Egypt were not dubious, that I was not an American agent or an informer of some sort. When they learned that my husband was not only a Muslim, but an Iranian, they implicitly knew I must be sympathetic to Egypt and Muslims ... that I would not flout Islamic, or rather, Eastern morals by acting as a sexual predator at the school. I could talk with male teachers without raising too many eyebrows or losing trust. I found that teachers generally held this misperception that Anglo Americans, even when they were married, were sexually free and that it was normal to have open relationships. The wife of a Muslim, however, would not be in such a relationship. (Email interview)

That the researcher was an 'object' of their attention can be seen in her description a little later in the chapter: 'Many teachers did their bit of proselytizing. The women who initially accused me of flirting now daily stressed that I should ask my husband to read the Quran aloud to me' (Herrera 1992: 15).

Friend of a friend

Shamim similarly finds that the role of 'friend of a friend' is more meaningful to the people in her setting that that of 'researcher'. It has already been noted that her attempt to establish the value of her research for them resulted in even more suspicion. Nevertheless, she perseveres and finally arrives at a way of presenting herself which suits the culture. To be accepted she has to take on a more 'informal' role: 'It was only after I started using culturally acceptable ways of gaining access as a friend of a friend of a friend that I was able to dispel the fears of the teachers and begin to be accepted as one of them' (1993: 96). She rationalizes this for herself by explaining that 'the role of the researcher was suspect in most cases. In contrast, the role of a friend is not only recognized socially but there is a general tradition of doing favours for friends without expecting anything in return' (1993: 113). Thus, the teachers were prepared to help 'as they would help a friend' to collect data for her thesis. 'In fact some teachers who had done a project or a thesis for their higher degrees (MA or MEd) realized just how difficult it was to collect data for research and were very sympathetic' (1993: 96).

This undertaking by the teachers to help Shamim get data began to take on forms which made her doubt the data's 'authenticity': 'Some even went to the extent of offering to do demonstration teaching for me so that I could get required data' (1993: 96). She describes various incidents of this:

> The following dialogue was overheard in the staff room at one site: 'Do we need to teach BEd [i.e. display teaching] style?' 'You can't teach that way for two weeks'. (Research diary: 5 1 91) ... One teacher told me that some students in her class asked her, after Phase 1 of my visit was over: 'Miss, now that Miss Fauzia is not here, can we stop this business of newspapers' (she had used newspapers to teach passive voice during my visit) and get on with some real work, i.e. preparation for their matriculation exams. (Research diary: 26 10 91) (Shamim 1993: 103)

Nevertheless, there was something to learn from this:

> I discovered that display teaching was done for a number of reasons: 1) because the teachers wanted to try a new technique and felt reassured at my presence (Nighat, site 2), 2) they wanted to display their knowledge of a particular technique for me (Salima, site 4), or 3) they did not want me to feel bored ... Sometimes teachers seemed to feel a sense of guilt if they thought their lesson had not provided any 'data' for me. (Shamim 1993: 108–109)

Notice here Shamim's reference to teachers by fictitious code name, and the number of the site where they are observed, and her reference to her research diary above.

Within the domain of the culture of dealing, as listed in the right of Figure 7.2, Herrera and Shamim find that they have to leave behind some of the more 'established' routines for qualitative researchers to go with the social roles which the people in the research setting prefer for them. Some researchers might find it morally difficult to agree to be associated with personas with which they would not normally want to be associated. The 'wife or mother' and 'friend of friend' labels can have anti-professional associations. The researcher cannot be expected to change her total self-image, which might anyway be seen as fraudulent play-acting. However, in all social interaction we need to respond to people according to how they see us – not to be people totally according to their terms, but to be ourselves in response to how we see that they see us, and to work with this scenario to achieve the images we want for ourselves. In my view, it is exactly the same in qualitative research. One would hope that Herrera and Shamim were able to work with the roles they were ascribed to become real people in their own right. I find Punch's advice generally very useful:

> One need not always be brutally honest, direct and explicit about one's research purpose, but one should not normally engage in disguise. One should not steal documents. One should not directly lie to people. And, although one may disguise identity to a certain extent, one should not break promises made to people. (Punch 1994: 91)

I do not think Herrera and Shamim are lying about who they are. They are not even deceiving anyone. They are simply bringing out aspects of their identities to play a certain role – as they may in any other new work or social situation. Essentially, they are not 'pretending'. Indeed, in the scenarios which they both describe so richly, if they did pretend it would be seen through immediately and all their credibility would be lost.

Behaving appropriately

Nevertheless, as professionals, researchers need to monitor their presence in a professional way. The next group of examples demonstrate how researchers account in writing for behaviour and procedures they adopt in response to the settings they have now learnt something about (the right of Figure 7.2).

Appearance and conduct

Once Shamim feels confident that she is beginning to understand the nature of the relationships she is forming, she can begin to monitor her own behaviour and appearance. Within the area Hammersley and Atkinson (1995: 83) refer to as 'impression management', she writes about how she adapted her appearance in her attempts to fit in:

> I took special care to dress up in such a way that I didn't appear very smart or fashionable but kept to a middle ground. The teachers at each site were very surprised to see me wearing a chaddar the first day. However, it seemed to help them to identify with me more easily. (Shamim 1993: 106)

She took care to prepare herself to try and participate in their world: 'I also began to keep track of popular TV programmes (it provided a good topic of conversation in the staff room) and picked up local speech patterns (e.g. referred to the Head as "Head Sir")' (1993: 106). Nevertheless, despite all her attempts, the pressure was never off: 'For me the balancing of relationships between the different power structures in the school (Head, teachers, students) was very exhausting and gave me the feeling of always walking on a tightrope – one false move and the whole game would be over' (1993: 114). Personal appearance is an important way for the researcher to improve the way in which she fits into the setting. However, decisions of this nature must depend on what has already been observed about its culture. Thus, Anderson writes about how he presented himself while observing lessons:

> I sat discretely at the side trying to make as little impact as possible dressed somewhere between the teachers (smart but casual – e.g. for males chinos and shirt) and the students (casual – jeans and trainers). I considered that my dress

fitted in and I was not aware that it affected my relationships with the participants. (Anderson 2002: 129)

In her methodology chapter, Honarbin-Holliday describes how she acquires an understanding of how to conduct herself within a politically dangerous Iranian system where she is an outsider, despite her Iranian nationality. She takes on an attitude of respectful humility:

> My conduct as a researcher, and the respect I hold for the institutions and the participants in Tehran constitute a very important part of my methodologies. ... I had been warned by so many that no institution in the Islamic Republic of Iran would be accessible; that the doors have been closed for the last 25 years ... that even if I were to be granted access and permission to conduct my research, it would not be safe and it would be interrupted and I would be accused of espionage; and that ultimately my data would be confiscated from me and I might end up in prison. None of these predictions have taken place. (Honarbin-Holliday 2005: 45)

She finds that a polite letter of introduction from a senior academic at her university to the senior person responsible for art education in Iran was 'the single most important step' in gaining access. She suggests that its reference to 'making a contribution to knowledge was appreciated'. This led to a series of introductions to important academic gatekeepers which culminated in 'a very short note of introduction to the Head of Visual Arts ... at Tehran University'. The subsequent interview led eventually to the final stages of her acceptance:

> He received me austerely but politely and the first question he asked me was about my studio work and artistic engagement. This was highly significant because I believe Tehran accepted me to proceed with my research primarily because I am a fellow practitioner, an artist. ... Three months later ... I was informed that I must also submit my research proposal for scrutiny. ... [After] a total of six weeks in two trips, I was officially a researcher at Tehran University and seconded to Al-Zahra University to carry out observations. (Honarbin-Holliday 2005: 46)

(The importance of her being a practising artist has already been noted in Chapter 6 in the way she interacted with art students and faculty.) The six weeks of waiting 'in lobbies and secretaries' offices' was not wasted, as it allowed her the space to investigate how she should behave and dress. The detail that she applies to this is further evidence of research rigour discussed in Chapters 1 and 2. She refers to 'a process of socialization and initiation into the field'; how she 'regulated' her 'use of language, analysed degrees of formality', familiarized herself with 'political and social discourses, and formed a deeper understanding of dress codes' of the wide variety of people who frequented government and university offices. From this, she was able to determine a policy for self conduct:

I had to work at the universities and with male and female lecturers and professors who were mostly political appointments and not museum curators and art critics. ... I was not an artist nor an art student in Tehran, I was primarily a researcher trusted by the Iranian Government. ... I chose a black headscarf for the universities and kept my long dark aubergine colour coat as a uniform. My large black shoulder bag could take all my equipment of several pens and notebooks, diaries, camera, tape recorder, photographs of my artwork, and some apple juice for those intervals in Ramadan, the month of fast. I did not find this dress code in anyway uncomfortable or unacceptable, it was part of the job, I simply got on with it. (Honarbin-Holliday 2005: 46)

Going with the politics

Delikurt (2005), in her doctoral study of the politics of educational reform in Northern Cyprus, has the not uncommon problem of being a researcher within a setting within which she has recently had the role of senior inspector; and many of the people she interviews are politicians with whom she has been hierarchically connected within a system characterized by issues of power and interest. She feels it important to follow a disciplined approach to interviewing, but has to do so in response to this scenario. In draft material which will contribute to her chapter on research procedures, she writes:

> The issue of 'multiple personae' was problematic ... in relation to both the interviewee and the interviewer ... I felt that I had to be clear about which personae of the politician I wanted to interview. ... Was I talking to the politician X, as Mr. X, the person or as Mr. X, the party leader or as the party itself? It was an arduous exercise. (Delikurt 2005: 160)

The issue was complicated by the way the politicians saw *her*. When she raised issues connected with an event within which she had had an official role herself, they responded as though she were still in this role, thus moving into old political-professional relations:

> For example, minister/inspector; or director of inspectorate/inspector; director of common services/teacher trainer. I found this as an inescapable constraint during some interviews and felt that respondents were creating the same hierarchical distance or role reversal from being an interviewer/interviewee. I realised that I was connected to my respondents within the context of history, culture, and societal structures that overlapped and interconnected. (Delikurt 2005: 161)

On one such occasion she notes, on visiting an office at the ministry, 'after having coffee with a politically appointed director':

> [Name] right away confided in me about the potential headmaster candidates for the new school. Apparently the minister asked him to shortlist some names.

He asked for my opinion. I was taken aback because this was confidential information with political repercussions. The list contained names I knew quite well – knew their political 'colour' too. He insisted that I gave my opinion as an ex-inspector (FN O6/4). (Delikurt 2005: 165)

Within their personae as politicians, they were naturally interested in using the opportunity of interview to speak as politicians. (Notice the coding she uses to distinguish her different respondents.) They were also interested to learn what other politicians had said – 'Some crafty questions were articulated in their attempts to discover what others have said. "Perhaps X has already told you about this but... (R3)"' (2005: 161).

Rather than try to control this, she decided, on the one hand, to go with the flow, making a special case for their special type of contribution. On the other hand, she could be more relaxed in the monitoring of her own 'power' during interviews because:

Politicians adopt a more Machiavellian style to map their own agenda to control the interview. ... They are elected to 'talk' on behalf of those who elect them. Preserving an effective public political persona and investing for future elections rely on their ability to make best use of every opportunity to 'talk'. As Ostander (1993) says this is a reflection of their position of power. (Delikurt 2005: 159)

(Notice how Delikurt uses reference to literature to support her point.) However, this extract demonstrates her decision to do what she can to respond to the needs of the people in her research setting, as she provides extra privacy:

The interview took place at my house. The setting was quite a private terrace. Our usual terrace table and chairs. There is a neighbour's house facing the terrace across the street but they have to come and sit on their balcony to be able to hear what was being spoken and during the interview nobody came out. The respondent could see that too. This rather private setting gave such an immense 'freedom' to R10 that he had no worries that somebody would be eavesdropping. I thought the noise of the thousand cicadas around us would be a nuisance but I don't think we noticed them after we really got onto 'heavy topics' (Research diary).

Using experience as data

The sixth point on the right of Figure 7.2 refers to the researcher using the experience of her relations with people in the research setting as data, not just within the ongoing process of improving her own relations, but to increase understanding of the culture generally, thus contributing to the whole investigation. It is still not common for studies to show this explicitly, although it can be seen within the fibre of the writing. Thus, Herrera includes her descriptions of relations with the teachers in the main body of the data analysis part of her study. It is also significant that the tone and detail of description are the same as that for any other part of her data – as description of behaviour or event (see Table 4.1). Later, she comments that:

> All of these reactions to me definitely constituted research data. They raised issues having to do with religion, culture, politics, sex and gender. In other words, they helped me to understand the social sensibilities, sensitivities, cultural practices and political perceptions of people in the school community. (Email interview)

Shamim, in a later working of her chapter on research relations, takes a more macro view concerning how such experience contributes to the wider task of understanding society and concludes that:

> It is essential, in my opinion, to continue to share our individual experiences in the field in order to enhance our understanding of different socio-cultural contexts and their implications for the collection and interpretation of our data. (Shamim 1996)

In my own study of Egyptian classrooms, I did make explicit use of the experience as data.

Being conspicuous

Like Delikurt, during the course of my study I am concerned with following what I see at the time to be established procedure, this time in watching classes and trying to be an unobtrusive observer, sitting somewhere inconspicuous at the back of the classroom. The following extracts are from the first data analysis chapter of my thesis, 'Non-pedagogic classroom culture', under the sub-thematic heading, 'Interaction with outsiders: hospitality'. Notice throughout how I separate my actual data from discussion by indenting it, refer to lecturers by code, and further anonymize by hiding gender.

On entering one classroom for the first time, I found that there was no room for me to sit at the back, but that its welcoming character seemed to make this unimportant:

> This notion of classroom hospitality suggests a classroom culture sufficiently *resilient* to cope with the intrusion of outsiders. An example of this was the apparent indifference on the part of the students in one class, when:
>
> > I entered the class after it had begun (late finding the place) and was sat on a chair on the plinth [at the front of the classroom designated for the lecturer]. There was no way I could have found a seat at the back; but I found that seeing the students' faces was a big advantage. The students did not seem to notice me too much. (Obs. 15, site 13)

This made the great care I had taken, in the earlier stages of my observations, to be unobtrusive by trying to sit at the back, seem redundant. (Holliday 1991: 257–258)

I go on to explain how this 'local' protocol of placing observers at the front worked when there were three present:

On one occasion: 'We three observers sat together at the front of the class to the left of the lecturer, on special seats brought by the students' (obs. 43, site 9, LL). ... However, once again, this did not seem to be an issue: 'The students did not pay much attention to *three* observers. We all sat at the front, this time on the left, on the stage' (obs. 23, site 13). (Holliday 1991: 258, original emphasis)

I then describe how my presence seemed to be used by senior people in the faculty to break what I had so far perceived the protocol to be, and get into other people's classes – especially those of the foreign lecturers they were obviously curious to see:

Some of the details of what happened with regard to observation 16 deserve attention, especially as the lecturer was an outsider expatriate:–

I had just been to pay a courtesy call on the dean with the head of department and had met a lecturer from the curriculum department. They both escorted me to the lesson, after showing me the library, and then asked if they could come in and watch. They seemed sensitive to the situation ... and asked me to go and ask BE if it would be all right. I did as they asked ... and s/he agreed. We sat in the front, on the left, to the side. ... (Obs. 16, site 13, BE) (Holliday 1991: 259)

Because she was an expatriate, I presumed that she would expect observers to sit at the back. At the same time I felt I should treat my two co-visitors as 'guests' on what I was perceiving to be *their* terms:

I attempted to pull us all as far as permissible into the corner. I did not feel that it would have been done to ask my 'important' fellow observers to sit at the back. I sat between them and laid out my copy of the material on my briefcase for them both to see. I explained things to them while the students were doing group work. (Obs. 16, site 13, BE) (Holliday 1991: 259–260)

I continue to make sense of this very complex scenario in the following way:

Supporting the notion of a resilient classroom culture was what appeared to be relaxed attitudes regarding the *sanctity* of the classroom. In observation 16, although my two co-observers were very keen to ask the lecturer's permission to let them in, they seemed to have no qualms about me having to interrupt the lecturer, who had already entered the class, in order to get the permission. (Holliday 1991: 260, original emphasis)

A further visit to the same expatriate lecturer with my 'local' co-observers reveals more. Here the co-observers seem to me not only to be trampling over the relationship of the lecturer with her students by arguing with them about her teaching, but also to be endangering our relationship with the institution (not theirs) that had agreed to let us come and watch:

> What I considered to be a considerable disturbance was created by my two colleagues, when, after the classes: –
>
>> ... without my knowledge, (my two local colleagues) asked BE if s/he would like them to go and talk to the students ... about their course material. ... They were in the class for about thirty minutes, and when they came out looked quite disturbed [... and] announced in a very loud voice in the middle of the staffroom that they had had a 'bloody battle' ... to defend the course. Apparently a lot of shouting had taken place. ... I was personally very worried.
>
> (Obs. 24, site 13, BE, LG, LH) (Holliday 1991: 261)

I then try to make sense of this in my discussion of the data:

> Rather than a trampling of protocol – my first gut reaction – this event may indeed have been an example of a type of *protocol* with which I was unfamiliar, which was *local* to this particular educational environment. Moreover, I was not able to see how this protocol worked because it was based in a *deep action* which was hidden to me as an outsider. (Holliday 1991: 262, original emphasis)

The use I make of this complex experience, within my overall research aim of learning about the classroom culture, can be seen in my final summary of the chapter, which in turn comes after considerable discussion of implications – 'd) The classroom culture was unexpectedly *hospitable* to outsiders and *resilient* to intrusion. There seemed to be a markedly relaxed local attitude regarding the *sanctity* of the classroom. The rules for local *protocol* were generally difficult to perceive by outsiders' (1991: 295, original emphasis). I then report on two further hypotheses, regarding the mechanics of education change, which also grow from this data:

> *Hypothesis 2*: The classroom culture is sufficiently used to crisis, hospitable, and yet resilient, to endure the trauma of change. ... *Hypothesis 7*: Because of the existence of deep action phenomena which are difficult to perceive by and sometimes strange to outsiders, innovation (a) can only be effectively managed in the long term by insiders and (b) needs to be verified by further investigation of the local cultures. (Holliday 1991: 296, original emphasis)

Disciplined learning

What binds all the above examples together is the discipline with which each researcher observes, makes sense of and learns from the cultural experience she gains as she interacts with the people she encounters in her research setting – the final point on the right of Figure 7.2. The quest is far from easy and involves personal dangers, for the researcher as well as for the people in the research setting, who find their lives being changed by the experience.

Although I have not focused specifically on ethical issues, I have demonstrated the dangers of the researcher simply trying to conform to a prescribed ethical code, trying to be sensitive to what is going on in the setting without realizing that this code may itself be a product of her own cultural ethnocentricity. As Appell warns us, the dangers are 'at an *interface* of ethical and epistemological systems, therefore posing unforeseen moral dilemmas' (1978: ix, my emphasis), and it is at this interface that researchers have to be especially careful. At this interface, the researcher must be prepared to relinquish the securing power of her own culture and discourse and be prepared to begin again, perhaps risking being an incompetent in the terms of the new culture – and learn anew how to be 'an acceptable incompetent' (Hammersley and Atkinson 1995: 99). At the same time the researcher must find the perhaps 'non-professional' social skills she has always had, which enable her everywhere to find ways of fitting in. She is thus 'intellectually poised between familiarity and strangeness', while 'socially … poised between stranger and friend … typically a "marginal native"' (1995: 112, citing Lofland, Powdermaker, Everhart and Freilich). But most important of all, she must write about it and thus account for what she does.

Summary

The following points have been made in this chapter:

- The presence of the researcher in the research setting is unavoidable and must be treated as a resource.
- Reflexivity provides a way of dealing with the issues arising from the knowledge that much of what the researcher sees is a result of her own presence.
- When entering the setting, the researcher is also bringing her own cultural baggage and discourse. The setting thus becomes a culture of dealing between this and the culture of the people there. It is a dangerous place where misconceptions of the foreign other can easily arise.
- The researcher must try to see through and liberate herself from the professional discourse she brings with her in order to establish relations with the people in the research setting on their own terms. They are there as people in their own right, not simply to participate in her research. Researchers must be prepared to take on roles that are meaningful to the culture, which may be alien to the professional research discourse.
- Writing about the complexities of this dealing therefore becomes an important part of showing the workings of the study, helping to account for the researcher's strategies in a disciplined way.
- The personal data the researcher collects in order to learn how to behave appropriately can also be important data for the study as a whole. Writing about relations can thus become part of the main discussion of data of the study.

CHAPTER EIGHT **Making**

• • • • • • • • **Appropriate**

Claims

In this final chapter I am going to address the issue of making appropriate claims about the people in the research setting. Throughout the book I have argued that researchers need to show their workings in their writing as explicitly as possible so that they can be fully accountable for *how* they have managed their own subjectivity, *how* they have responded to the worlds and sensitivities of the research setting and the people in it, and *how* the data they have chosen to present supports what they want to say. Another important ingredient of rigour and validity in qualitative research is making sure that the researcher's claims are appropriate to the data she has collected and the argument she has constructed around it – and that these claims are true to the people and their affairs within the setting, without exaggeration. Underpinning this entire process, the researcher must continue to account for her own ideology, professional-academic culture and discourse and monitor how far this influences the claims made.

I shall look at how the realities of the research setting and its people are easily distorted by the discourse of qualitative research itself, and reductive cultural overgeneralization, and at how researchers in my corpus struggle to overcome these problems. The main point of my discussion will be that making appropriate claims is not simply a matter of technical accuracy, but of creating images of the people we research which promote understanding of their humanity and do not reduce and package them. This is thus a deeper, ethical and indeed political issue.

─────────────────── **Allowing 'ordinary' voice** ───────────────────

Chapters 5 and 6 looked at the ways in which researchers as writers come out and assert the agendas which have formed their research, thus being open about how their own perceptions and biases influence what they see and find. There is another side, however, to do with the 'ordinary' world of the people in the research setting. The personal power of the writer is one thing, but perhaps more important and problematic is the personal power of those she writes about. No matter how open and sensitive the language used by the researcher, it will still have an irrevocable power, which critical, postmodern and feminist researchers continue to struggle to reduce. They 'dream of finding an innocent language in which to represent, without exploiting or distorting, the voices and ways of knowing' of people who always seem to be characterized as the 'subaltern "subjects"' of the research (Stronach and McLure 1997: 4). There is a sense of anguished realization here of a no-win situation. Hence, even the most progressive feminist ethnography becomes no more than 'the "practice of failure", urging researchers to abandon the "drive to innocent knowing" that, despite its good intentions and person-centred methods (indeed because of them), never succeeds in its mission to rescue the researched from epistemic violence' (1997: 4, citing Lather). I have already dealt, in Chapter 7, with the dangers of 'participant-centred methods' which are more to do with the discourse of the researcher than the world of the people in the research setting, and with how researchers are after all locked into being researchers, and can never really see the world as if they were not.

All that one can do is continue to problematize the genre, taking the postmodern line of constantly

> putting the Word in its place ... opening up to critical discourse the lines of enquiry which were formerly prohibited ... so that new and different questions can be asked and new and other voices can be asking them ... the opening up of institutional and discursive spaces within which more fluid and plural social and sexual identities may develop. (Stronach and McLure 1997: 6, citing Hebdige)

This requires great caution. Organizing raw data under thematic headings is an effective means of making sense. There is nevertheless a strong temptation here for the researcher to tie things up too neatly – packaging and repackaging to produce a finely coherent text in which the ragged edges of the original social setting are clipped off and disposed of.

Not making the participant abstract

A major source of distortion is in the academic, third-person detachment of traditional social science writing (see Chapter 6). Foley argues that, as well as making the author 'physically, psychologically, and ideologically absent from the text', this mode of expression suggests an 'all-knowing interpretive voice' which 'speaks from a distant, privileged vantage point in a detached, measured tone' and 'helps create a common denominator people of social archetypes and roles rather than complex, idiosyncratic individuals' (Foley 1998: 110). I think that this is certainly the case. It is indeed easy to create a sense of 'timeless space called the "ethnographic present"' and 'to write in an abstract, formalistic intellectual language which freezes ordinary people and everyday life into a neat, coherent, timeless portrait' (1998: 111).

A useful solution to this is reducing the sense of abstractness by bringing out the voice of the writer – using the first person, balancing theory and reference to litera-ture with personal experience, revealing personal 'interpretive perspective' in 'an autobiographical style', and reporting 'specific events and actual personal encounters rather than composite typifications' (Foley 1998: 112). All of these underlie the hon-esty, caution, humility and reserve which the researcher needs.

Foley makes some other suggestions which I would take more cautiously. Although 'jargon-filled descriptions' might be overdoing it, judiciously used technical terms, such as 'interpretive' and 'reflexive', can save long phrases of explanation. Using 'narrative' which is 'mutually produced' with the people in the research setting, again makes me wary of cases where such collaboration is the product of the researcher's own discourse. One also needs to ask on what basis the narrative style best represents the culture observed, and on what basis the researcher can presume the degree of empathy with the people in the research setting to claim joint author-ship. I would be cautious about putting 'theoretical/interpretive perspective in an appendix': this presumes that the narrative is sufficiently 'real' to stand alone, and that the researcher does not need to articulate how the particular meaning, which she has designed, has been arrived at. Telling the story of what one observes 'with a healthy dose of metaphor irony, parody, and satire' (Foley 1998: 112) seems to me to pretend to be 'telling it how it really is' and 'being there', which sit more with a naïve naturalism than with the critical position that Foley takes. There is the danger here of allowing subjectivity to run riot to the extent that the boundaries between data, discussion and argument become very blurred. This seems to move away from, rather than towards, an 'innocent language' which does not distort. I would nevertheless say that these are choices which *depend* on the nature of the setting and the researcher's relationship with it. Foley is perhaps talking very specifically about researching communities in which he gets deeply involved, with which he does feel he can achieve empathy.

Creating textual room

I agree that we must be very wary of 'the "writerly texts" of conventional academics' which project an 'unwavering authoritative voice free of guilt, angst and self doubt' (Foley 1998: 124, citing Fiske). We must instead engage with 'guilt, angst and self doubt' and think more about the implications of how we write. We must always ask the question, 'In whose voice do we write?', but must not be seduced by the presumption that we have the power to present the voices of others *as* they speak them. The answer to the question is certainly, 'Well, of course, our own' (Fine and Weis 1998: 27), as discussed in Chapter 6. But we can find ways within our own argu-ment and discussion to present other voices as *we* see them, while making it clear that it is *our* vision – to 'relentlessly create textual room for counter-hegemonic narratives' (1998: 27).

The approach with which I address these issues is therefore one of strategic, technical detachment from, rather than emotional joining with, the Other of the people in the research setting – 'an attitude of detachment towards society that permits the sociologist to observe the conduct of self and others' (Vidich and Lyman 2000: 38). This does not mean that I am now arguing against the coming out of the researcher, which I championed in Chapter 6. There is a delicate balance to be maintained here. On the one hand, as an indisputable part of the setting she has entered, the researcher, with all her cultural and ideological baggage, must 'come out' and reflexively deal with this. On the other hand, she must exercise immense constraint in what she reads into what she sees and hears. She is therefore coming out with respect to her own impact, but holding back with respect to her interpretation. She 'creates *textual room*' both for herself and, separately but at the same time, for the setting and the people in it. *For herself as the researcher:* she comes out and states ideological and cultural agency, by demarcating Self as 'I' from others, and acknowledging involvement from a position of individuality. *For the people in the research setting*: she acknowledges that the 'setting' is only her perspective on a larger, complex world because she only understands a little of what she sees and hears, by using strategic, technical procedures to ensure caution and restraint in interpretation.

Importantly, the creation of textual room is something which the researcher *does*. This does not mean that she actively strives to protect any aspect of the world of the people in her research itself. This would be very presumptuous, especially as it must be remembered that the way she sees the world of the people in the setting is a construction of the way in which she herself has demarcated the research setting. She has limited influence on that world, and is in no position, in her role as a researcher, to 'protect' it – though she may in other domains of her life, e.g. as a sport scientist, as an artist or as an educator. What she does have considerable power over is the way she writes. It is in her writing, rather than in the setting itself, that she thus strives to protect textual room.

At the same time, technical detachment does not mean that the researcher should not get close to the phenomena she is investigating. It simply means that she must be aware of, and account for, the implications of this involvement. She needs to be able to manage a '*heuristic* distancing', which allows for 'close scrutiny' and 'proximity to the action' (Gubrium and Holstein 1997: 41, their emphasis). This requires the same sort of demarcation between different aspects of what the researcher does and thinks – between mental caution and physical action – as in separating what she sees and hears, as data, and what she thinks about it; and between thinking as a researcher and thinking as a participant within the social mélange of the setting.

Cautious detachment

Achieving textual room for the setting involves cautious detachment and academic protocols, which often annoy the novice writer because they seem to 'cramp' her creative 'style'.

Hedging

Hedging is acknowledged by applied linguists as central to cautious detachment (e.g. Dudley-Evans and St John 1998: 76; Swales 1990: 112). The *Collins English Dictionary* definition of the term does not give it particularly positive connotations, as it is associated with avoidance or caution in gambling: 'to evade decision or action, esp. by making noncommittal statements', 'to guard against the risk of loss ... by laying bets with other bookmakers', 'to protect against financial loss through future price fluctuations' and 'to hinder, obstruct, or restrict'. However, its role is essential when dealing with the subjective, shifting, relative 'truths' confronted by qualitative research.

Dudley-Evans and St John suggest that one major function of hedging is 'distancing' – 'the use of a reporting verb such as *suggest, appear to, seem to, tend to* ... distance[s] the writer from the statement that s/he is reporting'. They compare the phrases 'The data quoted in the Financial Times *show* that the value of the dollar is rising' and 'The data quoted in the Financial Times *suggest* that the value of the dollar is rising' and maintain that 'in the first sentence the writer is aligning him/herself with the claim through the use of ... *show*, while in the second the use of *suggest* distances the writer from the claim and shows a neutral position' (Dudley-Evans and St John 1998: 76). Another function is 'softening':

> If a writer criticizes another by saying: 'Jones *appears not to have understood* the point I was making', the use of *appears* mitigates the criticism and is a politeness device rather than a distancing device. The writer is committed to the criticism, but follows the convention that criticisms are made politely. (Dudley-Evans and St John 1998: 76–77, their emphasis)

This type of cautious language is necessary in all qualitative statements based on *interpretation*, whether of data or, as in the second example, of literature. In the following examples from my corpus, I will show how this caution is maintained throughout the written study.

Setting a cautious scene

This extract comes from the introductory background section of Emami and Ekman's study of elderly immigrants in Sweden. The underlined hedging phrases serve to align their claims with what they actually know about the situation they are looking at. They skilfully mix their own impressions of the setting ('in many cases ... complaints') with what other researchers say in the literature:

> Early Iranian immigrants in Sweden <u>often</u> become isolated and lose contact with the outside world (Hajighasemi, 1994). <u>In many cases</u>, their only social contacts are with their children or other relatives. The absence of a broader social network leads to <u>other</u> problems, <u>many of which</u> are related to professional health-care. A <u>reduced</u> sense of well-being and <u>poor</u> self-confidence may

be the underlying reasons for many of the medical complaints. ... <u>According</u> to Hajighasemi (1994), the health problems of this immigrant population are <u>often</u> considered by medical professionals to be psychosomatic. (Emami and Ekman 1998: 184, my underlining)

The key here to making appropriate claims is expressing quantity without precise amounts – 'often' without saying how often, 'many' without saying how many, 'reduced' without saying how far reduced, and 'poor' without saying to what degree. The writers thus communicate that they have a reserved sense of the setting without getting into specifics which they cannot validate – reserved until they find out more during the course of their study. Also, the extract shows them using other research while at the same distancing themselves from it. Hence, 'according to' puts the full responsibility of saying that the health problems are 'often considered ... to be psychosomatic' fully with Hajighasemi (1994). Similarly, further on in their literature review, they place the responsibility on a range of other authors for suggesting that 'the migration process has been described as occurring in different phases (Sluki, 1979; Foster and Olkiewicz, 1984; Dten, 1986; Brink and Saunders, 1990)' (Emami and Ekman 1998: 185). Here, 'has been described' also considerably softens the claim by placing it in the passive and thus detaching it from specific authorship and dispersing it, as the subsequent dates show, over a period of time. The 'has been' clears away the past and creates space for Emami and Ekman to make their own, more assertive contribution.

Making restrained sense

The same type of caution is evident in this extract from Byrd's study of maternal care giving at the point where she describes, in the data analysis part of her paper, what happens when the single nurse she is observing prepares for a home visit:

Before first visits, information was <u>often</u> sketchy. <u>Data such as</u> 'young mother' and 'premature infant' raised <u>certain questions</u> about the mother's ability to understand and meet the special needs of a premature infant. <u>At other times</u>, the nurse used past knowledge. <u>For instance</u>, when contemplating a visit to a mother and her second baby, the nurse remembered her visits the previous year .... <u>She said</u>: 'I wasn't sure about this mother ...'. (Byrd 1999: 28–29, my underlining)

This is a complex piece of analysis as Byrd tries to make sense of the nurse making sense of the small amount of information she has been given. Byrd has been able to build a picture of the nurse through observation and interview over 'a period of 8 months' during '53 home visits' (1999: 27). Nevertheless, as she pieces together what she has seen and heard, she still has to exercise considerable caution, restraining herself from making more than approximate claims. Although she refers to data, questions and times, she restrains herself from being too specific with 'such as', 'certain' and 'other', providing instead an 'instance' to support these approximate claims by citing what the nurse says.

She continues in this vein as she describes what happens on 'entering the home' of one of the mothers:

> The very beginning of the visit was <u>often</u> symbolic of the confirming or doubting process beginning to unfold. ... The nurse <u>entered confidently</u>. This <u>kind of</u> set the tone for the confirming process that followed. <u>In contrast, another</u> mother <u>delayed opening</u> the door and <u>did not invite</u> us to enter. The nurse <u>moved hesitantly</u> through the door and into the home. This hesitancy seemed characteristic of the nurse's judgement about the mother's ability to care for the infant as well. (Byrd 1999: 29, my underlining)

Here there is a balance between fairly definite statements of what happened (broken underlining) and statements of restrained approximation (single underlined). Within this, 'in contrast another' (double underlining) is significant in the way it creates texture, in what might become a rather still sea of description calmed by hedging, by setting events with different characteristics against one another. The poignancy of qualitative description is indeed often in illuminating apparent contradictions which show the complexity and richness of social phenomena.

In both these extracts Byrd is not so much failing to be certain, as preserving the personal space of her central participant, the nurse, and the mothers she visits – not presuming to read too much into their actions and accounts, while still being able to establish an overall characterization of what is going on. This can be seen again in the discussion in the implications and conclusion part of her paper. In this extract she explains what her research project enabled her to find out, viz. 'Field research was helpful for understanding home visits from the viewpoint of an experienced nurse. Nursing processes and strategies during home visiting to the at-risk maternal-child population were made explicit' (Byrd 1999: 31). It is significant here that she is not claiming more than helpfulness in understanding. Moreover, she carefully defines what sort of understanding – from the viewpoint of her major participant, and of specific processes and strategies. She does not claim a great degree of understanding – simply that understanding was 'helped'.

This may seem a small achievement but it does enable Byrd to attach what she has seen to theory, as she comments that, 'to initiate and progress the home visiting process during a single visit, and to continue the process over a series visit, the nurse employed strategies based on notions similar to those from social exchange theory' (Byrd 1999: 31). Then, after expanding on the significance of this, she continues to link what she has understood with other work:

> Categories of outcomes are similar to those of previous studies (Byrd 1997b). However, we are made more aware of how distinct client–nurse interactive processes result in particular outcomes. Nurses may limit specific positive consequences when they doubt, rather than confirm the adequacy of maternal caregiving. (Byrd 1999: 31, my underlining)

Thus, while still being cautious, with 'similar' rather than 'the same', 'more' rather than stating exactly how much, and 'may' rather than 'does', she succeeds in showing how her study contributes to an advancement of understanding. It is significant that her claim to similarity to other studies is not the same as claiming replicability. To do that would fall within the domain of quantitative research, where a dominant aim is to test the validity of other work (see Table 1.1). As a qualitative researcher, Byrd is instead adding another instance to a developing picture.

Being careful with people's words

The classic approach to assuring textual room for the voice of the people in the research setting is through using their own verbatim accounts as the major data source. However, because the researcher must present this type of data, like all others, within her own commentary and argument, as much care must be taken about how it is selected and interpreted. Furthermore, verbatim data is as open as any other to distorting the world of the people involved (see Chapter 4). It can also serve to reduce, rather than enhance, the humanity of the participant. Tyler gives us a harsh warning that, despite our current intentions to escape from the nineteenth-century treatment of the 'research subject' as 'noble savage', researchers are still in danger of reducing her 'with the tape recorder'

> to a 'straight man', as in the script of some obscure comic routine, or even as they think to have returned to 'oral performance' or 'dialogue', in order that the native have a place in the text, they exercise total control over her discourse and steal the only thing she has left – her voice. (Tyler 1986: 127–128)

All of Shaw's data, in her study of the impact of the media on women's body images, comprises oral accounts collected through interview. In her concluding discussion, supported by reference of literature, she draws attention to the different ways in which this data can be interpreted:

> An over-simplistic feminist reading of the data could suggest that the women who expressed an influence from the media on their 'body image' and body-related behaviour ... are beguiled casualties of the beauty system in Western consumer society. However, the women working to 'beautify' their bodies in this research are not deluded 'cultural dopes' (Davis 1995). Rather, they are an active, interpreting, knowledgeable and diverse audience, who attribute meaning to cultural images of female 'beauty', and negotiate their relationships with their own bodies within the constraints of the 'fashion-beauty complex' (Bartky 1990). (Shaw 1998: 22)

Shaw thus takes on the difficult task of making sure that the reader gets the most positive message from the data she presents. The efforts to which she goes to represent the complex reality of the women in her study is shown in the following extracts.

Halfway through the data analysis part of her paper, Shaw is moving from looking at 'the women's perceptions of the female body in the media' to ask 'what impact ... these images' were 'perceived to have on women's attitudes towards their own bodies' (1998: 14). Here, she tries to make sense of the various responses she has collected:

> When the women talked <u>in a general way</u> ... <u>some differences</u> between the three groups emerged. <u>While</u> there were differences between the women within the groups, overall the 'alternative identity' women <u>seemed least sensitive</u> to influence from media images. <u>A key theme</u> which emerged was the comparison of one's own body with media images of the female body, which <u>seemed</u> to <u>feature more strongly</u> for the diet and fitness women:

> You might think ... 'Do I fit into that category?' (Diet, 2). (Shaw 1998: 14, my underlining)

The underlined phrases show how she hedges to maintain restraint from making more than qualitative claims – 'some', 'seemed least', 'more strongly'. At the same time, they also show a skilled movement from what appears 'in a general way', a possible conflict between accounts – 'while', 'overall' – and recognition of 'a key theme' that helps her make further sense. Very useful to keep track of are the names she has given to the different groups – 'alternative identity', 'diet' – which enable her to make quick reference. After providing fragments of data as evidence, Shaw then demonstrates how she pursued this potentially conflicting picture in her data collection to find a deeper 'truth': 'When the women were probed for more specific responses, the differences between the three groups became more subtle and complex, and three further themes emerged' (1998: 14). She then proceeds to describe the details of these themes, and to present more data fragments as evidence. Eventually, she arrives at the statement that:

> These women viewed living up to the media images ... as an 'impossibility', as 'unrealistic'. While they were aware of the images, and in some cases did express a desire to be thinner, they recognized and accepted the futility of using them as 'standards' for their own bodies. (Shaw 1998: 15–16)

Later on, she considers even more factors. Again, the underlined phrases show cautious, yet persistent sense making:

> However, it also seems that there are <u>some 'identity' factors at play</u>. The value that the majority of the women, particularly the diet and fitness groups, placed upon achieving a healthy, fit body <u>suggests</u> that working on the body <u>plays a key role</u> in maintaining a positive self-view. This is <u>reflected</u> in the comments of one fitness woman who said:

> > I do a lot of keep fit and it's got to the stage now if I don't go I feel let down in myself ... I'm thinking 'You should have gone tonight, that's terrible, why didn't you go' (Fitness, 3).

> <u>In contrast</u>, 'self respect' as a reason for body-related behaviour was given uniquely by some of the 'alternative identity' women. <u>This arguably reflects</u> an

attitude of 'stewardship' towards the body: the body as an entity which these women feel they have a responsibility to care for.

'Arguably reflects' is a key phrase in showing that Shaw is doing no more than making claims on the basis of sufficient evidence to support an argument.

These extracts show that Shaw is not simply interested in reporting what the women say, but in searching around, and 'probing', both while collecting the data and while analysing the data she has, until she finds the deeper meanings that make more sense. It is also clear that *themes* are used not simply to organize the data, but as pegs upon which the researcher can hang her own thoughts during the process of the research itself.

Suspending judgement

Hedging can be seen as a linguistic device to ensure caution. At a deeper, method-ological level, though very much involving hedging, *bracketing* is a means for look-ing at the social world in a particular way and 'making the familiar strange'. I have already noted in passing that this refers to the way in which documents can be seen as artefacts of culture rather than as information. In their discussion of ethno-methodology and phenomenology, Gubrium and Holstein thus define bracketing as a means to 'temporarily suspend all commonsense assumptions' in order to 'make visible the practices through which taken-for-granted realities are accomplished' (1997: 40, citing Schutz).

Culturism

An area where such suspension of judgement is necessary is in the major quest of the qualitative researcher to avoid reducing the people she is investigating to something less than they are, by *othering* the 'different' or 'foreign' as simplistic, easily digestible, exotic or degrading stereotypes. There are various manifestations of this danger. Fine (1994) draws attention to the othering of gender, class, race and ethnic groups. I shall approach this area from an angle which is close to my own experience, and focus on *culturism* – similarly constructed to sexism and racism in that it reduces people, not so much to prescribed gender or racial stereotypes as to prescribed cultural stereo-types (Holliday 2005a: 17).

This is a far deeper issue than those not familiar with the literature to do with othering may think. Apart from the ease with which all of us can fall into reductive discourses, there is an inherent culturism within the history of social science, and especially in the tendency in which nineteenth-century Western anthropology justi-fied colonialism, as already described in Chapter 1. This can be traced back to a dom-inant 'methodological nationalist' sociology which grew out of a nineteenth-century European nationalism (Schudson 1994: 21) and the modernist construction of 'national-level "imagined communities"' (Dobbin 1994: 124). The dangers are however not left in the past. In a post-colonialist era there are still 'unequal narratives' that create an 'unreciprocal interpretation of other non-Western cultures' (Sarangi 1995, citing Asad and Said). Edward Said's Orientalism thesis states that the East is still constructed by the Western popular and literary psyche as dark, immoral, lascivious, despotic and so on (Said 1978, 1993). Especially after September 11, we have seen a reconfirmation of Said's assertion that the vast complexity of Middle Eastern society is reduced to a simplistic notion of Islam (Said 2003).

Within modern multicultural societies the colonialist legacy of essentialist cultural chauvinism also underlies the way in which we construct 'foreign' minority cultures resident in the West (Sarangi 1995: 11). Thus, the behaviour of British 'Asians' is reduced by the media, government and popular discourses to being 'a consequence' of their 'Asianness', their 'ethnic identity', or the 'culture' of their 'community'. It is on this basis that we can 'claim to speak "for" them, "represent" them' and 'explain them to others' (Baumann 1996: 1, 6). 'Even in the modern (or postmodern?) era, the state still has a direct interest in promoting research that provides it with facts for the purpose of social regulation' (Jordan and Yeomans 1995: 393). Indeed there are always going to be successive layers of critique, where 'feminist anthropologists have criticized the new ethnography for ignoring the long tradition of feminist theory on ethnography in favour of postmodernism' and 'this has led, they argue, to merely exposing power relations within texts rather than overcoming these relations in the field' (1995: 395).

It is my view that culturism underpins much of this thinking in that it is dependent on an essentialist view of culture which presumes 'that particular things have essences which serve to identify them as the particular things that they are' (Bullock and Trombley 2000: 283). 'Cultures' thus become coincidental with countries, regions and continents, implying that one can 'visit' them while travelling and that they contain mutually exclusive types of behaviour, so that people 'from' or 'in' French culture are essentially different to those 'from' or 'in' Chinese culture. This psycho-geographical picture also presents a hierarchical onionskin relationship between a national culture and elements within it, so that 'Egyptian school culture' is a subset or subculture of 'Egyptian education culture' and so on. At the more macro level, 'Kenyan culture' becomes a subset of 'African culture'. Common variations on this geographical theme are the association of 'cultures' with religions, political philosophies, ethnicities and languages, where 'Islamic culture', 'black culture' and 'English language culture' take on the same essence of containment (see for example Keesing 1981, 1994; Holliday et al. 2004).

Much of this essentialism will seem natural and normal to many readers, because it is in many ways the default way of thinking about how we are different to one another. It is however problematic because if we think of people's behaviour as defined and constrained by the culture in which they live, agency is transferred away from the individual to the culture itself, so that we begin to think that 'German culture believes that ...', and that 'she belongs to German culture, therefore she ...' – which is only a short, easy distance from chauvinistic statements like 'in Middle Eastern culture there is no concept of individualized critical thinking'.

Avoiding easy answers

The sensitivities expressed in Chapter 7 may address to a degree the politics of the presence of the researcher, where they are in danger of adding to and exacerbating inequalities within particular research settings (Cameron et al. 1992; Shamim 1993; Gieve and Magalhães 1997); but researchers must also be ever vigilant in monitoring the chauvinistic ideologies deep within their own language in the written study.

I am using 'ideology' here, as already defined in Chapter 1, to mean something that can be present in everyday '"common sense" assumptions' that certain states of affairs or being, often represented by 'relations of power' are 'natural' (Fairclough 1989: 2). This fits with current discussions in critical discourse analysis – that racism, sexism or, indeed, culturism can become naturalized in our own everyday language to such an extent that we become 'standardly unaware' of their ideological impact (Fairclough 1995: 36). What is needed is a self-disciplining methodology of prevention.

Clown or compere

To illustrate the dangers of falling into the culturist trap in writing, it is necessary to move away from my corpus of written studies for a moment and look at some work in progress. The following extract is draft material from Grace's study of an international curriculum project in a Chinese university. (Grace is a fictitious name. I do not cite the study of which this is work in progress to protect the identity of the researcher, who realized the unintentional culturism in her language and made moves to put it right before producing the final work.) It is the last two lines of a description of a classroom event, in which students are doing oral presentations in front of the class, followed by a connection she makes with her experience of television and stage in the wider Chinese society:

> It seems most obvious in the case of male–female pairs ... the students are behaving like the comperes whom I have seen in Chinese variety shows! In Chinese television and stage shows there are usually two comperes: a man in a tight-fitting white blazer and a girl in a large flouncy ballroom gown. They adopt a stiff, ballet-like posture, pinching their buttocks together and puffing their chests out. With their left hands they hold the microphone flat against their chests. Meanwhile they hold their right palms out to the audience in magnanimous gestures of welcome. They both wear fixed cheesy grins and heavy rouge. They take turns sing-song to speak with an intonation, the man in a low dignified tone and the woman in a high-pitched nasal whine. As one speaks, the other looks on lovingly and nods approval after each utterance. The exact same appearance and behaviour are imitated by students in university stage shows. (My underlining)

When Grace presented this extract at a research seminar, it invited considerable comment from other people there, who saw in it culturist language which Grace had clearly not intended, but which is in fact there. A very probable reading of this text is that the description of Chinese comperes is sarcastic, as characterized by phrases (underlined) that depict 'clown-like' behaviour. A Chinese informant took exception to this (apparent) representation, and explained that Chinese comperes do not intend to be clown-like, and that the 'white blazer' and 'ballroom gown' are 'normal' symbols of the formality expected on stage and television. Thus, 'flouncy', 'cheesy', 'heavy', sing-song' and 'high-pitched nasal whine' represent Grace's own derogatory spin on events which are not normally considered to be derogatory.

Grace's response to this was that she was indeed unaware of any sarcasm in her text, that she had simply described what she thought she had seen, and had certainly not intended to make the behaviour she was describing appear 'clown-like'. She also knew all along that Chinese compares did not *intend* to be clown-like.

It does not matter whether Grace intended to be sarcastic or not, or knew whether or not Chinese comperes intend to be clowns. What is important is that what she actually wrote does include phrases which make Chinese comperes appear, if not 'clown-like', at least 'ridiculous' – and that now she can see this herself. The important implication here is that there is ideological content in her text of which she was initially unaware, and therefore had not accounted for.

What makes Grace's description *culturist* is the way in which behaviour in the classroom event is linked with what happens on television and stage elsewhere in society. On the one hand, comparison adds richness. Although the setting of Grace's research is within the university, some reference to its locatedness within a wider social setting can enhance thick description. However, on the other hand, she is allowing herself to imagine a degree of cultural homogeneity which may not exist – seeing the students in the classroom as primarily Chinese, according to a pre-defined, reduced notion of 'culture', rather than primarily students. This fronting of 'Chineseness' then enables a direct link to comperes who are, in the same way, characterized as primarily Chinese, rather than primarily comperes. (The equivalent in sexist writing would be to characterize their behaviour as, say, 'feminine', and to validate this by comparing it with 'feminine' behaviour elsewhere.) In addition to this, because of the language embedded in the text which signals 'ridiculous', the overall, apparent implication is that Chinese student behaviour is somehow substandard and is generalized to substandard elements characteristic of Chinese 'culture'.

Moreover, Grace's use of very exact statements of comparison (broken underlining) – '*are* behaving like' and '*exact* same' (my emphasis) – implies a jumping to easy conclusions which bracketing would try to avoid. One of the seminar participants commented that whatever was happening in the classroom was likely to have nothing at all to do with being 'Chinese' or being like 'Chinese comperes'.

'Children' or ' people'

Another example of culturist language in a description of behaviour, of which the author was initially unaware, is in my own work in progress. The following extract is from my description of my own students' behaviour while I was teaching them. The students are Hong Kong Chinese of between 18 and 21 years old. Ironically, the reason I was carrying out the research was because I wanted to debunk a significant amount of culturism in current applied linguistics research which characterizes language students from the Far East as 'passive'. It was not until I looked at what I had written, presumably with great sensitivity, weeks later, that I saw the ideological implications of the phrases (underlined):

> I was determined <u>to get them</u> into choosing topics for projects by the end of the morning. ... The students <u>arrived in dribs and drabs</u> late. They <u>arranged themselves</u> around the cluster of tables <u>fairly haphazardly</u>. Some of them were beginning to turn on computers and I told them not to, to sit straight down – fearing that <u>they were going to get onto their chat-lines</u>. (I had got the impression previously that they spent every moment of 'free' time on chat lines.) ....
> Then I left them for 30 minutes to devise ideas for projects. ... When I returned <u>they were remarkably on task</u>. Some of them <u>perkily</u> looked round to say they were 'on-time'.

It may be difficult for the reader to see the traces of culturism here. I can because I know my own preoccupations while writing – or, to put it differently, when I see what I wrote, it enables me to excavate the preoccupations which were there, but too deep for me to notice, at the time of writing. 'To get them' implies a superior teacher trying to change culturally 'inferior' behaviour of the object other 'them' (rather than 'us'). 'Dribs and drabs', 'fairly haphazardly' and 'they ... chat-lines' implies confirmation of this *expected* behaviour. 'Arranged themselves' implies a sense of degenerate self-indulgence – nothing better to do than to 'display' themselves 'ornamentally'. 'Get them ... by ...' also reveals the objectives-led control element of a so-called 'student-led' pedagogy, within which students are in reality operatives to be 'improved' by a controlled treatment. Hence, I found it 'remarkable', on returning to the class after leaving to get something, to find that 'they' were actually doing the things I had set them – whereas there was no reason at all why they should not. Nevertheless, I still refer to them as being 'perky' – like 'children' rather than adult people.

Bracketing

Largely because of the understandings which I achieved through this scrutiny of my own writing, I attempted to reduce the chauvinism in my view of the Hong Kong Chinese students by employing the phenomenological discipline of bracketing. This forces the researcher to think again and hold back from the explanation which most easily springs to mind. It requires her to recognize where her particular prejudices lie and to discipline herself to put them aside. I took advice from Baumann's account of his ethnography of the multicultural London borough of Southall. To avoid explaining the behaviour of British Sikhs in terms of reduced 'ethnic' stereotypes, he made himself think of them first as Southallian, and only considered their 'Sikhness' or caste if it *emerged* independently from the data. He thus succeeded in putting 'ethnic culture' as explanation in its place and began to discover the way in which 'culture' was used as a cultural artefact in different 'dominant' and 'demotic' discourses within the suburb (Baumann 1996: 2, 10).

In the methodology section of my written study of the Hong Kong students, I therefore wrote about how I had been influenced by a particular professional discourse which focused on essentialism notions of 'Chinese culture'. This awareness helped me to consider the fact that they were students first and to consider their Chineseness as an explanation of their behaviour only if it emerged (Holliday 2001: 124; Holliday 2005a: 88). This discipline of thinking enabled me to arrive at fresh understandings. In the following description of the same students in a lecture in their university in Hong Kong, I find further evidence not only of the way in which I had infantilized them when they were in my classes in Britain, but also of how the apparent lack of 'autonomy' which had been attributed to their 'Chinese culture' was connected to the amount of 'private space' they had been allowed in the British language classroom:

> From the back of the large theatre, and slightly to the side of the students I noticed that the rows which they inhabited seemed to offer a sense of *private space*; and the distance from the lecturer afforded them the possibility of sharing notes and quiet comments while the lecture was in process. The students tended to sit near each other and not in places arranged by the lecturer. Also because of the size of the room, with a door from the back as well as from the front, the students were able to come and go once the lecture was in session without too much disruption. The students tended to enter from the back of the room, while the lecturer entered from a door at the front. The students *seemed more adult* than when they had been on the immersion programme in the UK. (Holliday 2005a: 94-95, my emphasis)

Separating data from judgement

I do not intend to argue that researchers should not pass any judgement on what they observe, but that when they do, they should be careful that it *emerges* through their *submission* to *data* (Figure 7.2), and that it should then be expressed within the domain of *argument* which is explicitly grounded in and accountable to specific data. The demarcation within the written study that this requires has already been discussed in Chapter 5. In the previous section I have argued that this requires considerable self-awareness and discipline on the part of the researcher.

An example from my thesis demonstrates how this can be achieved, though still not perfectly. The following extract begins with a piece of descriptive data recording my local colleague's negative reaction to accompanying me on a visit to an expatriate lecturer who was working with a new language laboratory at one of the universities in my setting, and then continues with a commentary which links this reaction to another similar case:

However, on the way back:

> [My local colleague] said that her/his time had been wasted and that s/he had learnt nothing and that s/he had been brought on the visit under false pretences, that s/he had been led to believe that ... [the expatriate lecturer] was an expert. (Obs. 38, site 7, LH)

> This reaction was repeated when this local colleague was introduced to another expatriate lecturer who had considerable experience with language laboratories and had collected a lot of material which s/he was prepared to share (note to obs. 38, site 7). (Holliday 1991: 372, original square brackets and gaps – showing my then changes to the original notes)

The language in both the descriptive data and the commentary is relatively neutral, relating events and reactions as simply as possible. Only the phrase leading into the data – 'however' – indicates that this was not what I had expected – that my local colleague would find the visit useful because 's/he' – I use the neutral gender label to further anonymize – was developing materials for language laboratories, and I had thought s/he would like to see what other people were doing. I then follow this with an analysis (argument) of why my colleague had *not* reacted as expected, which is in turn supported by further reference to data, and then a continuation of my argument:

> On both occasions <u>I had seen</u> my local colleague as a recipient to useful ideas as a result of meeting the expatriate lecturers. However, my local colleague: –

> > ... [saw] her/himself in each case as the consultant and expert, a perception not shared by the expatriate lecturer[s], who felt that ... [they] had been asked to the meeting[s] to advise. (Note to obs. 38, site 7, LH)

> <u>I interpreted</u> my local colleague's misconception (<u>in my terms</u>) regarding the aims of our professional relationship, as a difficulty, <u>on her/his part</u>, in accepting practical experience as valuable. <u>I felt</u> that s/he saw her/himself as already expert because of her/his PhD, and ... was only prepared to learn from somebody more expert. The credentials of somebody more expert <u>would be seen</u> only in terms of theoretical knowledge. The credentials of the expatriate lecturer at site 7, who considerably played down what s/he knew, very much putting forward the image of 'amateur tinkering' (obs. 38, site 7, BF), were not sufficient <u>in my local colleague's terms</u>. (Holliday 1991: 372–373, square brackets and gaps in the original data fragment; added to the argument, my underlining)

Not only is what I felt about the event reserved for the analysis, I also distance myself from what I noted, and probably felt quite strongly about, at the time of the event described in the data fragment. This can be seen in the use of the underlined phrases which refer to my own thoughts, 'seen', 'interpreted' and 'felt' in the past. 'Would be seen' signals the hypothetical consequence of what *I* thought. 'In my terms' also makes it clear that my comments on the 'difficulty, on his/her part' are entirely my own. However, I am not so successful in making it clear whether or not 'in my local colleague's terms' is my own interpretation or theirs.

What is important here is that the extract is an example of my recognition, as a researcher, that there are three distinct voices at work which correspond to the second, third and fourth discussed near the end of Chapter 6. Voice 2 is myself making a neutral record of what I see and hear, as represented by the data; voice 3 is myself making judgement (comment) about what I see at the time; and voice 4 is myself making judgement about 2 and 3. An example of voice 2 can also be seen in the data fragment cited near the beginning of this extract. Unlike the data fragments in the previous extract, this one is from a footnote to my observation record because it was seen at the time as comment rather than description and therefore kept separate.

Pursuing 'local perceptions'

The reader may think that this is all unduly complicated, and prefer a straightforward account of what happened and what it meant. The point is that 'what happened' is never straightforward, and neither is the researcher's telling of what happened. I see it as the researcher's responsibility to unpeel the complexity, no matter how complicated it might get.

The thematic subheading for the part of my thesis that these extracts come from is 'Local lecturer perceptions of the curriculum project'. Within this subtheme I pursue 'local' perceptions through several 'points of focus', looking at the issue from different directions thrown up by the data. The analysis I have just dealt with comes under *Who are the experts?* The next point of focus is *Territory and status*, where, after looking at several more pieces of evidence from data, I present the following argument. It is based on a theoretical distinction, following Bernstein, between two types of education cultures, integrationist, or more skills oriented, and collectionist, or more academic subject oriented:

> My integrationist motives ... had been to involve local lecturers in the curriculum discussion and development process – the area of expertise upon which the professional-academic culture of the curriculum project was capitalizing. The local lecturers were prepared to enter into this process, but for different reasons. For them it seemed to be an arena for asserting professional-academic status and territory. It would be hasty to suggest that this local pre-occupation was only to be found in this particular local situation. It may well be shared by academics throughout the world, where academic reputation and expertise are a basis for promotion and respect. (Holliday 1991: 376, my underlining)

Again, I am analysing my own behaviour as well as 'theirs', and use the education culture distinction as a possible explanation for my own conflict with my 'local' colleagues, which I was seeing repeatedly in the data. Hence the contrast between 'my ... motives' and 'for them' (underlined). On this basis, I am able to theorize about what 'seemed' to be *their* motives. Nevertheless, I continue to 'bracket' – to restrain from indulging in culturist statements about what might have seemed at the time 'Egyptian' characteristics, which I would probably have associated with 'Byzantine duplicity', or some other such stereotype – with 'it would be hasty'. Instead, I use the education, rather than national, cultural distinction to suggest that *their* behaviour 'may well' be shared by (collectionist) academics elsewhere.

It is therefore by applying a complexity of checks and balances on one's own pre-occupations that such an analysis can proceed, striving to find the reality of the people in the setting, which is not confined to easy extensions of ethnic or national cultural explanation. A refreshing example of breaking away from the easy explanation is Herrera's final comment in her ethnography of an Egyptian girls' school (Holliday 1999: 239). She was initially enticed into the research by the strangeness of the place, which then made her rethink the way she presented herself as a researcher. Nevertheless, through all this she is able to see it as 'a school' rather than simply 'an Egyptian school':

> It is Egypt, it is the East, it is also a developing country. But it is also humanity. Beyond my initial fascination with the exotic protocol, drills, sounds and system, it became just an ordinary school. ... I cannot count the times I felt myself transformed over six thousand miles and more than a decade away to the parochial school in downtown San Francisco that I attended as a child. Superficially the two schools are vastly different. ... Yet despite their specific features [one can] ... join them together in the world community of schools. (Herrera 1992: 80–81)

People in relationships

Especially in the later chapters in this book, but also throughout, I have tried to characterize the qualitative researcher as one person amongst others in the social setting where she is carrying out her research. As such, she is a person who is trying to understand others, but must do this through the way in which they interact with her (Chapter 7) – just like anyone who is relating to new people, or indeed friends and colleagues she has known for longer but whom she must still struggle to understand. In everyday life we have always to remember that how people are to us has a lot to do with how we are with them. They react to the complex baggage that we bring with us; and we also see them in terms of this baggage.

This means that what happens around us is not plain to see. We have to work hard to organize our thoughts and experiences to discover what is going on. In Chapter 4 I invoked the argument that thick description is not so much a collection of interconnected data as the result of the researcher's intent and strategy in sorting out 'the winks from the twitches' and in actively making sense of the data. This image of the qualitative researcher is very evident in some of the examples in this chapter – as someone who really needs to *do* something, to sort out what is really going on. This can be seen especially with Grace, who needs to work to get through the haze and illusions created by her own ideological and cultural baggage. Shaw too has to work hard to find ways to present her data to show a message that is different to the dominant expectation of her readers.

Showing the workings (Chapter 3) thus becomes a way of saying to the unbelieving: look, *this* is where I got my ideas from but you have to see them in *this* way in order to see what I have seen – and the evidence *I* want you to notice (Chapter 7) is *not* what you would see with *your* preoccupations if *you* were there: it is *this* evidence and *this* evidence, and *this* is what *I* want you to notice about each fragment (Chapter 5). The image of the stranger (Chapter 1) is important here, as someone who can see what others cannot. Seeing the familiar as strange is however a difficult discipline, which requires special strategies to push aside easy answers both in ourselves and in those we write for.

Qualitative research is thus a struggle to see and a struggle to explain; and it must be so if it is to be a defence against the dominant, easy, racist, sexist and culturist discourses of our society. What is significant about Herrera's conclusion about the Egyptian girls' school is that she engages with the 'foreign' in all its complexity, and indeed makes it special, but so deeply that we can see there people just like ourselves.

Summary

The following points have been made in this chapter:

- The claims the researcher makes must be appropriate to the data she has collected and true to the ordinary world of the people in the setting.
- The researcher must struggle to allow textual room for the people in the research setting. This involves putting her preoccupations, discourse and ideology in their place, and appreciating how little she knows.
- Hedging can be used as a technical strategy to ensure caution and restraint in interpreting what is seen (descriptive data), and interpreting and presenting data (descriptive and verbatim) in commentary and argument.
- Care must be taken not to other or reduce the people in the setting through prescribed racist, sexist or culturist stereotyping. This requires strategic use of bracketing to avoid 'easy' explanations.
- Researchers must be wary of unintentional racist, sexist or culturist phrases embedded in their own language.
- Evaluation or judgement must be restricted to commentary and argument, leaving description of what is seen or heard as neutral as possible.
- Researchers must struggle to pursue the deeper perceptions of the people in their setting.

········ **Topics for Discussion**

These questions are to help novice and other qualitative researchers to find their way around the examples and principles presented in each chapter. Although in each case I refer to a specific part of the chapter, I hope this reference will stimulate wider reading in the vicinity. Where questions invite readers to evaluate their own work, this will be an invitation to go back and improve.

Chapter 1

1 Locate the items in Tables 1.1 and 1.2 and use them to determine the degree to which written studies with which you are fJamiliar are qualitative or quantitative.
2 Use Table 1.3 in a similar way to determine how far the studies employ naturalist or postmodern paradigms.
3 Consider Examples 1.6 and 1.7, and any experience you have of progressive focusing – where the findings from one research event lead to the setting up of another research event. What did you learn in the first event which led you into the second?
4 Consider Examples 1.8 and 1.9 and instances from your own experience of having approached a new small culture. (a) What understandings of this culture did you gain which insiders did not seem to have? (b) At what point did you stop seeing things strangely and become part of the 'thinking-as-usual' world?

Chapter 2

1 Consider Table 2.2, Figure 2.2, and the description of selecting a setting in Holliday's research project in Egypt. In a current research project, in what sense is the research setting bounded and the data you are collecting interconnected?
2 Look at the way in which Anderson develops his research questions. How, and with what stimuli have research questions developed in a project with which you are familiar?

3 Look at some written studies. (a) How far do the authors describe the process of selecting a research setting? (b) How does this affect validity?

Chapter 3

1 Compare some written studies with the plan in Figure 3.1. (a) How far do they deal with the items listed there? (b) Considering their research aims, how adequately do they show their workings?
2 Map some other written studies onto Figure 3.2. Considering their research aims, how adequately do they deal with the issue of ideology?
3 Consider Figure 3.3 and a current research project. How are you going to catalogue, code and then refer to your own data?
4 Consider the section on articulating issues. Is it true that you can do anything as long as you can articulate your reasons for doing it?

Chapter 4

1 Compare Table 4.1 and Figure 4.3 with some written studies and your own research. (a) What types of data are being collected? (b) How do these types interconnect to build pictures? (c) What pictures are being built?
2 Consider what Herrera and Celik choose to describe in the Egyptian school and in McDonald's. How far do your own descriptions (a) detail the richness of the phenomenon in question, (b) remain neutral, (c) make the familiar strange?
3 Consider verisimilitude and the value of illuminating instances. Show some of your own data to colleagues. How far does it (a) appear 'true' to them, and (b) illuminate something they had not previously thought of?
4 What types of visual image could you include as data in your research project? What could they say to the reader of your study which other forms of data could not? What would you need to say about them in the written study?

Chapter 5

1 Consider the difference between commentary, data and argument, and between showing and telling. Look at the data analysis section in your own work. (a) How far do you succeed in demarcating these elements? (b) When you show your work to colleagues, how far do they get the point you wish to demonstrate?
2 Consider the issue of organizing data thematically (Figure 5.1), and look at how this is done in written studies. How satisfactorily do authors (a) explain how they do this, and (b) account for their departure from 'reality'?
3 Map the details of your own research onto Figure 5.2. How far (a) have your own preoccupations responded to what is going on in the setting, and (b) have you accounted for this in your writing?

4   Consider Figures 5.2 and 4.3, and a selection of written studies. To what extent do the latter succeed in presenting thick description convincingly?

5   Using ideas from Wu's and Ovenden's work, think of alternative ways of representing your data in your written study. Assess how far they would be successful in making it clear what you wish to say about the data.

Chapter 6

1   Find examples of academic writing in which (a) footnotes are used for referencing, (b) brackets are used for referencing, and the first person is not used, and (c) the first person is used, and consider the discussion on mixed messages and new thinking. How far do the examples correspond with (i) humanities, (ii) positivistic and postpositivist naturalism, and (iii) postmodernism? What is the policy of your department, profession or discipline on the use of the first person? How does this compare with expectations in your earlier educational background? How do you now feel about this?

2   Look at some written studies and the discussion about the use of the first person. (a) How far do the researchers succeed in personalizing their argument? (b) How exactly do they do this; and is the rigour of their approach compromised?

3   Look at a written study and work out (a) how many of the five voices are present, and (b) the success with which they are demarcated and used.

Chapter 7

1   Look at Figure 7.1 and consider a current research project. (a) What are the different characteristics of the researcher, setting and setting cultures? (b) Are there any potentials for conflict? (c) Which of the three cultures are likely to dominate the others? (d) Are there any other cultures that influence the situation?

2   Following the discussion through the chapter, consider your own research project. From the way in which the people in the setting respond to your presence, what can you learn (a) about the culture of the setting, (b) about your own culture, and (c) about how you therefore ought to behave?

3   Consider your own research writing. How necessary is it for you to write about your relations with your people in the research setting? What is the connection between this activity and (a) being rigorous in showing your workings and (b) the need to capitalize on all available data?

Chapter 8

1   Consider the section on allowing ordinary voice, and some written studies. How far do the studies (a) create an abstract reality in which real people do not exist, (b) show the person of the researcher as distinct from the people she is writing about?

2   Consider the section on cautious detachment, and find examples of hedging in written studies, (a) in literature review, (b) in description of events, (c) in commentary and

argument based on verbatim data. How precise is the hedging in (i) creating a realistic picture, (ii) preventing distortion that might be caused by the preoccupations of the researcher, and (iii) showing evidence of searching enquiry?

3   Consider the section on suspending judgement and some of your own descriptive writing. (a) Is there any evidence of sexism, racism or culturism in your writing? (b) What are the preoccupations or prescriptive theories about people that have caused it to be there? (c) What strategies can you use to prevent it?

4   Look at your own work and other written studies. What evidence is there of real effort to pursue and make sense of the complex perceptions of the people in the research setting?

•••••••• Written Studies Used as Examples

Albert, E. (1999) 'Dealing with danger: normalizing the risk in cycling', *International Review for the Sociology of Sport,* 34(2): 157–171.

Anderson, C. (2002) 'The dominant discourse in British EFL: the methodological contradictions of a professional culture'. Department of Language Studies, Canterbury Christ Church University.

Berman, H. (1999) 'Stories of growing up amid violence by refugee children of war and children of battered women living in Canada'. *Image: Journal of Nursing Scholarship,* 31(1): 57–63.

Broadley, S. (1999) 'Behind closed doors in a small "hardcore bodybuilding gym"'. Unpublished undergraduate dissertation. Department of Sports Science, Canterbury Christ Church University.

Byrd, M. (1999) 'Questioning the quality of maternal caregiving during home visiting,' *Image: Journal of Nursing Scholarship,* 31(1): 27–32.

Çelik, N.C. (1999) 'McDonalds'. Unpublished undergraduate assignment. Department of Language Studies, Canterbury Christ Church University.

Delikurt, P. (2005) 'Revolution or evolution in educational change: the intended policy–actual policy–policy in use continuum revisited. A case study in the English language teaching and learning context of the Turkish Republic of Northern Cyprus'. Department of Language Studies, Canterbury Christ Church University.

Duan, Y.P. (in process). 'The influence of the Chinese university entrance exam (English)'. Unpublished PhD thesis, Department of Language Studies, Canterbury Christ Church University.

Emami, A. and Ekman, S. (1998) 'Living in a foreign country in old age: life in Sweden as experienced by elderly Iranian immigrants'. *Health Care in Later Life,* 3(3): 183–198.

Goulimaris, R. (in process) 'Television news and the construction of meaning: super-themes in the Greek media landscape'. Unpublished thesis, Department of Media, Canterbury Christ Church University.

Hayagoshi, H. (1996) 'British teachers' perceptions of Japanese students, in contrast with Japanese students' perceptions of their own needs and wants'. Unpublished master's dissertation. Department of Language Studies, Canterbury Christ Church University.

Herrera, L. (1992) 'Scenes of schooling: inside a girls' school in Cairo', *Cairo Papers in Social Science* 15, Monograph 1.

Holliday, A.R. (1991) 'Dealing with tissue rejection in EFL projects: the role of and ethnographic means analysis'. Unpublished PhD thesis, Department of Linguistics and Modern English Language, University of Lancaster.

Honarbin-Holliday, M. (2005) 'Art education, identity and gender at Tehran and al Zahra Universities'. Unpublished PhD thesis, Media and Cultural Studies, Canterbury Christ Church University.

Linehan, A. (1995) 'A search for a suitable context for writing: developing students' writing through self-access'. Unpublished master's dissertation. Department of Language Studies, Canterbury Christ Church University.

Maguire, J. and Mansfield, L. (1998) '"No-body's perfect": women, aerobics, and the body beautiful'. *Sociology of Sport* 15: 109–137.

Ovenden, C.A. (2003) 'The socio-cultural construction of learner independence in a tertiary EFL institution'. Unpublished PhD thesis, Institute of Education, University of London.

Pierson, C.A. (1999) 'Ethnomethodologic analysis of accounts of feeding demented residents in long-term care'. *Image: Journal of Nursing Scholarship*, 31(1): 127–131.

Scholl, C. (1999) 'Description of a small culture: tourists in a church'. Unpublished undergraduate assignment. Department of Language Studies, Canterbury Christ Church University.

Shamim, F. (1993) *Teacher–learner behaviour and classroom processes in large ESL classes in Pakistan.* Unpublished PhD thesis, International Education, University of Leeds.

Shaw, A. (1998) 'Images of the female body: women's identities and the media', in J. Richardson and A. Shaw (eds), *The Body in Qualitative Research*. Aldershot: Ashgate.

Talbot, M. (1992) 'The construction of gender in a teenage magazine', in N. Fairclough (ed.), *Critical Language Awareness*. London: Addison Wesley Longman: 175–199.

Wu, Z. (2002) 'Teachers' "knowledge" and curriculum change: a critical study of teachers' exploratory discourse in a Chinese university'. Unpublished PhD thesis, Department of Linguistics and Modern English Language, University of Lancaster.

References

Adler, P.A. and Adler, P. (1994) 'Observational techniques', in N.K. Denzin & Y.S. Lincoln (eds), *Handbook of Qualitative Research*. Thousand Oaks, CA: Sage. pp. 377–392.

Albert. E. (1999) 'Dealing with danger: normalizing the risk in cycling', *International Review for the Sociology of Sport* 34(2): 157–171.

Allwright, R.L. (1988) *Observation in the Language Classroom*. London: Longman.

Anderson, C. (2002) 'The dominant discourse in British EFL: the methodological contradictions of professional culture'. Department of Language Studies, Canterbury Christ Church University.

Appell, G.N. (1978) *Ethical Dilemmas in Anthropological Enquiry: A Case Book*. Waltham, MA: Crossroads Press.

Asad, T. (ed) (1973) *Anthropology and the Colonial Encounter*. London: Ithaca Press.

Atkinson, P (1990) *The Ethnographic Imagination*. London: Routledge.

Atkinson, P. and Coffey, A. (1995) 'Realism and its discontents: on the crisis of cultural representation in ethnographic texts', in B. Adam & S. Allan (eds), *Theorizing Culture: an Interdisciplinary Critique after Postmodernism*. London: UCL Press. pp. 41–57.

Atkinson, P. and Delamont, S. (2005) 'Analytical perspectives', in N.K. Denzin & Y.S. Lincoln, (eds), *Handbook of Qualitative Research*, 3rd edn. Thousand Oaks, CA: Sage. pp. 821–840.

Atkinson, P. and Hammersley, M. (1994) 'Ethnography and participant observation', in N.K. Denzin & Y.S. Lincoln (eds), *Handbook of Qualitative Research*. Thousand Oaks, CA: Sage. pp. 248–261.

Bailey, C., White, C. and Pain, R. (1999) 'Evaluating qualitative research: dealing with the tension between "science" and "creativity"'. *Area* 31(2): 169–183.

Ball, M. and Smith, G. (1999) *Analyzing Visual Data*. London: Sage.

Ball, M. and Smith, G. (2001) 'Technologies of realism? Ethnographic uses of photography and film', in P. Atkinson, A. Coffey, S. Delamont, J. Lofland & L. Lofland (eds), *Handbook of Ethnography*. London: Sage. pp. 302–319.

Barmada, W. (1994) 'Developing an institutional self-evaluation scheme in an ESP centre in the Arab world: rationale, experimentation and evaluation', Unpublished PhD thesis, Deapartment of Linguistics, University of Leeds.

Barton, A.H. and Lazarsfield, P.F. (1969) 'Some functions of qualitive of quantitive analysis in social research', in G.J. McCall & J.L. Simmons (eds), *Issues in Participant Observations*. Reading, MA: Addison Wesley. pp. 163–195.

Barua, F. (1996) '19th century Poona district gazetteers.' Unpublished paper presented at the Confronting South Asia seminar, University of Pune, India.

Baumann, G. (1996) *Contesting Culture*. Cambridge: Cambridge University Press.

Beals, A.R., Spindler, G. and Spindler, L. (1967) *Culture in Process*. New York: Holt, Rinehart & Winston.

Becker, H.S. (1997) 'Visual sociology, documentary photography, and photojournalism: it's (almost) all a matter of context', in J. Prosser (ed.), *Image-Based Research: a Sourcebook for Qualitative Researchers*. London: Falmer.

Bell, J. (1993) *Doing your Research Project*. Milton Keynes: Open University Press.

Berman, H. (1999) 'Stories of growing up amid violence by refugee children of war and children of battered women living in Canada'. *Image: Journal of Nursing Scholarship*, 31(1): 57–63.

Block, D. (2000) 'Problematizing interview data: voices in the mind's machine?', *TESOL Quarterly* 34(4): 757–763.

Bloor, M. and Bloor, T. (1991) 'Cultural expectations and socio-pragmatic failure in academic writing', in A., Adams, B. Heaton & P. Howarth (eds), *Socio-Cultural Issues in English for Academic Purposes*. London: Modern English Publications, The British Council. pp. 1–12.

Broadley, S. (1999) 'Behind closed doors in a small "hardcore bodybuilding gym"'. Unpublished undergraduate dissertation. Department of Sports Science, Canterbury Christ Church University.

Bullock, A. and Trombley, S. (eds) (2000) *New Fontana Dictionary of Modern Thought*. London: HarperCollins.

Byrd, M. (1999) 'Questioning the quality of maternal caregiving during home visiting', *Image: Journal of Nursing Scholarship*, 31(1): 27–32.

Cameron, D., Frazer, E., Harvey, P., Rampton, B. and Richardson, K. (1992) *Researching Language: Issues of Power and Method*. London: Routledge.

Canagarajah, S. (1999) *Resisting Linguistic Imperialism*. London: Oxford University Press.

Celik, N.C. (1999) 'McDonald's'. Unpublished undergraduate paper. Department of Language Studies. Canterbury Christ Church University.

Clark, R. and Ivanič, R. (1997) *The Politics of Writing*. London: Routledge.

Clark, R., Cottey, A., Constantinou, C. and Yeoh, D.C. (1990) 'Rights and obligations in student writing', in R. Clark, N. Fairclough, R. Ivanič, N. McLeod, J. Thomas & P. Meara (eds), *British Studies in Applied Linguistics 5: Language and Power*. Cardiff: BAAL, CILT. pp. 85–102.

Clifford, J. (1986) 'Introduction: partial truths', in J. Clifford & G.E. Marcus (eds), *Writing Culture: the Poetica of Politics of Ethnography*. Berkeley, CA: University of California Press. pp. 1–26.

Coffey, A. (1999) *Ethnographic Self*. London: Sage.

Collier, M. (1979) *A Film Study in Classrooms in Western Alaska*. Fairbanks: Center for Cross-Cultural Studies. University of Alaska.

Comaroff, J. and Comaroff, J. (1992) *Ethnography and the Historical Imagination*. Boulder, CO: Westview Press.

Crabtree, B.F. and Miller, W.L. (eds) (1992a) *Doing Qualitative Research: Research Methods for Primary Care, Volume 3*. Newbury Park, CA: Sage.

Crane, D. (1994) 'Introduction: the challenge of the sociology of culture to sociology as discipline', in D. Crane (ed.), *The Sociology of Culture*. Oxford: Blackwell. pp. 1–19.

De Brigard, E. (1975) 'The history of ethnographic film', in P. Hockings (ed.), *Principles of Visual Anthropology*. The Hague: Mouton. pp. 13–44.

Delikurt, P. (2005) 'Revolution or evolution in educational change: the intended policy – actual policy – policy in use continuum revisited. A case study in the English language teaching and learning context of the Turkish Republic of Northern Cyprus'. Department of Language Studies, Canterbury Christ Church University.

Denzin, N.K. (1994) 'The art and politics of interpretation', in N.K. Denzin & Y.S. Lincoln (eds), *Handbook of Qualitative Research*. Thousand Oaks, CA: Sage. pp. 500–515.

Denzin, N.K. and Lincoln, Y.S. (eds) (2000a) *Handbook of Qualitative Research*, 2nd edn. Thousand Oaks, CA: Sage.

Denzin, N.K. and Lincoln, Y.S. (2000b) 'The discipline and practice of qualitative research', in N.K. Denzin & Y.S. Lincoln (eds), *Handbook of Qualitative Research*, 2nd edn. Thousand Oaks, CA: Sage. pp. 1–30.

Denzin, N.K. and Lincoln, Y.S. (2005) 'The discipline and practice of qualitative research', in N.K. Denzin & Y.S. Lincoln (eds), *Handbook of Qualitative Research*, 3rd edn. Thousand Oaks, CA: Sage. pp. 1–32.

Dobbin, F.R. (1994) 'Cultural models of organization: the social construction of rational organizing principles', in D. Crane, (ed.), *The Sociology of Culture*. Oxford: Blackwell. pp. 117–141.

Duan, Y.P. (in process) 'The influence of the Chinese university entrance exam (English)'. Unpublished PhD thesis, Department of Language Studies, Canterbury Christ Church University.

Dudley-Evans, T. and St John, M.J. (1998) *Developments In English for Specific Purposes.* Cambridge: Cambridge University Press.

Elley, W.B. (1989) 'Tailoring the evaluation to fit the context', in R.K. Johnson (ed.), *The Second Language Curriculum.* Cambridge: Cambridge University Press. pp. 270–85.

Ellis, C. and Bochner, A.P. (2000) 'Autoethnography, personal narrative, reflexivity', in N.K. Denzin & Y.S. Lincoln (eds), *Handbook of Qualitative Research*, 2nd edn. London: Sage. pp. 733–768.

Emami, A. and Ekman, S. (1998) 'Living in a foreign country in old age: life in Sweden as experienced by elderly Iranian immigrants', *Health Care in Later Life*, 3(3): 183–198.

Emerson, R.M., Fretz, R.I. and Shaw, L.L. (2001) 'Participant observation and fieldnotes', in P. Atkinson, A. Coffey, S. Delamont, J. Lofland & L. Lofland (eds), *Handbook of Ethnography.* London: Sage. pp. 352–68

Erlandson, D.A., Harris, E.L., Skipper, B.L. and Allen, S.D. (1993) *Doing Naturalistic Enquiry.* Newbury Park, CA: Sage.

Fairclough, N. (1989) *Language and Power.* London: Addison Wesley Longman.

Fairclough, N. (1995) *Critical Discourse Analysis: The critical study of language.* London: Addison Wesley Longman.

Fine, M. (1994) 'Working the hyphens', in N.K. Denzin & Y.S. Lincoln (eds), *Handbook of Qualitative Research.* Thousand Oaks, CA: Sage. pp. 70–82.

Fine, M. and Weis, L. (1998) 'Writing the "wrongs" of fieldwork: confronting our own research/ writing dilemmas in urban ethnographies', in G. Shacklock & J. Smyth (eds), *Being Reflexive in Critical Educational and Social Research.* London: Falmer Press. pp. 13–35.

Foley, D. (1998) 'On writing reflexive realist narratives', in G. Shacklock & J. Smyth (eds), *Being Reflexive in Critical Educational and Social Research.* London: Falmer Press. pp. 110–129.

Gee, J.P. (1997) 'A discourse approach to language and literacy'. Forward to C. Lankshear, P.J. Gee, M. Knobel & C. Searle (eds), *Changing Literacies.* Buckingham: Open University Press.

Geertz, C. (1973) *The Interpretation of Cultures: Selected Essays.* New York: Basic Books.

Geertz, C. (1993) *The Interpretation of Cultures: Selected Essays.* London: Fontana.

Gieve, S. and Magalhães, I. (eds) (1997) *Power, Ethics and Validity: Issues in the Relationship between Researchers and Researched.* Centre for Research in Language Education (CRILE), Lancaster University.

Golden-Biddle, K. and Locke, K.D. (1997) *Composing Qualitative Research.* Thousand Oaks, CA: Sage.

Goulimaris, R. (in process) 'Television news and the construction of meaning: super-themes in the Greek media landscape'. Unpublished thesis, Department of Media, Canterbury Christ Church University.

Guba, E.G. and Lincoln, Y.S. (2005) 'Paradigmatic controversies, contradictions, and emerging confluences', in N.K. Denzin & Lincoln, Y.S. (eds), *Handbook of Qualitative Research*, 3rd edn. Thousand Oaks, CA: Sage. pp. 191–215.

Gubrium, J.F. and Holstein, J.A. (1997) *The New Language of Qualitative Research.* New York: Oxford University Press.

Gummesson, E. (1991) *Qualitative Methods in Management Research.* Newbury Park, CA: Sage.

Hammersley, M. and Atkinson, P. (1983) *Ethnography: Principles in Practice.* London: Tavistock.

Hammersley, M. and Atkinson, P. (1995) *Ethnography: Principles in Practice.* London: Routledge.

Harper, D. (2000) 'Re-imagining visual methods', in N.K. Denzin & Y.S. Lincoln (eds), *Handbook of Qualitative Research*, 2nd edn. London: Sage. pp. 717–767.

Harper, D. (2005) 'What's new visually?', in N.K. Denzin & Y.S. Lincoln (eds), *Handbook of Qualitative Research*, 3rd edn. London: Sage. pp. 747–762.

Harrison B. (2002) 'Photographic visions and narrative inquiry', *Narrative Inquiry* 12(1): 87–111.

Hayagoshi, H. (1996) 'British teachers' perceptions of Japanese students, in contrast with Japanese students' perceptions of their own needs and wants'. Unpublished master's dissertation, Department of Language Studies, Canterbury Christ Church University.

Herrera, L. (1992) 'Scenes of schooling: inside a girls' school in Cairo', *Cairo Papers in Social Science* 15, Monograph 1.

Holliday, A.R. (1991) 'Dealing with tissue rejection in EFL projects: the role of and ethnographic means analysis'. Unpublished PhD thesis, Department of Linguistics and Modern English Language, University of Lancaster.

Holliday, A.R. (1992a) 'Tissue rejection and informal orders in ELT projects: collecting the right information', *Applied Linguistics* 13(4): 404–424.

Holliday, A.R. (1992b) 'Intercompetence: sources of conflict between local and expatriate ELT personnel', *System* 20(2).

Holliday, A.R. (1996) 'Developing a sociological imagination: expanding ethnography in international English language education', *Applied Linguistics,* 17(2): 234–255.

Holliday, A.R. (1999) 'Small cultures', *Applied Linguistics,* 20(2): 237–264

Holliday, A.R. (2001) 'Finding social autonomy', in P. Bodycott & V. Crew (eds), *Language and Cultural Immersion: Perspectives on Short Term Study and Residence Abroad.* Hong Kong: Hong Kong Institute of Education. pp. 123–131.

Holliday, A.R. (2005a) *The Struggle to Teach English as an International Language.* Oxford: Oxford University Press.

Holliday, A.R. (2005b) 'How is it possible to write?', *Journal of Language, Identity, and Education,* 4(4): 304–309.

Holliday, A.R. (2006) 'The value of reconstruction in revealing hidden or counter cultures', *Journal or Applied Linguistics,* 1(3): 275–294.

Holliday, A.R. and Hoose, J. (1996) 'Middle ground: collaborative research and recognition of researcher-researched sub-cultures'. Unpublished paper, Canterbury Christ Church University.

Holliday, A.R., Hyde, M. and Kullman, J. (2004) *Intercultural Communication.* London: Routledge.

Holloway, J. and Wheeler, S. (1996) *Qualitative Research for Nurses.* Oxford: Blackwell.

Holman Jones, S. (2005) 'Autoethnography: making the personal political', in N.K. Denzin & Y.S. Lincoln (eds), *Handbook of Qualitative Research,* 3rd edn. London: Sage. pp. 763–791.

Holstein, J.A. and Gubrium, J.F. (2005) 'Interpretive practice and social action', in N.K. Denzin & Y. S. Lincoln (eds), *Handbook of Qualitative Research,* 3rd edn. Thousand Oaks, CA: Sage. pp. 483–506.

Honarbin-Holliday, M. (2005) 'Art education, identity and gender at Tehran and al Zahra Universities'. Unpublished PhD thesis, Media and Cultural Studies, Canterbury Christ Church University.

Hoyle, E. (1970) 'Planning organizational change in education', *Research in Education,* May: 1–22.

Ivanič, R. and Roach, D. (1990) 'Academic writing, power and disguise', in R. Clark, N. Fairclough, R. Ivanič, N. McLeod, J. Thomas & P. Meara (eds), *British Studies in Applied Linguistics 5: Language and Power.* London: BAAL and CILT. pp. 103–119.

Janesick, V.J. (2000) 'The choreography of qualitative research design: minuets, improvisations, and crystallization', in N.K. Denzin & Y.S. Lincoln (eds), *Handbook of Qualitative Research,* 2nd edn. Thousand Oaks, CA: Sage: 379–399.

Jenkins, D. (1986) 'An adversary's account of SAFARI's ethics of a case study', in M. Hammersley, (ed.), *Controversies in Classroom Research.* Milton Keynes: Open University Press. pp. 220–227.

Jordan, S. and Yeomans, D. (1995) 'Critical ethnography: problems in contemporary theory and practice', *British Journal of Sociology of Education,* 16(3): 389–408.

Kabbani, R. (1986) *Europe's Myths of Orient: Devise and Rule.* London: MacMillan.

Keesing, R.M. (1981) *Cultural Anthropology.* Orlando, FL: Harcourt Brace.

Keesing, R.M. (1994) 'Theories of culture revisited', in R. Borofsky (ed.), *Assessing Cultural Anthropology.* New York: McGraw-Hill. pp. 301–312.

Kress, G. and Hodge, R. (1979) *Language as Ideology.* London: Routledge.

Kress, G. Leite-García, R. and van Leeuwen, T. (1997) 'Discourse semiotics', in T.A. van Dijk (ed.), *Discourse as Structure and Process.* London: Sage. pp. 257–91

Kubota, R. (1999) 'Japanese culture constructed by discourses: implications for applied linguistics research and ELT', *TESOL Quarterly,* 33(1): 9–35.

Kuhn, T.S. (1970) *The Structure of Scientific Revolutions.* Chicago: University of Chicago Press.

Kyeyune, R. (1996) 'Identifying the preconditions for implementation of change: a focus on the teachers' articulation of constraints on innovation in English language education in Uganda'.

Unpublished doctoral thesis, Department of Language Studies, Canterbury Christ Church University.

Lankshear, C., Gee, P.J., Knobel, M. and Searle, C. (1997) *Changing Literacies*. Buckingham: Open University Press.

Linehan, A. (1996) 'A search for a suitable context for writing: developing students' writing through self-access'. Unpublished master's dissertation. Department of Language Studies, Canterbury Christ Church University.

Longinotto, K. and Mir-Hosseini, Z. (1999) *Divorce Iranian Style*. Channel 4 Television.

MacDonald, B. (1971) 'The evaluation of the humanities curriculum project: a holistic approach', *Theory and Practice*, 10: 163–7.

MacDougall, D. (1975) 'Beyond observational Cinema', in Hockings (ed.), *Principles of Visual Anthropology*. The Hague: Mouton. pp. 109–25.

Maguire, J. and Mansfield, L. (1998) '"No-body's perfect": women, aerobics, and the body beautiful'. Sociology of Sport, 15: 109–137.

Marcus, G.E. (1986) 'Contemporary problems of ethnography in the modern world system', in J. Clifford & G.E. Marcus (eds), Writing Culture: the Poetics and Politics of Ethnography. Berkeley, CA: University of California Press. pp. 165–193

Marcus, G.E. (1994) 'What comes just after "post"? The case of ethnography', in N.K. Denzin & Y.S. Lincoln (eds), *Handbook of Qualitative Research*. Thousand Oaks, CA: Sage. pp. 563–574..

McNiff, J. (1988) *Action Research: Principles and Practice*. London: Macmillan.

Meinhof, U.H. and Galasinski, D. (2000) 'Photography, memory, and the construction of identities on the former East–West German border', *Discourse Studies* 2(3): 323–353.

Miller, S.M., Nelson, M.W. and Moore, M.T. (1998) 'Caught in the paradigm gap: qualitative researchers' lived experience and the politics of epistemology', *American Educational Research Journal*, 35(3): 337–416.

Mills, C.W. (1970) *The Sociological Imagination*, Harmondsworth: Pelican.

Morawska, E. and Spohn, W. (1994) '"Cultural pluralism" in historical sociology; recent theoretical directions', in D. Crane (ed.), *The Sociology of Culture*. Oxford: Blackwell: 45–90.

Nunan, D. (1990) 'The teacher as researcher', in C. Brumfit & R. Mitchell (eds), *ELT Documents 133: Research in the Language Classroom*. London: MEP, The British Council. pp. 16–32.

Nzimiro, I. (1979) 'Anthropologists and their terminologies: a critical review', in G. Huizer & B. Mannheim (eds), *The Politics of Anthropology: From Colonialism and Sexism towards a View from Below*. The Hague: Mouton. pp. 67–83.

Ovenden, C.A. (2003) 'The socio-cultural construction of learner independence in a tertiary EFL institution'. Unpublished PhD thesis, Institute of Education, University of London.

Pelto, P.J. and Pelto, G.H. (1970) *Anthropological Research: The Structure of Enquiry*, 2nd edn, New York: Harper & Row.

Pierson, C.A. (1999) 'Ethnomethodologic analysis of accounts of feeding demented residents in long-term care', *Image: Journal of Nursing Scholarship*, 31(1): 127–131.

Pink, S. (2001) *Doing Visual Ethnography*. London: Sage.

Punch, M. (1994) 'Politics and ethics in qualitative research', in N.K. Denzin & Y.S. Lincoln (eds), *Handbook of Qualitative Research*. Thousand Oaks, CA: Sage. pp. 83–97.

Reason, P. (1994) 'Three approaches to participative enquiry', in N.K. Denzin & Y.S. Lincoln (eds), *Handbook of Qualitative Research*. Thousand Oaks, CA: Sage. pp. 324–339.

Richards, K. and Skelton, J. (1991) 'How critical can you get?', in A. Adams, B. Heaton & P. Howarth (eds), *Socio-Cultural Issues in English for Academic Purposes*. London: Modern English Publications, The British Council. pp. 24–40.

Richards, T.J. and Richards, L. (1994) 'Using computers in qualitative research', in N.K. Denzin & Y.S. Lincoln (eds), *Handbook of Qualitative Research*. Thousand Oaks, CA: Sage. pp. 445–462.

Richardson, L. (1994) 'Writing: a method of enquiry', in N.K. Denzin & Y.S. Lincoln (eds), *Handbook of Qualitative Research*. Thousand Oaks, CA: Sage. pp. 516–529.

Richardson, L. and St Pierre, E.A. (2005) 'Writing: a method of enquiry', in N.K. Denzin & Y.S. Lincoln (eds), *Handbook of Qualitative Research* 3rd edn. Thousand Oaks, CA: Sage. pp. 959–978.

Robson, C. (1993) *Real World Research*. Oxford: Blackwell.

Rose, G. (2001) *Visual Methodologies*. London: Sage.

Roy, A. (2002) *Come September: in Conversation with Howard Zinn*. Audio recording, Lensing Performing Arts Centre, Santa Fe. Lannan Foundation.

Ruddock, J. and Hopkins, D. (eds) (1985) *Research as a Basis for Teaching: Readings from the Work of Lawrence Stenhouse*. Oxford: Heinemann.

Said, E. (1978) *Orientalism*. London: Routledge & Kegan Paul.

Said, E. (1993) *Culture and Imperialism*. London: Chatto and Windus.

Said, E. (2003) 'Preface to Orientalism', *Al-Ahram Weekly Online*, 650, 7–13 August. Accessed at: http://weekly.ahram.org.eg/2003/650/op11.htm

Sangari, K. (1994) 'Relating histories: definitions of literacy, literature, gender in early nineteenth century Calcutta and England', in S. Joshi (ed.), *Rethinking English*. Delhi: Oxford University Press.

Sarangi, S. (1995) 'Culture', in J. Vershueren, J. Östman & J. Blomaert (eds), *Handbook of Pragmatics*. Amsterdam/Philadelphia: John Benjamins.

Scholl, C. (1999) Description of a small culture: tourists in a church'. Unpublished undergraduate assignment. Department of Language Studies, Canterbury Christ Church University.

Schudson, M. (1994) 'Culture and the Integration of National Societies', in D. Crane (ed.), *The Sociology of Culture*. Oxford: Blackwell. pp. 21–43.

Schutz, A. (1964) 'The stranger', *Collected Papers*, Vol.2. The Hague: Martinus Nijhoff. pp. 91–95.

Schutz, A. (1970) *On Phenomenology and Social Relations*. Chicago: University of Chicago Press.

Scott, D. and Usher, R. (1999) *Researching Education*. London: Institute of Education Press.

Shamim, F. (1993) 'Teacher–learner behaviour and classroom processes in large ESL classes in Pakistan'. Unpublished PhD thesis. International Education, University of Leeds.

Shamim, F. (1996) 'The process of research: a socio-cultural experience'. Unpublished paper, Department of English, Karachi University.

Sharpe, K. (1994) 'An examination of some conditions of educational homogeneity in French primary schooling'. Unpublished PhD thesis, Department of Education, Canterbury Christ Church University.

Shaw, A. (1998) 'Images of the female body: women's identities and the media', in J. Richardson, & A. Shaw (eds), *The Body in Qualitative Research*. Aldershot: Ashgate.

Smyth, J. and Shacklock, G. (1998) 'Behind the "cleansing" of socially critical research accounts', in G. Shacklock & J. Smyth (eds), *Being Reflexive in Critical Educational and Social Research*. London: Falmer Press. pp. 1–12.

Spradley, J.P. (1980) *Participant Observation*. New York: Holt, Rinehart & Winston.

Stake, R.E. (2005) 'Qualitative case studies', in N.K. Denzin & Y.S. Lincoln (eds), *Handbook of Qualitative Research*, 3rd edn. Thousand Oaks, CA: Sage. pp. 443–466.

Stenhouse, L. (1985a) 'The illuminative research tradition', in J. Ruddock & D. Hopkins (eds), *Research as a Basis for Teaching: Readings from the Work of Lawrence Stenhouse*. Oxford: Heinemann: 31–32.

Stenhouse, L. (1985b) 'The case-study tradition and how case studies apply to practice', in J. Ruddock & D. Hopkins (eds), *Research as a Basis for Teaching: Readings from the Work of Lawrence Stenhouse*. Oxford: Heinemann. pp. 52–55.

Strauss, A. and Corbin, J. (1994) 'Grounded theory methodology', in N.K. Denzin & Y.S. Lincoln (eds), *Handbook of Qualitative Research*. Thousand Oaks, CA: Sage. pp. 273–85.

Stronach, J. and McLure, M. (1997) '... Opening ...', in J. Stronach & M. McLure (eds), *Educational Research Undone*. London: Open University Press. pp. 1–13.

Swales, J. (1990) *Genre Analysis*. Cambridge: Cambridge University Press.

Talbot, M. (1992) 'The construction of gender in a teenage magazine', in N. Fairclough (ed.), *Critical Language Awareness*. London: Addison Wesley Longman. pp. 175–199.

Thornton, R.J. (1988) 'The rhetoric of ethnographic holism', *Cultural Anthropology*, 3(3): 285–303.

Tyler, S.A. (1986) 'Post-modern ethnography: from document of the occult to occult document', in J. Clifford & G.E. Marcus (eds), *Writing Culture*. London: University of California Press. pp. 122–140.

Usher, R. and Edwards, R. (1994) *Postmodernism and Education: Different Voices, Different Worlds.* London: Routledge.

Van Lier, L. (1988) *The Classroom and the Language Learner.* London: Longman.

Vidich, A.J. and Lyman, S.M. (2000) 'Qualitative methods', in N.K. Denzin & Y.S. Lincoln (eds), *Handbook of Qualitative Research,* 2nd edn. Thousand Oaks, CA: Sage. pp. 37–84.

Walford, G. (1991) 'Reflexive accounts of doing educational research', in G. Walford (ed.), *Doing Educational Research.* London: Routledge. pp. 1–17.

Wallace, C. (1992) 'Critical literacy awareness in the EFL classroom', in N. Fairclough (ed.), *Critical Language Awareness.* London: Addison Wesley Longman. pp. 59–81.

West, L. (2001) *Doctors on the Edge: General Practitioners' Health and Learning in the Inner City.* London: Free Association Books.

Wu, Z. (2002) 'Teachers' "knowledge" and curriculum change: a critical study of teachers' exploratory discourse in a Chinese university'. Unpublished PhD thesis, Department of Linguistics and Modern English Language. University of Lancaster.

Index

action research, 17, 30, 31, 32, 33,
        52, 87, 100
Adler, P., 63, 79, 89, 115
Adler, P. A., 63, 79, 89, 115
Albert, E., 85, 86, 98, 127, 128, 129
Allwright. R. L., 38
Anderson, C., 26, 33, 34, 140, 160,
        161, 187
Appell, G. N., 167
Argument, xii, 21, 22, 61, 64, 67, 92, 93,
        94, 95, 96, 97, 98, 101, 102, 103, 104,
        105, 107, 108, 109, 110, 116, 120, 123,
        125, 127, 128, 130, 132, 137, 154, 168,
        170, 175, 177, 182, 183, 184, 185,
        186, 188, 189, 190
Asad, T., 14, 178
Atkinson, P., 15, 17, 18, 19, 20, 23,
        25, 33, 38, 40, 43, 78, 79, 80,
        115, 123, 130, 131, 137, 141,
        160, 167

Bailey, C., 9, 80, 123
Ball, M., 68, 69
Barmada, W., 87, 88
Barton, A. H., 33
Barua, F., 14
Baumann, G., 41
Beales, A. R., 12
Becker, H. S., 68
Bell, J., 3, 31
Berman, H., 55, 88, 97
Block, D., iii, 63
Bloor, M., 121
Bloor, T., 121
Bochner, A. P., 135
bracketing, 21, 106, 131, 133, 134,
        135, 177, 180, 181, 186
Broadley, S., 24, 30, 59
Bullock, A., 178
Byrd, M., 132, 133, 173, 174, 175

Cameron, D., xiii, 10, 179
Canagarajah, S., 74
case study, 18, 30, 31, 46, 47, 48, 52,
        54, 78, 88
cataloguing, iii
Celik, N. C., 26, 27, 30, 34, 35, 36, 37, 41,
        50, 72, 81, 82, 83, 87, 188
Clark, R., xiii, 118, 119, 120, 121, 123, 124
Clifford, J., 20
co-construction, 68, 97, 114, 115
coding, 15, 19, 54, 56, 61, 81, 107, 122, 145,
        159, 162, 163, 164, 167, 188
Coffey, A., 78, 123, 136, 137
Collier, M., 69
Comaroff, J., 14
conceptual framework, ix, x, 43, 48, 49, 50,
        53, 61, 149
conventions, viii, 15, 117, 121, 122, 124,
        129, 172
Corbin, J., 17
Crabtree, B. F., 24
Crane, D., 12, 143
culture
    of dealing, ix, 142, 143, 144, 147, 148,
        155, 156, 159, 167
    small, viii, 13, 30, 31, 35, 41, 142, 143,
        144, 147, 154, 187
culturism, cultural chauvinism, xiii, 179,
        180, 185, 186

data, iii, vii, viii, ix, x, xi, xii, xiii, 4, 9, 13,
        14, 16, 17, 19, 20, 21, 24, 26, 29, 32,
        33, 35, 36, 39, 40, 42, 43, 45, 46, 47,
        49, 54, 55, 56, 57, 58, 60, 61, 62, 63,
        64, 67, 68, 69, 70, 71, 73, 74, 75, 76,
        77, 78, 79, 80, 81, 82, 83, 84, 85, 86,
        87, 88, 89, 90, 91, 92, 93, 94, 95, 96,
        97, 98, 99, 100, 101, 102, 103, 104,
        105, 106, 107, 108, 109, 110, 111,
        112, 114, 115, 116, 122, 123, 124,

125, 127, 128, 129, 130, 131, 132, 133, 134, 135, 136, 137, 138, 141, 144, 148, 149, 151, 152, 158, 159, 161, 163, 164, 166, 167, 168, 170, 171, 172, 173, 175, 176, 177, 182, 183, 184, 185, 186, 187, 188, 189, 190
accounts, 7, 14, 19, 60, 74, 84, 85, 86, 88, 89, 98, 103, 104, 114, 115, 120, 127, 136, 138, 151, 174, 175, 176
analysis, 32, 47, 54, 56, 58, 61, 92, 93, 96, 97, 99, 101, 103, 108, 109, 116, 124, 128, 130, 131, 134, 164, 173, 175, 188
artefacts, xii, 13, 15, 72, 125, 137, 138, 182
corpus of, xiii, xiv, 1, 20, 23, 26, 27, 63, 70, 72, 81, 92, 93, 94, 96, 97, 101, 107, 108, 109, 110, 116, 117, 127, 137, 141, 142, 149, 168, 172, 179
description, vii, xii, 19, 39, 48, 52, 53, 54, 55, 56, 57, 61, 62, 63, 66, 67, 68, 69, 71, 72, 73, 74, 77, 78, 80, 81, 82, 85, 86, 87, 88, 89, 90, 91, 101, 102, 103, 104, 106, 109, 112, 115, 116, 136, 137, 138, 144, 152, 158, 164, 174, 179, 180, 181, 182, 184, 186, 187, 189
discussion of, 43, 56, 92, 93, 94, 107, 149, 167
documents, 63, 72, 73
drawings, 41, 45, 68, 73, 80, 82, 118, 138, 154
  interconnecting, 35, 42, 188
  oral, 40, 85, 86, 88, 102, 103, 104, 105, 132, 138, 175, 179
  photographic, 69, 73, 76, 114
  raw, 93, 94, 95, 96, 107, 108, 109, 116, 169
  reconstruction of, 135
  verbatim, xiii, 19, 63, 66, 67, 69, 70, 86, 89, 102, 103, 175, 186, 190
  visual, xi, 63, 68, 69, 70, 71, 73, 137, 141, 188
Delamont, S., 79
Delikurt, P., 162, 163
Denzin, N., 14, 15, 18, 19, 20, 78, 79, 148
Derrida, 40, 138
Dobbin, F. R., 178
Duan, Y., 40, 114
Dudley-Evans, T., 172

Edwards, R., 154
Ekman, S., 128, 133, 172, 173
Elley, W. B., 87
Ellis, C., 135
Emami, A., 128, 133, 172, 173

Emerson, R. M., 20
Erlandson, D. A., 98
everyday life, vii, xi, 9, 10, 11, 13, 24, 47, 72, 86, 97, 129, 130, 139, 170, 179, 185

Fairclough, N., 13, 72, 74, 117, 118, 147, 148, 153, 154, 179
Fictionalization, 112, 113, 118, 153
Fine, M., xiv, 124, 170, 177
first person, 22, 111, 122, 123, 124, 127, 128, 131, 139, 170, 189
Foley, D., 169, 170

Galasinski, D., 69
Gee, J. P., 13, 126
Geertz, C., 42, 77, 78, 79, 80, 87, 94, 116
Genre, 45, 73, 117, 118, 119, 120, 122, 124, 126, 131, 132, 138, 139, 169
Gieve, S., 179
Golden-Biddle, K., 103, 119, 122, 123, 125
Goulimaris, R., 70, 71, 72
grounded theory, 18, 30, 119
Guba, E. G., 19, 98
Gubrium, J. F., 11, 14, 17, 19, 20, 21, 79, 141, 171, 177
Gummesson, E., 24

Hammersley, M., 17, 18, 19, 20, 23, 25, 33, 38, 40, 79, 80, 130, 131, 141, 160, 167
Harper, D., 68, 69, 110, 114
Harrison, B., 69
Hayagoshi, H., 49, 50, 107, 128
Herrera, L., 27, 47, 58, 63, 64, 66, 67, 70, 71, 75, 76, 77, 80, 81, 82, 83, 101, 102, 103, 104, 105, 129, 130, 140, 149, 150, 151, 152, 154, 156, 157, 158, 159, 160, 163, 185, 186, 188
Hodge, R., 13
Holliday, A. R., ii, iii, 4, 11, 13, 32, 38, 39, 40, 41, 42, 46, 56, 57, 60, 65, 68, 69, 95, 99, 108, 110, 114, 130, 131, 134, 136, 143, 144, 147, 155, 165, 177, 178, 182, 183, 184, 185, 187
Holloway, J., 26
Holman Jones, S., 135
Holstein, J. A., 11, 14, 17, 19, 20, 21, 79, 141, 171, 177
Honarbin-Holliday, M., 39, 55, 67, 68, 69, 70, 80, 111, 114, 137, 138, 161
Hopkins, D., 24
Hoyle, E., 87

Instances, 10, 87, 88, 173, 174, 175
interpretive paradigm, 6, 11, 12, 18, 40, 68, 99, 123, 137, 169, 170

Interviews, xiii, 3, 6, 19, 26, 28, 31, 32,
    33, 35, 37, 38, 52, 53, 63, 65, 66,
    71, 75, 83, 84, 85, 88, 94, 96,
    97, 100, 107, 114, 136, 137, 144,
    158, 161, 162, 163, 164, 173, 175
Ivanič, R., xiii, 118, 119, 121, 123, 124

Janesick, V. J., 20, 21, 30, 48, 79
Jenkins, D., 155
Jordan, S., 154, 178

Keesing, R. M., 178
Kress, G., 13, 68, 72
Kuhn, T., 14
Kullman, J., 70
Kyeyune, R., 58

Lankshear, C., 11, 13, 14, 117, 126
Lazarsfield, P. F., 33
Lincoln, Y. S., 14, 15, 18, 19, 20, 98,
    148, 156
Linehan, A., 27, 30, 31, 100, 101, 129, 133
literature review, 15, 29, 31, 43, 46, 47,
    48, 52, 53, 54, 57, 58, 59, 63, 95,
    103, 105, 107, 109, 116, 118, 119,
    120, 121, 122, 127, 128, 129, 130,
    131, 132, 133, 135, 151, 152, 163,
    170, 172, 173, 175, 177, 189
Locke, K. D., 103, 119, 122, 123, 125
Longinotto, K., 79, 80
Lyman, S. M., 171

MacDonald, B., 87
MacDougall, D., 142
Magalhães, I., 179
Maguire, J., 28, 29, 30, 31, 32, 36, 37, 41,
    45, 49, 50, 52, 83, 84, 127
making the familiar strange, 13, 26, 29, 40,
    62, 72, 74, 177
Mansfield, L., 28, 29, 30, 31, 33,
    36, 37, 41, 45, 49, 50, 52, 83,
    84, 127
Marcus, G. E., 39, 141
Marginality, 40, 68, 167
McLure, M., 169
McNiff, J., 32
Meinhof, U. H., 69
Methodology, 12, 20, 43, 48, 49, 52,
    53, 58, 63, 95, 112, 141, 149,
    161, 179, 182
Miller, S. M., 20, 24, 95, 119, 123, 156
Mills, C. W., 21
Mir-Hosseini, Z., 79, 80
Moore, M. T., 70
Morawska, E., 14

narrative, viii, 15, 55, 66, 112, 113, 122,
    135, 136, 170
    personal, xi, 63, 135, 136
Nunan, D., 24
Nzimiro, I., 14

observation, 5, 6, 17, 18, 26, 28, 31, 35, 36,
    39, 40, 45, 54, 56, 58, 60, 63, 67, 73, 75,
    76, 80, 81, 85, 86, 88, 89, 92, 94, 98, 99,
    100, 106, 107, 109, 114, 131, 134, 153,
    165, 173, 184
othering, xii, 14, 24, 137, 144, 145, 171, 177
Ovenden, C. A., 66, 112, 113, 114, 135, 189

participants, 17, 18, 25, 26, 28, 35, 38, 45,
    49, 52, 53, 66, 103, 111, 137, 140, 153,
    154, 155, 169, 171, 174, 175
Pelto, G. H., 63
Pelto, J. P., 63
people in the research setting, xi, 8, 9, 12,
    14, 17, 18, 25, 26, 28, 35, 38, 45, 49,
    52, 53, 55, 58, 63, 64, 66, 68, 74, 79, 91,
    103, 104, 111, 114, 117, 123, 136, 137,
    140, 141, 143, 144, 148, 149, 150, 153,
    154, 155, 156, 157, 159, 163, 167,
    168, 169, 170, 171, 174, 175, 185,
    186, 189, 190
personal knowledge, 69, 112, 116
Pierson, C. A., 86, 87, 88, 104, 105, 106,
    109, 127, 128, 129
Pink, S., 69, 114
postmodernism, xi, xii, 14, 19, 20, 21, 79,
    96, 113, 119, 123, 135, 139, 140, 156,
    169, 178, 187
Punch, M., 159

quantitative research, vii, xiii, 1, 2, 4, 5, 7, 8,
    20, 23, 29, 30, 31, 32, 34, 62, 88, 118,
    123, 125, 140, 175, 187
questionnaires, 3, 6, 62, 66, 88

Reason, P., 17, 25, 32
reflexivity, 17, 20, 33, 58, 62, 104, 125, 141,
    150, 170, 171
research
    diaries, 63, 64, 65, 66, 100, 111, 159,
        162, 163
    questions, vii, 21, 23, 26, 29, 30, 33,
        34, 37, 45, 53, 75, 76, 100, 187
    setting, vii, xii, 4, 5, 6, 8, 9, 10, 11, 12,
        14, 15, 19, 20, 21, 22, 23, 24, 26, 27,
        30, 31, 33, 34, 35, 36, 37, 38, 39, 40,
        41, 42, 45, 46, 47, 48, 49, 50, 52, 53,
        54, 55, 58, 59, 60, 61, 63, 64, 66, 68,
        69, 71, 75, 76, 78, 79, 82, 83, 84, 85,

86, 87, 88, 89, 91, 92, 94, 96, 101,
  108, 112, 113, 116, 119, 130, 135,
  138, 140, 141, 142, 143, 144, 148,
  149, 150, 151, 152, 153, 154, 155,
  156, 157, 158, 160, 162, 163, 167,
  168, 169, 170, 171, 172, 173, 174,
  180, 182, 185, 186, 187, 188, 189
researcher
  as insider, 52, 85, 111, 112, 140, 152
  as outsider, 4, 13, 46, 52, 108, 150, 151,
    161, 165, 166
  as stranger, vii, 10, 12, 13, 21, 26, 40, 71,
    114, 148, 167, 186
Richards, K, 121
Richards, L., 79
Richards, T. J., 79
Richardson, L., 14, 79, 119, 122, 123, 125
rigour, xi, xii, 1, 7, 8, 21, 22, 23, 24, 30, 43,
    55, 60, 67, 114, 117, 126, 137, 156, 161,
    168, 189
Roach, D., 121
Robson, C., 48
Rose, G., 68
Roy, A., 113
Ruddock, J., 24

Said, E., 122, 178
Sangari, K., 14
Sarangi, S., 14, 178
Scholl, C., 26, 34, 36, 37, 54, 59, 70, 82, 140
Schudson, M., 14, 177
Schutz, A., 10, 12, 14, 21, 177
science, xi, xii, xiii, 1, 7, 8, 9, 13, 14, 17, 19,
    24, 28, 55, 61, 72, 79, 94, 114, 118, 119,
    122, 123, 124, 126, 131, 132, 135, 139,
    141, 148, 150, 169, 177
Scott, D., 19, 124
Shacklock, G., 141, 149
Shamim, F., 150, 151, 152, 153, 154, 156,
    157, 158, 159, 160, 164, 179
Sharpe, K., 71, 73, 74
Shaw, A., 49, 51, 53, 54, 59, 100, 105, 107,
    109, 129, 130, 175, 176, 177, 186
showing the workings, xii, 8, 15, 22, 39, 43,
    45, 54, 59, 60, 61, 75, 95, 103, 104,
    109, 111, 117, 149, 156, 167, 168,
    186, 188, 189
Smyth, J., 141, 149
sociological imagination, xii, 21, 39, 83, 139

Spohn, W., 14
Spradley, J. P., 20, 25, 33, 34, 35, 38, 58
St John, M. J., 172
St Pierre, E. A., 79, 119, 123, 125
Stake, R. E., 17, 18, 78, 88
Stenhouse, L., 78, 88
Strauss, A., 15, 17, 18, 53, 128
Stronach, J., 169
subjectivity, 135
submission, xiii, 96, 111, 116, 155, 182
Swales, J., 172

Talbot, M., 29, 30, 31, 37, 51, 52, 73, 74,
    133, 134
themes, xii, 8, 25, 45, 63, 93, 94, 96, 97,
    98, 99, 100, 102, 103, 104, 108, 109,
    112, 116, 140, 149, 151, 164, 169, 176,
    178, 184
thick description, vii, ix, xii, 40, 62, 68, 77,
    78, 79, 80, 81, 84, 85, 86, 88, 91, 92, 99,
    101, 103, 104, 105, 106, 108, 110, 116,
    123, 137, 180, 185, 189
thinking-as-usual, 12, 72, 187
Thornton, R. J., 94
Trombley, S., 178
Tyler, S. A., 175

Usher, R., 19, 154

validity, 2, 3, 8, 33, 35, 39, 45, 62, 68, 77,
    82, 113, 151
van Lier, L., 38
verisimilitude, 79, 80, 113, 126, 188
Vidich, A. J., 171
voice, viii, 20, 45, 63, 67, 68, 69, 95, 112,
    117, 119, 121, 122, 123, 124, 125, 126,
    128, 130, 131, 135, 136, 137, 139, 141,
    145, 146, 147, 153, 156, 159, 166, 168,
    169, 170, 175, 184, 189

Walford, G., 7
Wallace, C., 72
Weis, L., 124, 170
West, L., 88, 113, 178
Wheeler, S., 26
White, C., 14, 128
Wu, Z., 110, 111, 112, 114, 189

Yeomans, D., 154, 178